CELEBRATING CHRISTMAS
AROUND THE WORLD

BOOKS BY HERBERT H. WERNECKE
Published by The Westminster Press

Celebrating Christmas Around the World
Christmas Stories from Many Lands
Christmas Customs Around the World
Christmas Songs and Their Stories

CELEBRATING
CHRISTMAS
AROUND
THE WORLD

Edited by Herbert H. Wernecke

Philadelphia
THE WESTMINSTER PRESS

Republished by Omnigraphics • Penobscot Building • Detroit • 1999

Library of Congress Cataloging-in-Publication Data

Celebrating Christmas around the world / edited by Herbert H.
Wernecke.
 p. cm.
 ISBN 0-7808-0306-X (lib. bdg. : alk paper)
 1. Christmas. I. Werneke, Herbert II. (Herbert Henry),
1895–1975.
GT4985.C37 1999
394.2663 — dc21   99-27454
                                                            CIP

This book is printed on acid-free paper meeting the ANSI Z39.48 Standard.
The infinity symbol that appears above indicates that the paper in this book
meets that standard.

Printed in the United States

Contents

EUROPE

FOREWORD

"ONE WORLD OR NONE" is a stern challenge that compels us to stop and think in our day as never before. For almost two thousand years the Christmas message has resounded year in, year out. Millions upon millions of people have sung the songs of the Nativity in anthem, hymn, and carol forms. Yet, it seems as if mankind has made no genuinely significant progress in that direction throughout the past centuries.

We must agree, however, "Christianity has not failed; it has not even been seriously tried." To encourage sympathetic understanding and greater intercommunication among peoples and nations and groups within nations, to increase our appreciation of all countries and peoples on this planet—or shall we say, "to seriously try Christianity"?—is the chief reason for continuing the series of "Around the World" volumes that have been so cordially received. They now include: *Christmas Stories from Many Lands, Christmas Customs Around the World,* and *Christmas Songs and Their Stories,* as well as their very modest forerunners which, however, breathed the same spirit, namely, *Carols, Customs and Costumes Around the World* and *Favorite Christmas, Folk, and Sacred Songs.* This new volume describes further the celebration of the Christmas festival as reflected in customs and stories from many lands, in five continents.

The typists, Mrs. Hulda Lutz and Mrs. Ruth Southern, whose prompt and efficient work made it possible to complete this volume relatively soon after *Christmas Stories from Many Lands,* deserve our special thanks.

May this volume, along with its predecessors in the series, make the angels' song increasingly real: "Glory to God, Peace on Earth, Good Will to Men."

H. H. W.

ACKNOWLEDGMENTS

THOUGH THE MATERIALS included in this volume were gathered over a period of years and in several cases from out-of-the-way places, practically all the authors and publishers concerned could be located. If any errors have crept in as to crediting copyrighted material, kindly notify the editor and prompt corrections will be made.

Special acknowledgment is made and appreciation expressed to the following:

Augsburg Publishing House, for the following material reprinted from *Christmas: An American Annual of Christmas Literature and Art:* "Christmas from Boston to Alaska" ("Christmas in Uncle Sam's Attic"), by John T. Faris, Vol. 6 (1936), pp. 36 ff.; "Christmas at Bethlehem" ("In Bethlehem for Christmas"), by Madeleine Sweeny Miller, Vol. 8 (1938), pp. 69–72; "The Christmas City of America," by Burnette Thompson, Vol. 11 (1941), pp. 31–35; "A Christmas Salute to West Point and Annapolis" ("Annapolis and West Point Christmas Festivities"), Anonymous, Vol. 13 (1943), pp. 39–41; Sweden, from "Christmas in Scandinavia" ("The Swedes Love Christmas"), by Marie Malmin Meyer, Vol. 22 (1952), pp. 18 ff.; "A Pennsylvania Dutch Christmas," by Jean Louise Smith, Vol. 26 (1956), pp. 12–24.

The Belgian Tourist Bureau, for "Christmas in Belgium."

The Board of World Missions, the Presbyterian Church in the United States, for "Christmas in the Congo"; "Christmas Fiestas in Spain"; "How to View Christmas" (Korea); "Christmas in Taejon" (Korea); "Christmas at Campinas" (Brazil).

The Board of World Missions of the Reformed Church in America, for "A Universal Christmas in India"; "A Bonfire in the Courtyard and in the Church" (Iraq).

Mr. Willy Breinholst, for "Christmas in Denmark."

Kenneth Irving Brown, for "The Christmas Guest," from *A New Christmas Treasury,* by Robert and Maria Lohan (The Stephen Daye Press, 1954), pp. 278–285.

The Christian Board of Publication, St. Louis, for "Christmas in Puerto Rico," by Frances M. Hill, from the *Junior World,* November 23, 1958.

Doubleday & Company, Inc., for "Aniela's Birthday and Christmas" (Poland), from *Up the Hill,* by Marguerite de Angeli, copyright 1942 by Marguerite de Angeli; and for "Christmas in Matabeleland" (Southern Rhodesia), by Stuart Cloete, copyright 1942 by Stuart Cloete and reprinted by permission of William Morris Agency, Inc.

Friendship Press, for "We Want to Stay Here for Christmas" (China), from *Missionary Story Hour,* by Nina Millen, pp. 41–48.

D. C. Heath & Company, for "Christmas and Three Kings' Day," from "Letters from Guatemala," by Delia Goetz (1941), pp. 34–39.

The Macmillan Company, for "Christmas in Provence," from *Little Tonino,* by Helen Hill and Violet Maxwell (1928); "Christmas Upon a Greenland Iceberg," from *The Children's Book of Christmas,* by J. C. Dier (1927), pp. 59–61.

David McKay Company, Inc., for "A Navaho Christmas," from *Waterless Mountain,* by L. A. Armer (1931), pp. 60–66.

The Norwegian Information Service, for "Old and New Christmas Traditions in Norway."

Stewardship Council, United Church of Christ (formerly, Missions Council of the Congregational Christian Churches), for "How Missionaries Contribute to the Christmas Celebration" (Japan); "Songs, Gifts, and Love" (Korea); "Christmas at a Hospital" (Korea); "Christmas at Ponape in the Caroline Islands" (Micronesia).

The University Publishing Company, for "Christmas in Armenia," from *Tales of Olden Days,* by Hazel G. Kinscella (1939), pp. 145–146.

The Viking Press, for "Fiddler, Play Fast—Play Faster," from *The Long Christmas,* by Ruth Sawyer. Copyright 1941 by Ruth Sawyer. Reprinted by permission of The Viking Press.

William L. White, for "A Christmas Broadcast from the Trenches, 1939" (Finland).

Whiteside, Inc., and William Morrow & Company, Inc., for "'Here Is Joseph, Here Is Mary,'" by Annie B. Kerr, from *So Gracious Is the Time,* pp. 23–31.

AFRICA

CONGO

Christmas in the Congo

PREPARATION for Christmas in the Congo begins when some group is designated to prepare the annual Christmas pageant. Sometimes it will be a school group; sometimes it will be the elders or deacons of the church. Christmas Day itself begins with groups of carolers walking to and fro through the village, along the roadway, by the houses of the missionaries, singing the lovely carols known the world around. Often one is awakened by some caroling group that passes under his window just before dawn when the group of carolers is beginning to converge at the house of worship. The entire Christian group is found at dawn at the church for a service of prayer where once again everyone will join in the singing of the carols and where the day's big service will be properly announced. Then everyone goes home to make final preparation as to his best clothes and also to be sure to prepare his offering for the Christmas service. Now the most important part of their Christmas worship service is the love offering, which is their gift in honor of Jesus. At about eight or nine o'clock not only will every Christian who is not ill find his way to the house of worship but many non-Christians who have been caught up in the joyous spirit of the day will also come and join in the celebration of the birthday. Of course, there will be the usual Scripture and the singing of all the carols and many, many special musical numbers by groups who have done their best to prepare some bit of music for this service,

5

and then the part of the service that is probably the most important of all is the march-around offering. Everyone in the service will be expected to go forward and lay his gift upon the raised platform near the Communion table—his gift to Jesus on this, His birthday. Not a person will come to the service without something in his hand to be offered as his gift on this day. Those who do not have money will bring some article they have made, or something from their garden, or some fruit from their trees; and in many cases where there is no other gift available, some old lame person has often hobbled forward with a cup and saucer or a knife, fork, and spoon that he took off his table rather than come to this service without his gift.

Always, of course, there is a Christian sermon, following much the same theme as we would follow in such a message here. This service may last as long as two hours and has in some cases lasted three hours, but never too long for the African Christian. For them, it is one of the most joyous days of the year, and by their worship they indicate it is Jesus Christ who has brought this unusual joy into their lives.

In recent years, following the Christmas service many of the people have had Christmas dinners, preparing tables out in front of their home and inviting many of their intimate friends to share then around the table in a continuation of the joyful spirit which is found in every heart throughout this day. And so as the missionaries gather for their Christmas dinner together, likewise the African Christian, out in front of home after home, will gather with his friends and continue the rest of the day in a mood of singing, gratitude, and joyfulness. And so as the sun sets on Christmas in the Congo, the entire population of village after village will have felt the impact of the spirit of joy, hope, and brotherhood that is felt the world around because Jesus was born a long time ago and is continually reborn in the lives of people the world around today.

Kanda's Christmas in the Congo

MRS. DONALD F. BOBB

(Bulope Mission, Africa)

A S KANDA SAT on the backless bench, his little chalk slate slid to the ground unnoticed, for he was far, far away! Each day he found it increasingly difficult to keep his mind on his schoolwork. The teacher had already looked at him rather sternly this morning, as though he knew the mind of a fourteen-year-old boy three weeks before Christmas!

There would be no lighted tree, but there was the light of God in his heart! There would be no expensive gifts, but the gift of God's love was his today and always. There would be no elaborate meal, but he would feast at the Lord's own Table. He had nothing to give his father or mother, but he had his Joy Gift tucked safely away at home in a little earthen vessel —how he had saved to make this offering on Christ's birthday!

Strains of the "Hallelujah Chorus" ran through his head. Was there ever a song so majestic, so thrilling to the heart of an African boy! Kanda had always loved to sing, and knew many a hymn in entirety from memory. When a fellow doesn't own a hymnal, he, of necessity, learns from sheer repetition.

He worked so hard on the "Hallelujah"! The missionary had played the English record and every choir member was eager to claim this magnificent musical masterpiece for his own. It was hard work, even for those who read a little music, but Kanda, who knew no notes, had to learn his tenor part by rote. But it was worth it!

And the pageant—it would be the best in years! One of the missionary ladies had just received her boxes from the States and there was aluminum foil to make new wings for the angels this year. White hospital gowns, borrowed from the "White Cross" supplies, made wonderful robes for the "heavenly host"!

Mary, Joseph, and the Wise Men would be elegant, since

every missionary on the station had searched his attic trunks for old bathrobes, bedspreads, and curtains for costumes. Herod and his soldiers would be handsome in their cardboard helmets, swords, and shields.

Kanda prayed especially hard that the station generator would run well on the "big night," for the colored cellophane spotlights made the scenes perfect.

As the eventful day drew nearer, joy and expectation mounted in Kanda's heart. The night of the final rehearsal, Kanda's step was light and sure as he headed for choir practice. He didn't even wait for the second drum call, as was often his habit, but set out with the first. His heart was so full of praise and joy that he did not complain of the mile-and-a-half walk in the dark to the big church.

He was friendly and cheerful as he met smaller children and women with their babies on their hips, all scurrying along the semidark path to "God's House." They did not mind that they had to come night after night in order to learn the difficult songs.

Strains of bass, tenor, alto, and soprano wafted on the warm night air. All were singing or humming their favorite, the "Hallelujah." They were dispelling any doubt that the missionary had had that they were incapable of learning this difficult piece.

Finally the "big night" arrived and the church was filled. Soft exclamations of *"Ka! Ka!"* fell from parted lips as newcomers beheld the once barren church now transformed by a lovely array of palms and flowers. The pageant was wonderful; the lights really did work; not too many babies cried; and Kanda tingled with joy such as he had never felt before when he stood with his two hundred African brethren singing "Hallelujah."

This was thrill enough, but wonder of wonders! When all was over, the missionary had a "machine" which, with a push of a button, played back the very music they had just sung.

That night as he lay awake on his mat, hearing the deep breathing of his parents who slept nearby, he suddenly felt more grateful than ever for them. It had not been easy for them to follow Christ all the way, but they had, and had striven to nurture him in His ways.

His father had been laughed at when he entered the school for evangelists when he was "older." Other women had mocked his mother when she enrolled in the mission school for adult women to learn to write and read God's Word. They had been faithful in teaching him all the "affairs of God."

Before the sun had risen Christmas Day, the first drum was calling: "Come to worship God; come to worship God." Every morning Kanda awoke to this drum call and went with his father and mother to the village chapel for morning prayers. This was the normal beginning of a Christian's day.

But today was special! The missionary was coming with the fascinating "magic pictures" as a special treat, and then there would be the final culmination of his Christmas—Kanda would give his Joy Gift! The only gift he had was for the Christ himself, but to Kanda this was the most natural thing in the world, for after all it was Christ's birthday. Christ *was* Christmas to this Congo boy!

SOUTH AFRICA

Christmas Throughout South Africa

CHRISTMAS in the Union of South Africa is a summer holiday. For most people it is an out-of-town day. In December, the southern summer brings glorious days of sunshine that carry an irresistible invitation to the beaches, the rivers, and the shaded mountain slopes. Then the South African holiday season reaches its height. Schools are closed for the long summer vacations, and camping is the order of the day. If South Africa has no snow at Christmas, it has flowers, many beautiful varieties of cultivated and wild flowers being in their full pride to flame as brightly as a yule-log fire.

In many ways South Africans cling to the Christmas customs of the Old World. Shop windows are draped with sparkling cotton wool and tinsel to give the traditional Christmasy setting familiar to, say, shoppers in London and New York. Even Father Christmas, a South African prototype of St. Nicholas or Santa Claus, braves the sunny side of the street in his customary robes—cotton wool trimmed cloak and hood to simulate snow—and points the way to the elaborate "toylands" in the big stores. In the shops he is seen helping parents to choose their gifts and spreading fun among the children.

Christmas greeting cards, complete with robin and snow-decked cottages, are exchanged during the season. In the cities and towns carol singers make their rounds on Christmas Eve. Church services are held on Christmas morning. Christmas Eve celebrations in larger centers include "Carols by Candle Light" and special screen and floor shows.

Homes are lavishly decorated, usually with pine branches, and all have the decorated Christmas fir tree in a corner, with presents for the children around. Holly is missing, as none grows in the warm South African climate. Sometimes a local type of mistletoe is hung up in a strategic position, but more often imitation mistletoe has to do. At bedtime on Christmas Eve, children may also hang up their stockings for presents from Father Christmas.

Some streets are colorfully lighted up at night, with floodlights on prominent buildings and a sparkling Christmas tree on the city square.

For many South Africans, Christmas dinner is an open-air lunch. For many more, it is the traditional dinner of either turkey, roast beef, mince pies, or suckling pig, yellow rice (tumeric) with raisins, vegetables, and plum pudding, crackers, paper hats, and all. In the afternoon, families go out into the country and usually there are games or bathing in the warm sunshine, and then home in the cool of the evening. Boxing Day is also a proclaimed public holiday usually spent in the open air. It falls on December 26 and is a day of real relaxation.

For the non-European races of South Africa, Christmas is a holiday, a day of good eating and of lively exchange and enjoyment of gifts. On Christmas Day, the Cape Colored "Coons" in their gay and fanciful costumes commence their weeklong carnival of singing, dancing, and parading the streets with pipe and string bands.

Christmas was observed in South Africa as a purely religious festival until, by way of Victoria and Albert's England, Teutonic customs began to be introduced. It was originally a day of prayer and quiet meditation, the day above all others when the mother church was crowded with young and old alike who had come to worship and who immediately after the service exchanged small Christmas presents. The settlers who came to the Eastern Province in 1820 brought the ways of old England with them. Although these people had often neither cause nor means to rejoice, they did their best to mark Christmas with a repast a little better than the ordinary fare of the pioneer. When the military villages of Woburn and Johannesburg were raided by the Kaffirs and burned on a Christmas Day in the 1850's, Christmas dinner was being prepared, and some time later in one gutted cottage, where the roof had fallen in on the oven without crushing it, a plum cake was found cooked to perfection.

Christmas in Cape Town

YOU CAN THANK the Cape *Argus* (probably aided by Charles Dickens) for Christmas as we know it in Cape Town. It was a slow growth, but one that can be traced easily enough in the newspaper files.

Book after book by Charles Dickens, filled with the Christmas spirit, had been arriving in Cape Town during the '40's and '50's of the last century. Yet it was not until 1859 that any Cape Town newspaper thought of wishing its readers a merry Christmas. There was no Christmas shopping rush, because the custom of giving presents had not become widely established. Thus, during the week before Christmas in 1859, only two advertisements with a Christmas flavor appeared in the Cape *Argus*—one suggesting French flower vases as presents, the other offering Westphalia hams for the Christmas dinner.

On December 24 that year the Cape *Argus* came out with a leading article discussing Cape Town's apathy and pleading for a new outlook: "In accordance with the genial and time-honored custom of Old England, we wish our readers A MERRY CHRISTMAS. It must be confessed that in the Southern Hemisphere, with the thermometer standing at something like one hundred degrees, merriment is not precisely the condition either of mind or body which most readily associates itself with the idea of Christmas. [In 1859 Christmas week was "blazing, flaring, scorching, nose-blistering and red-hot."] When beef and turkey cannot be coaxed into keeping for longer than one night, and the recollection of plum pudding is distasteful, and the bare idea of mince pie and brandy throws one into a perspiration—it seems something like an unfeeling mockery to grasp your friend by the hand and hope he may have a merry Christmas.

"Seriously, Christmas at the Cape does lose much of the peculiar interest which attaches to it in northern climates. Certain it is that Christmas Day is lightly regarded here. We hope that we shall not be trespassing on very dangerous ground if we plead for the better observance of Christmas and urge the superiority of its claim to that of the unmeaning New Year's Day. And so we heartily wish our readers a merry and hospitable Christmas."

In the same issue the Cape Town Theater announced the first Christmas pantomime in South Africa—"The Babes in the Wood." "Christmas will not pass over without an endeavor to keep up the good old English custom of good old English pantomime founded on one of the oldest ballads in the language," advertised Mr. Sefton Parry, proprietor and manager. "An attempt of this kind upon so small a stage, with so many disadvantages to contend against, may seem at first almost impracticable; but Mr. P. trusts to perseverance and determination to ensure success. The scenery, painted expressly for the occasion, is of the most gorgeous description; the masks, properties, and tricks are of unusual excellence; and the dresses all that money and good taste could secure."

Christmas fare was plentiful and cheap. During that week in 1859, householders paid 30s. for a fattened pig and 9s. for a sucking pig. A fowl cost 1s., a turkey 4s. 6d., and oranges were 7s. a 100.

It was not until twelve years later, in 1871, that Christmas trees appeared in the shops. One leading store transformed its whole fancy department into a "Bazaar and Christmas Tree." Another shopkeeper drew up a special advertisement headed with a woodcut of the Royal Arms. It read: "Oh, Pa! Oh, Ma! Do go and pay Mr. Long a visit and buy me some toys—they are so fine, so unique, so instructive. Oh do, dear Pa! We will be such good children hereafter."

The campaign by *The Argus* was showing results at last. Christmas had come to Cape Town.

Christmas on the Farms of South Africa

"THE LADY OF THE HOUSE will hand around cakes and tarts." The last line of Hofmeyr's song is by no means an anticlimax: cakes and tarts were regarded as great luxuries among the farming community in South Africa little more than fifty years ago. The population of the land was predominantly rural and very conservative in outlook. The customs connected with the celebration of religious holidays and festivals had changed little through the centuries. The cakes and tarts were always part of the traditional Christmas or New Year meals as the Boer farmers had known them for more than a hundred years.

The small, round sweet cakes were made of rolled dough cut into shapes with a cup or a glass. The recipe for this luxury undoubtedly came from Holland with the earliest settlers, for Dutch emigrants to America have left behind them the custom of baking similar "cookies" on important days. The tarts were small pastries; they are often called *handtertjies* in modern speech to distinguish between them and the much larger tarts which had to be cut into slices, such as *melktert*. They were made of rolled pastry cut into circles and filled with jam. The edges of the pastry were stuck together by means of a beaten egg mixture and then crimped with a fork.

Different shapes were sometimes used to add variety to these two basic luxuries. Occasionally the dough would be cut out in the shape of a man; cracknel pastry in plaited shapes was also baked and served with the cakes and tarts. Plaited pastries have long formed part of Christmas and New Year meals; they can be traced back to the heathen feasts of our ancestors in Europe. They were symbolic offerings to the gods. When they were straight they represented plaits of hair, and when circular they symbolized the sun and its rays, or the bracelet with which the Germanic tribes buried their dead.

Throughout this story we are dealing with the Christmas customs of the farming communities living in the interior of South Africa—customs which were observed more than fifty years ago. Christmas to the rural Afrikaner was then much simpler than it tends to be today. Isolated from other influences, the farmers and their families kept Christmas much as an ordinary Sunday, except that cakes and ginger beer—luxuries normally reserved for birthdays, weddings, and celebrations—were available.

Yet the history of Christmas goes back deep into the past.

December 25 and January 1 have always been important dates. History and legend make mention of the Feast of Twelve Nights between our Christmas Day and January 6, the Feast of the Three Kings. Among our Germanic ancestors this period of merrymaking started on December 25 with the Midwinter Feast, the day of rejoicing in honor of the gods of the fertile earth and in honor of the dead. On this day, cattle were slaughtered to provide meat for the feasting and nourishment for people who still had to face two more months of winter snow. The results of the winter sacrifices could now be seen: the sun had ceased its southward wandering. Its rays were increasing in strength and the sap was beginning to rise almost imperceptibly in the plants and trees. Some of our ancestors seem to have celebrated this day in honor of the sun, a feast marking the winter solstice and the rebirth of light. Offerings were also made to the spirits of fertility.

This time of fructification, these twelve sacred nights, has left traces in the modern celebration of Christmas (*Weihnachten*) in Germany. But such ancient celebrations were not confined to the Germanic tribes. The Romans, among whom Christianity began, celebrated December 25 as the last day of the Saturnalia Festival; later on, the same day concluded the feast in honor of Mithra, the Persian sun god, who was also worshiped in Rome.

Those who wish to preserve the religious simplicity of the Christian Christmas festival regret the tendency noticeable in the larger cities of the Union, where the holy day has become nothing more than a noisy holiday, entirely unconnected with the birth of Christ. For many commercial interests, Christmas is a peak season; South Africa shares the internationalized Christmas and all its conventions with the Western world. The days before Christmas are regarded as having value only as shopping opportunities, while financial worries attached to providing lavish "traditional" Christmas entertainment tend to leave little room for peace and good will.

Half a century ago Christmas in the *platt land* was quite a different institution. In the strongly Calvinistic environment Christmas, in contrast to New Year's Day, was observed as a quiet religious festival, usually marked by the celebration of Holy Communion. In many country areas this pattern remains essentially the same today, little changed even by the improved communications. Baking cakes for the family was originally more often associated with New Year than with Christmas, although in some areas it had been advanced to Christmas Eve. Whatever the choice, cakes were usually made only once a year. It was customary to give the children small presents bought from traveling salesmen or from a store.

On Christmas Eve the children hung their stockings on the bedposts for the offerings of Father Christmas. This custom had reached even the most isolated parts of South Africa before the turn of the century. Such influences on the Boer republics had come from the English community, which had brought most of the Christmas customs unchanged from England. The legend of Father Christmas found favor and soon became part of the celebration of December 25.

Christmas Day itself would begin with the usual greetings between members of the family and their neighbors. Christmas wishes were exchanged personally—Christmas cards were never used. At about eleven o'clock a service would be held in the town churches; on the farms there were readings from the Bible, just as if it were an ordinary Sunday. After the service or the readings, the main Christmas meal was begun. For those families accustomed to celebrate New Year's Day as the main festival the meal would be an ordinary one of meat, rice, vegetables, and perhaps some little luxury such as they might occasionally have on a Sunday. In its most elaborate form Christmas dinner—or rather "lunch"—included a stuffed turkey or perhaps a sucking pig, followed by a Christmas pudding, the English plum pudding which in Afrikaans is simply *poeding*. Apart from visits to neighboring friends, the family celebration of Christmas ended with the meal.

In the towns a more elaborate pattern of Christmas celebrations began to develop. Even in the most sedate communities the church bell would be rung from midnight on the night before Christmas. Clusters of people went from house to house singing psalms and carols on Christmas Eve. Gradually more variety was introduced. Churches would erect Christmas trees, often decorated with fairy lights and hung with presents for the children. The German Christmas tree soon became an integral part of the festivities in South Africa, in schools, at functions, and in the home. Father Christmas joined the festivities, usually handing out the presents.

It seems likely that it was in the Western Province that the celebration of Christmas first became more elaborate than that of an ordinary Sunday. One can still see the relatively complex Christmas celebration on Boland farms. Early in the week a Christmas tree is provided for the Colored farm workers; on it is a present for each one.

On Christmas Eve the family and relatives of the owner dress their own Christmas tree for themselves and their friends. Then the presents are handed around. The Christmas meal has quality and substance. After an uncooked sucking pig is displayed, an apple or an orange in its mouth, for the comments of the diners, a sizzling turkey is whisked from the oven to the table. The pig then takes the place of the turkey in the oven, and local wine is served. After the main part of the meal is over, the Christmas pudding is carried on and cut at the head of the table.

It was not until the fourth century that the East began to celebrate the birth of Christ on December 25; the West followed this example a hundred years later. In respect of the development of culture and the change in customs, much has happened since that day became recognized as the day for rejoicing at the birth of Christ. South Africa shares with the Western world the same origin of her culture and customs. Beneath the familiar fabric of Christmas traditions as we know them today lie deep-rooted customs and conceptions, many of which go back far in the history of man.

SOUTHERN RHODESIA

Christmas in Matabeleland

STUART CLOETE

IT WAS FULL SUMMER. The grass was high, tall with the thunder rains. The cows sleek, contended with their calves at foot; the bulls and oxen somnolent with fat. In the gardens, the mealies stood like green maidens with long, tasseled hair, immobile in the breathless heat, while the women worked among them. Women with babies on their backs. Women with babies lying on breyed goatskins under the shade of trees. Women heavy with child, and young girls. Other women moved in long, black, shining lines to the river, with red earthen pots upon their heads.

In the kraals the men sat with their assegais beside them. The women worked. The men thought great thoughts of women and war. The blood spilled in winter was dry. The winter wounds were healed. When the summer was over and the harvest garnered, there would be war again; and women again—a by-product of war.

Little children herded the cattle and played. They threw small kerries at the birds they put up—the quail, the partridges, the pheasants, the guinea fowl that rose on whirring wings—and at the hares.

It was full summer. All Africa ran with milk and honey. The air was fragrant with hot blossom and the scent of wood fires and the smell of cooking meat.

In a hut rather larger than the others, and apart from them, Barnard, the Ivory Hunter, sat on a stool. He was figuring things out. He made it, as near as he could tell, Christmas. It must be about Christmas because it was so hot. The sun burned down out of an incandescent sky. "Hot, that's what it was. And Christmas; or it might be Christmas Eve."

At home they'd be eating turkey and plum pudding and mince pies. There'd be things in the pudding—money, half crowns, florins, sixpences, but no threepenny bits. Mother would never allow them. They were too small and might be swallowed. Carols . . . Presents, all tied up in parcels and marked with names: for John—that was his own name; for Katie, his sister; for James, his brother. Mother . . . Father. Funny, thinking like this. They'd all been dead for years. That was why he didn't like to pay any attention to Christmas. And he'd found it out only by accident. He'd been trying to work out the day that last lot of ivory should reach the coast. That was what had started him with the pencil and the paper and the calendar.

Christmas was not for men. It was for children.

Christ had been born on Christmas Day, in a manger, in Bethlehem. Yes, it came back when you thought about it. The whole thing. The story. His mother. Sunday School. The old church with ivy on it. The gravestones, some of them leaning sideways. That was at home, in England, Nottinghamshire. Hunting country. Men in pink. His father in pink. That was what?—nearly fifty years ago, and he was the last of them. He thought of the ivory again. A nice lot. Most of the tusks seventy pounds and over.

Not far away an old warrior sat.

"The old one licks his wounds," those who passed him said. And it was true. He sat in the sun outside his hut waiting for the shadows to lengthen, licking his wounds, thinking angrily of the past, staring at the distant horizon, and then looking down at his withered foot. Looking up; looking down with anger in his heart. He had come over that horizon. They all had come over it long ago. Young men, naked but for their assegais and shields, and the small ornaments on their legs that they wore for war.

Mosilikatze's Impis, soldiers of T'Chaka, Renegades from Zululand. There lay Zululand, where he stared over the horizon. Over the blue hills, the valleys, the rivers. Over it they had come. Young men leaping naked, beating their spears against their shields, hissing between their teeth. Warriors.

He looked at the huts of his kraal. Seven of them. The homes of his seven wives. Women taken in war but not one of them a Zulu. Old now, he pined for a Zulu maid. For the sound of his tongue spoken by a woman.

His children played in the dust. His bastards. Not Zulus. Half Zulus. The Matabele, that is what we are now, he thought. Matabele, who were once Zulus, the terror of the world. His bigger sons were soldiers in the army. His bigger girls married. The cattle the young men had paid for them grazed with his herd. But he was not content. He pined for the hills of his home, for his tongue spoken softly by a woman.

He pined for his lost strength, for the foot which had betrayed him. Up he looked at the horizon. There was Zululand many days away. Down he looked at his foot. And there would be war again. The messengers would go running from kraal to kraal with the bleeding tail in their hands to warn all men, to call them. He picked up his spear and rubbed its blade on a soft stone. The old one licked his wounds. *Aaie,* he licked his wounds, and he sharpened his spear. There would be war again. Lobengula, son of the black elephant Mosilikatze, would send out the messengers of war. The spears of the young men were thirsty for blood. They cried out. *Aaie,* the spears of his nation cried out. The spears of the old ones like himself who had been T'Chaka's men and Mosilikatze's cried out. Soon they would fight once more, with their bastard sons beside them. Zulus and half Zulus, old regiments and new.

It was hard to be crippled. To be called "the old one who licks his wounds." To be a lion lying in the long grass unable to come out. Able only to wait. Hard to be the father of the sons of captured women. To hear no soft Zulu voice. What had these women, these girls, to do with him? Young, one woman was as good as another. Old, it was not so. He spat on the blade of his spear and rubbed again. The lion does not only lick his wounds, he thought. He also sharpens his claws. One more fight. If only he could have one more fight.

In one of the huts a woman moaned.

The old one looked up when the white man came.

"I see you," he said.

"I see you," Barnard said. The old one was one of his friends.

"You are thinking, Old One," he said.

"*Aaie,* I am thinking. I am thinking of war and of my people and my sons that have not been born."

"You have many sons."

"I have many sons but they are not Zulus. They talk my tongue with lips of their mothers. I am old. I am sick. I pine for my home—for the green hills and rivers of my land."

"Today I too have thought of my land," Barnard said. "Because my heart was sore I came to speak to my friend."

A yellow dog with long ears moved out of the sunshine into the shade of the hut, scratched himself, and sat down.

"Behold the dog," the old one said. "He does what he wills. He is hot. He moves from one place to another as he wills. There is more freedom for a dog than a man." He pointed to his foot. "I am tied by the riem of disability. I can fight no more, travel no more."

A woman brought them beer in a pot. It was thick as porridge, gray-white, and strong. She was a young woman. A black deer of a woman. She whispered something to him.

He looked up at Barnard. "A child is born to me," he said. "A son. It is for this that I was waiting here. For the news of this birth."

A cock called to his hens, telling them of food he had found in the dust. A naked child crawled toward the cock.

"A child," Barnard said. "A boy. Have you a name for him?"

"I have no name. It is not seemly to name the unborn, nor to speak of the dead. Name him, White Man. Name him for the 'old one,' your friend."

"Call him Christmas," Barnard said. "That is the name of this day in my land over the great water."

"And what happened on this day that it is named?" the old one asked.

"On this day a child was born. A boy."

"Was he a warrior?"

"He was a great warrior. The greatest the world has ever

seen. Long ago he died, and still men fight with his name upon their lips."

"Tell me the tale."

Barnard sat down. The tale. How long was it since he had heard the story? Would it come back to him?

"A long time ago," he said, "there was a man and a woman. She was with child and they were pursued." Had Joseph been pursued?

"There was no place for them to go when they reached the great kraal to which they were traveling, and the woman gave birth among the cattle to a son. He was named Jesus. And the day of his birth was named Christmas Day. Word of his birth had gone forth and wise doctors came to see him. The king wished him killed."

"That was wise of the king."

"But he was not killed, nor was his father. His father was God."

"I have heard of God, though here we have him not. Here we have only Mosilikatze. And then what happened to the child?"

"He grew wise and strong. So great was he that he commanded all the peoples of the earth. He called and they came."

"Then that name will I give my son. The name of the day this great king was born. Christmas shall be his name."

They drank more beer.

At home they were having turkey and plum pudding and mince pies. There would be money in the pudding but no threepenny bits. At home there would be snow on the ground, and holly red with berries, and young men and girls kissing beneath the white drops of the hanging mistletoe.

It was full summer here; and a child had been born and named. Because of this he would never be able to forget Christmas Day again, for each day when it came the boy would have a birthday and there would be a feast with meat and beer. How little he remembered of the story, but it had been enough.

Christmas had come to stay in Africa. But he wished he

had remembered the story better. It was a finer tale than that. The finest in the world perhaps.

The naked baby had fallen asleep with his head on the back of the yellow dog. The cock and the hens had gone.

The women were bringing water back from the river. A shining string of tall black women with red pots upon their heads.

ASIA

ARMENIA

Christmas in Armenia

H. G. KINSCELLA

"How DID YOU CELEBRATE CHRISTMAS when you lived in Armenia?" asked Albert of his new schoolmate and friend, who had lived in far-off Armenia at one time.

It was the day before Christmas, and both boys had been having a very jolly time looking into the windows of the city's stores and guessing what they would receive for presents the next day.

"Christmas was quite different in our country," answered his friend. "We had no Christmas trees and no Santa Claus, but we lighted candles and set them, while burning, in the center of our table.

"Each child always had a present for each of his friends. Then when these had been exchanged, we would all go around to the homes of our aunts and uncles, or older friends, taking apples with us. Each of our older friends, when we wished them a Merry Christmas, would give us a present by sticking a small piece of money into the side of the apple we were carrying. We always had a very jolly time seeing who would get the most apples stuffed with the precious coins.

"Sometimes we collected presents from those who we knew wished to give us Christmas gifts in another way. We would climb upon the housetop and then lower a basket, tied to the end of a long rope, down the neighbor's chimney. The people in the house had already heard us climbing onto the house and were ready for us. They would fill the basket with candy and

24

other homemade gifts, and when we thought it was all ready for us, we would pull it up through the chimney again.

"Your Santa Claus is supposed to come down through the chimney. This was our way of playing Santa Claus to ourselves and to our friends."

CHINA

We Want to Stay Here for Christmas

GERTRUDE JENNESS RINDEN

IN THE WAITING ROOM of the foreign hospital, Shu-ying leaned as hard as she could against her mother's blue cotton shoulder—so hard that Mother would have moved over a little, but there was Shu-lan pressing his head just as hard on the other side.

Shu-ying, who was ten, sniffed the strong, clean smell of disinfectant. "Go home," she begged her mother. And her meaning was. "Let us all three go home this minute." Shu-ying kept her eyes on the big door through which more and more patients kept coming. If only her mother would take them out through that door! Or if only the foreign doctor would quickly hand her mother a paper of good medicine as a Chinese doctor would do, then they could hurry at once to their crowded little home where everything was cozy and familiar.

Shu-lan, who was six, looked wide-eyed at the white walls of the big room and at the many narrow benches full of strangers. "Go home," he whimpered.

But Mother folded her arms with determination. It had been

hard enough to decide to come to the foreign hospital. Now that she had the children here, she was not turning back.

Shu-ying and Shu-lan had the itch. They had had it for a long time. Now it was all over their bodies, and oh! so itchy that they could never be comfortable, not even for a minute, in the thick-padded garments that they must wear in the cold December weather of North China. Even while they waited, both children kept jumping down from the bench to twist and turn in their gray padded coats and their black quilted trousers.

"The money—is it ready?" asked Shu-ying.

"That, of course," said her mother, as she felt again for the pocket inside her blue cotton coat. "But remember, you must first let the doctor look at you. It is that way at hospitals."

"*Ai-yoh!*" wailed Shu-ying, clutching her mother's arm. Shu-lan crowded closer, and his eyes looked as frightened as those of the baby rabbit when his mother had stepped on its foot under the brick stove at home.

"But see," said Mother, trying to be cheerful, "see those others. They are not afraid." Shu-ying looked at the other people waiting. "Even that baby—"

Just in front of them was a round-faced baby on its mother's shoulder, peering at them out of its red satin hood. Any other time, Shu-ying would have reached out her hand and patted those fat cheeks. But today her hand was frozen with fear, like the rest of her.

"See! The mother is taking the baby in to the doctor now. Surely the foreign woman doctor must be kind if such a baby comes. It will be our turn next."

Before they knew it, it was their turn to go into the doctor's office. A Chinese girl, with a white cap on her black hair, was smiling and inviting them in. Why should anyone smile so much at such a dreadful time as this? thought Shu-ying, as she reluctantly followed her mother.

Shu-ying and Shu-lan had never seen a foreign woman, but they had heard a great deal about how all foreigners looked. Tien-min, a boy who lived in their court, had told them. "They have yellow hair like corn husks, and round eyes that are blue instead of black, and worst of all, long, long noses that stick way out in front of them." Truly Shu-ying and Shu-lan had expected to see something as frightful as the paper faces on the idols that were paraded in the streets on feast days. They stared at the doctor and decided that while this woman was strange, she was not so grotesque as an idol. Her hair was brown, so that it looked as though it might once have been a good black color like all people's, but now it had faded. Her eyes were round like marbles, as Tien-min had said, instead of long, like ordinary eyes, but they were brown. And her nose—yes, it was long and thin.

But there was no time to think about these things, for out of the woman's mouth were coming Chinese words. It couldn't be true, and yet it was true.

"How old are you?" she was saying to Shu-ying.

"Ten years old," answered Shu-ying, still keeping safely behind her mother.

"This little girl is also ten," said the doctor, taking a picture from her desk. "It is my niece in America." Shu-ying looked and looked. She liked the face of the little girl, but the hair— why had the mother not combed it neatly and braided it before taking the picture? It was all fluffy around the face. Every which way, thought Shu-ying, and for the barest minute she forgot herself while she pitied that child whose mother let her have a picture taken without having combed her hair.

Shu-ying did not know it, but while she was looking at the picture the American doctor was looking at the itch. Now she was saying something that was too terrible to believe.

"There is just one thing to do," said the doctor. "When the itch is as bad as this, we say that children must stay here in the hospital for two days and two nights, covered with a kind of medicine. That is the time required to cure this itch."

If the doctor had sat there and said, "Now a tiger is coming through the door," Shu-ying and Shu-lan could not have cried out any louder. Shu-lan began to shout and kick and bang his head against his mother in a tantrum of fear.

"Would you like to see the nice place the children stay all together in the hospital?" asked the doctor. At this, both children set up a tremendous wail, meaning that they certainly would not. They did not want to see anything in the hospital, and only because their mother followed the doctor and they were clinging to her did they drag along.

The truth was that Mother felt like crying just as loud as Shu-ying and Shu-lan, but being a mother she could not open her mouth and let the crying come out that way. She had to keep it all inside and act as though the hospital were just the nicest place in the world. "Hush," she said. "Do not frighten the other children." For now they had come through a door and were standing inside a long room full of white beds in a row. On those beds were boys and girls, every one with black hair and black eyes just like Shu-ying and Shu-lan. Such a sight! Even in all their fear, these two could not shout aloud any more but had to sniff and snuff and try to swallow and gulp the great lumps of crying back inside them. Moving among the beds were three big girls, called nurses, with white caps on their black hair.

As the doctor hurried away, one of these nurses came nearer. "I wonder who would like to sleep here tonight?" she said, pointing to the two narrow empty beds nearest the door. Of course, she meant Shu-ying and Shu-lan. Both of them began to cry out loud again. But Shu-ying was truly ashamed to cry, for in the very next bed to the empty one was a girl who had to lie very still with her leg bound to a long board that was held slanting upward by some ropes and straps. Her face was covered with smiles. In her hands, though she was lying flat on her back, were red paper and scissors, only now she wasn't cutting, just looking all smiles at Shu-ying and Shu-lan. Shu-ying could not take her eyes off that girl's strapped-up leg and her happy face.

"When you have medicine on your body, you may talk with that girl," said the nurse. "Come, let us give you a bath and put the medicine on quickly." Mother stayed with the children while they had a hot soapy bath and oh! such a thorough scrubbing.

"This itch is caused by tiny parasites that bore under the skin," said the nurse as she scrubbed. "They like dirty skin, and they do not like clean skin, nor good medicine. This is the medicine the itch does not like."

The nurse set a brown jar of yellow salve on the stool beside them. "Now you must help me," she said, and she gave each one a flat bamboo stick with which to take the thick salve from the jar. "With this we must cover you all over. And the more you rub it in, the quicker you can go home. It is of first importance," said the nurse, "that again and again we cover you with this salve." So she began to rub it on them. Shu-ying began to rub it on her stomach, and Mother rubbed it on her back, where she couldn't reach. Even Shu-lan took a stickful into his fat hands and began to squash it through his fingers until he almost laughed.

When the children were covered with salve and dressed in funny old cotton pajamas, the nurse took them back to the children's ward. The jar of salve went too and was set on a stool between their beds. There were lights everywhere now, and Mother knew that it was dark outside and that she must go quickly. When she had gone, Shu-lan cried louder than ever. Shu-ying wanted to cry too, but she could not because of all those other children. So she just turned her back and sobbed. Through her tears she could see the swinging door and the nurses coming and going. She wondered if she and Small Brother could slip through that door. Could she find her way along the strange halls and passages to the big gate? And once out in the dark, could she find her way across the town to their home?

"Do you want to cut some red paper? You may use my scissors." It was the girl in the next bed talking to them. Shu-ying turned to see. "It's for Christmas."

Hospital—doctor—nurse—bath—salve—and now Christmas! So many strange new words in one day! Shu-ying just stared.

"Don't cry, don't cry, Small Brother. After rice there will be the Christmas story," said the girl who couldn't move. "But take my scissors and cut some strips."

Shu-lan could not resist the shiny little scissors and the red paper, so he reached up for them and tried to cut the strips.

Only every strip he cut stuck to a different sticky finger until it was so funny that the girl in the bed chuckled and Shu-ying began to giggle.

"Never mind, then. I will make a Christmas chain to decorate your bed. And you can hear the story, even if you are sticky," said the girl.

"The story?" asked Shu-ying, because she wanted to talk to this girl.

"Yes, the Christmas story in the Bible. It's that big book over there on the table between the candles. Can you read?"

"Certainly not," said Shu-ying, shaking her head.

"Never mind. The nurse tells us the story," said the girl.

Now the nurses began to bring the evening rice. The rice was warm and white and fluffy. The nurses were friendly, like big sisters. The room was light and warm. The children in the beds were smiling or chatting gaily. Shu-ying could see that everything was all right. If only that big lump of fear inside her would go away and let her believe that she and Small Brother were safe.

As soon as the rice bowls were taken away, one of the nurses lighted the tall red candles on either side of the Book. Everyone in all the beds watched and waited. Then standing beside the Book and the candles, the nurse told a story. Oh! it was a wonderful story. It was about a Baby and about angels, and about shepherds and lambs who went to see the Baby. And about Wise Men who rode on camels to carry gifts to the Baby. When the story was over, Shu-ying had forgotten all about her fears, and when she looked at Shu-lan, she saw him solemn and wide-eyed but happy.

The next day there was talk of Christmas from every bed. Shu-ying learned that among the Christians it was a great festival, as great as New Year's.

"In two days it will be Christmas. In two days it will be Chrismas," every child was saying. And each one made something to decorate his bed—a star that the story told about, or a red chain for happiness. Some cut out red pagodas to paste on the windows. In the afternoon, Shu-ying and Shu-lan edged over near the Bible. They just wanted to see the Book from

which the story came. They held their sticky hands behind
them as they tiptoed up and looked at the Book between the
candles.

"You will hear the story again tonight," said the girl who
had to lie so still. And that was true. After supper the pretty
nurse lighted the candles and told the story again. This time
Shu-ying and Shu-lan enjoyed it more than the first time.

Early the next morning, the morning of the day when Shu-
ying and Shu-lan could go home, the nurse who told the
Christmas story came in to take care of the children. She was
going from bed to bed, putting the shiny thermometer into the
mouth of one child after another. Suddenly she noticed Shu-
ying and Shu-lan standing close together between their beds,
with their backs turned. She looked more carefully.

"What under all of heaven!" she exclaimed aloud, for she
could not believe what her eyes saw. Both children were using
the sharp edges of their flat bamboo sticks to scrape the salve
from their bodies. The nurse rushed over.

"What are you doing?" she asked impatiently.

That was a silly question because she could see plainly that
the salve was all off one of Shu-ying's arms and partly off the
other. And Shu-lan was scraping his salve off just as fast as
he could.

"Didn't I tell you it is of first importance to keep covered
with the salve? Here you are almost cured. If you scrape away
the salve, the itch will come back again."

Shu-ying spoke for them both. Slowly but firmly she said it.
"We don't want to be cured."

"Don't want to be cured!" The nurse almost dropped her
thermometer and her alcohol bottle.

"Don't want to be cured," repeated Shu-lan, his big, solemn
eyes looking straight into the eyes of the story nurse.

"Don't want to be cured!" exclaimed the nurse. "But this is
the day you go home."

"But we don't want to go home," said Shu-ying. "We want
to stay here for Christmas."

Then the story nurse laughed so hard that she had to sit
down on Shu-ying's bed, and while she laughed, both children

looked at her, wide-eyed and wondering. She wanted to lean over and hug them both, and would have, had it not been for her spotless white uniform and their sticky little bodies. She just couldn't wait to tell the doctor, so she went hurrying through the halls and soon came back with the happy news. "You may stay for Christmas. Only put the salve back on, and tomorrow you will have baths and put on your own clean clothes. We will send a message to your mother, and you will stay right here for Christmas."

The Christmas Lantern

CORNELIA SPENCER

"WHAT ARE YOU MAKING?" the American boy asked. He was watching the slender yellow fingers of a Chinese man as they carefully slit a length of bamboo into fine, supple strips.

"A lantern," Mr. Fu answered, smiling as he glanced up.

"How can you make the pieces so thin and even?" Edward asked again. "It must be very hard to do, yet it seems easy to you."

"My father made lanterns before me, and his father, also," the Chinese man replied. "Our family has always made lanterns. You know the shop down where the street branches to the east? That is the Fu Lantern Shop."

"Yes, but you are not making this one in the shop. You are making it here in the church courtyard. Why is that?"

"I wanted to see the place where it was to hang. Besides, this one will not be for sale."

"You mean you will not get any money for it?"

"No, because, you see, it is to be a Christmas lantern."

"A Christmas lantern? A Christmas present, you mean?"

"Yes, a present to the Pagoda Street Church. This is my

church, and I want to make a present."

"That's very nice," the boy murmured. He did not say any more. He was watching as Mr. Fu bent the strips and tied them firmly and neatly with fine cord. The shape was beginning, and he wondered what it would be. Perhaps a Christmas star or a Christmas tree. It did not seem to look like either. He sat down on one of the stone church steps and waited.

One part was finished. It was a cylinder about a foot and a half high. Now Mr. Fu was carefully shaping a roof for it. It had six pointed eaves. How could anyone's fingers move so easily and neatly! Edward was full of envy. "It is like one of the roofs of the pagoda," he said softly. "But I can't think how pagodas are connected with Christmas." A frown wrinkled his brow and yet he did not want to seem impolite.

"I have to make it the way that it seems beautiful to me," Mr. Fu said quietly. "I have made this kind many times before, only with different figures inside. But you must wait—until the candle is lighted." He paused and then added, as if to explain what he had first said: "You see, our most beautiful roofs have points, so this roof must have points. Christmas in China must be celebrated in a Chinese way. Isn't that as it should be?" He stood up from his crouching position and stretched himself a moment. The tails of his long gown were tucked up under his sash to be out of the way and his sleeves were rolled high on his wrists. He was neither a working man who would have worn a jacket rather than a gown, nor a gentleman who would have worn no sash and certainly not have tucked his tails under it.

"Of course, we Americans always try to make things about Christmas look like we think they did in Jesus' country," Edward said, still confused and yet not wanting to say much about it.

"You mean with the Christmas trees and the Old Christmas Father?" Mr. Fu asked and now he looked straight at Edward, puzzled too, before he stooped to his work again.

"Oh no, of course I don't mean the tree or Santa Claus," the boy answered. "I don't think they had those when Jesus was born in his country. I guess those are just ways of celebrating that have been added by different people." He felt a little silly because of what he had said.

"Well then, we shall have to add some Chinese ways of celebrating," Mr. Fu said with a touch of emphasis. "That is right, isn't it? Jesus lived for everyone, so we should all celebrate his birthday after our own ideas. . . . Now watch. I will make the bottom part into which this that I have done will fit. It will be like a balcony at the base of the whole thing, with points to match those of the roof."

Soon the frame was all finished. It was only a skeleton, but its shape was clear—a six-sided cylinder with a pointed roof, fitted down into a base which repeated the points. It didn't look Christmasy to Edward, but he could not help thinking it was terribly clever.

"I will do the rest in the shop," Mr. Fu said, "and you will not see it until the Christmas Eve program. Then you must look carefully because you will see something strange." He gathered up his small sharp knife and the lantern frame, gave a short bow, and went out of the great gate of the garden where Edward's house and the church stood.

All the day before Christmas, Edward watched the decorating in the church. He liked the cedar rope that swung across the building, and the great gilt characters embedded in masses of white cotton, for snow, which were hung against the walls. He studied them. That one was for *love* and that one for *believing* and that one for *kindness.* His father had taught him those. And those four words there, above the stage, meant *Jesus' Birthday.*

Here came Mr. Fu. He was carrying the lantern. Only the shape was recognizable, for now it was beautifully covered with fine transparent paper in several shades. Edward ran quickly to him. "Please let me see it," he said excitedly. The Chinese man held it down for him to see. "There's something down inside now," the boy said. "Look, it moves just from your carrying the lantern! And there are figures of people fastened to it in a circle!"

Mr. Fu lifted the lantern suddenly high. "You are not to see more now," he said. "You must wait until it is lighted for the celebration tonight. Then you can look all you like."

"Where does the candle go?" Edward asked. He would have liked very much to have had one more good look at the inside. "On that point down in the very center?"

"Yes, on the pin in the center. . . . Can you wait until to-night?"

"Of course, but I am going to get one of these seats right here where I can see what happens. Sometimes there is such a crowd—I'll come early." He thought of last Christmas. So many poor children had come. They had crowded forward. He had been with his playmates Li San and Wen Do. They had gotten cross because they were pushed about so much. He himself had given one boy in a dirty jacket a hard shove, and the boy had turned and looked at him. He still remem-- bered that look. The memory made him uncomfortable even yet. The boy hadn't said anything. He had just moved a short distance away and then tried again to see the Christmas play that was going on on the stage.

"There will be a crowd again tonight," Mr. Fu said, gazing up at the place where the lantern was to hang in the exact center of the large hall. "Everyone like fun, and a lot of these children don't have much of it. Then they have heard that the Lord Jesus liked children. You can't blame them for crowding in."

"No, of course not—not blame them," Edward said quickly. That boy's face came back. The eyes had seemed to accuse him. "I wish everyone could have a nicer Christmas," he added slowly.

"It will be nice tonight," Mr. Fu said cheerfully. "There's a program with a play, and music, and a speech—and look at the decorations!" His free hand swept the room to point out everything.

"Yes, but we Americans will have presents," Edward said. "I'm going to get a bicycle." For a moment he felt ashamed of it, and yet it was better to tell Mr. Fu.

"But a toy one," the man put in, not expecting an answer.

"No, a real one," Edward said under his breath. "Of course, Li San and Wen Do will ride it too—but most of the boys can't. How can everyone ride it?"

As if he had not heard, Mr. Fu went on. "We give our presents at New Year's. We give new shoes and hats and caps and packages of dainties, and everyone visits everyone. It is very lively. Now I must get the stepladder and hang this up." He went quickly away.

Edward and Li San and Wen Do were there early that night but not as early as many other children. Mr. Fu was on the stepladder just lighting the candle in the lantern. Edward flew to him. "You are lighting it!" he said breathlessly. He waited. Mr. Fu put a match to the red candle in the center of the lantern, pushed the part that locked it in place, and then stepped down. He stood below waiting for the flame to grow to its full size. His face was satisfied.

The children crowded around him and watched too. Now they could see the figures—people on camels, men in long robes, men with flocks of sheep. From the other side of the watching circle someone shouted, "On this side there is a star above a house!" From beside Edward, Li San said, "The ones with the robes are the Wise Men—and the ones with the sheep are the shepherds!"

Mr. Fu stepped back among the children. Some grown people had joined them.

"They're moving!" Edward said suddenly. "Look! They're going slowly around and around in the central part of the lantern."

"The heat of the candle makes them move," Mr. Fu said.

"They're going toward the star," a girl said in a high, clear voice.

"They're looking for the baby Jesus," a shabbily dressed boy announced. His eyes were fixed on the lantern and its light showed that his face was dirty and that his hair needed cutting.

"Of course! That's it," Edward said at once, looking across at the boy. "They are all going to the place where Jesus was just born. It's neat!" He looked back at the moving silhouettes. That boy's face—where—of course! It was the boy whom he had pushed away last year. He dropped his eyes from the lantern again to look at the boy and found the Chinese boy gazing at him. "You were smart to know so quickly what the lantern meant," Edward said. The boy grinned back at him. "On my side I could see the star before the moving began. That told me," he said and brushed back his hair and straightened down his soiled jacket, embarrassed.

"Where's Mr. Fu gone?" someone said.

"I'm here," the man answered. The crowd was gathering and people began to pour into the building for the program. Mr. Fu had been lost for a moment. Now the children rushed up to him. "It's beautiful—and clever—it has meaning." All kinds of praise came from them.

"There's only one trouble with it," a boy's voice said. "The seekers never reach the place where the star is." Edward turned to look. It was that boy again.

"You musn't say that," Mr. Fu said at once. "Not even a master lantern maker can do everything in a lantern. To make the figures step out of their places would be impossible." He sounded a bit cross, then his voice cleared and he added more gently: "Just remember, they are going in the right direction. They are following the star. Now if they turned back, you could truly complain." He smiled his sudden smile and went quickly away.

The seats were filling and the boys took some nearest the lantern. Edward leaned over to Li San and said softly, "What's the name of that boy who guessed the meaning?"

"I think they call him 'Tatters.'"

"We can't have him called that, you know," Edward said seriously. "We'll have to find out about him—and—and see if he needs our help."

"Yes, yes, of course." Li San nodded vigorously and whispered the message to Wen Do.

INDIA

A Universal Christmas in India

CHRISTMAS is truly universal, for Jesus Christ came to seek and to save all who believe. So, with relatives in America and Oman and friends throughout the world, we as a family joined the heavenly host singing and praising "Glory to God in the highest, and on earth peace among men with whom he is pleased."

Christmas was universal, or at least international, for us in another respect. Our tree came from Germany, the ornaments from America, the lights from Japan, the stand from India, cards from Japan, Germany, England, Ceylon, Iraq, Pakistan, the Persian Gulf, India, and America, presents from countries already mentioned, a wooden crèche from Italy, another from Jerusalem, a book from Greece, and even caviar from Russia.

We express our appreciation to friends and supporting churches whose innumerable greetings and gifts gladdened us at this season. We pray that you support the total program of the church as loyally as you remember us. May God bless richly our joint efforts in the work of his Kingdom, as individuals and as families.

Christmas was quieter than we would have wished. We missed the snow and evergreens of the Midwest, the white church spires of Colonia, N. J., the festive air and magical store-front decorations of the big city. Instead we had warm, sunny skies and flaming poinsettia trees. But most of all we missed friends and family and the church life so vital a part of Christmas. Here we are not only separated from home, but also from the church we came to serve, as we are in Mysore rather than the Rayalaseema Diocese of the CSI, to which we are assigned, and the local church leaders do not use us to best advantage.

We heard little of the familiar Christmas carols except in church and from our phonograph. However, we were serenaded by different local Indian church groups, singing in Tamil and Telegu. The largest group had forty children, brightly dressed and accompanied by pastor, teachers, and *bajana,* or orchestra of drums, cymbals, and harmonium. The children performed group dances and sang Indian lyrics, using gaily colored sticks and tambourines.

We were surprised to learn that because of the English influence, people of all religions observe Christmas as a time of greeting, of buying new clothes and exchanging gifts, as well as a time when the postmen, milkmen, municipal peons, sweepers, and others expect *baksheesh.* We gave Kamala, the *ayah,* a week with her relatives, but our cook, Sam, a Hindu, greeted us Christmas morning in his surf-white new waiter's jacket, with brass buttons, a warm smile, garlands of jasmine and marigolds, and that special token, a lemon (not an April Fool's joke out of season), a symbol here of high esteem, bearing wishes for long life and prosperity, as he carefully explained to us.

Both boys were up early for the big day. Kenny got a head start, with Bobby the Menace right behind in his walker, and exclaimed, "Oh ho, Santa," "Myst Tree," "Beeeg Bear," "*Bike*!" It took him little time to undo all his parents' efforts wrapping and tying gifts Christmas Eve. Grandparents are grandparents, whether with us or far away, for their surprises were abundant. The biggest surprise, however, is yet to come —"Blacky," a Labrador Retriever, still too young to leave his mother.

IRAQ

A Bonfire in the Courtyard and in the Church

MOST OF THE PEOPLE of Iraq are Mohammedans, but there are a significant number of Christians. In the Christian homes, Christmas is observed with religious significance.

There is an unusual ceremony held in the courtyard of the home on Christmas Eve. One of the children in the family reads the story of the Nativity from an Arabic Bible. The other members of the family hold lighted candles, and as soon as the story has been read a bonfire is lighted in one corner of the courtyard. The fire is made of dried thorns and the future of the house for the coming year depends upon the way the fire burns. If the thorns burn to ashes, the family will have good fortune. While the fire is burning, a psalm is sung. When the fire is reduced to ashes, everyone jumps over the ashes three times and makes a wish.

On Christmas Day a similar bonfire of thorns is built in the church. While the fire burns the men of the congregation chant a hymn. Then there is a procession in which the officials of the church march behind the bishop, who carries an image of the infant Jesus upon a scarlet cushion. The long Christmas service always ends with the blessing of the people. The bishop reaches forth and touches a member of the congregation with his hand, putting his blessing upon him. That person touches the one next to him, and so on, until all have received "the Touch of Peace."

At Home and in the Hospital in Iraq

THE FIRST SIGN that Christmas is approaching in Iraq comes in August when the mission family get out the Montgomery Ward catalog and scan the pages for the gifts they must order early so that they will arrive by Christmas. Two weeks before the Advent season, the manger scene is placed in the mission living room to depict vividly to all visitors the Christmas story. Christmas in Arabia is like any other day to the neighbors who hear the prayer call five times a day on that day too. There are no decorations in the bazaar and no Christmas spirit even for one day. Christmas is not kept by the Moslems. For the missionaries and the Christian community, however, it is a full and wonderful season, for the activities last several days. For many years in Muscat it has been the custom to visit the homes of all the employees of the mission and sit and talk with each family.

Carols are sung and the Christmas story is read to them. This may be the first time the wife in the family has ever heard the Word of God read, for some of the women are not allowed to visit the women's meetings. As the day wears on and twilight covers Muscat, some Arab friend will lead the way with his kerosene lantern. It lights the way for those who take to them the Light of Lights.

Christmas Day begins at dawn in the mission home, when the children awaken to the filled stockings and are tempted to peek into the Christmas tree room. Early breakfast is served, and after the story is read from the Gospel of Luke as a family, the gifts from home and each other are opened. The neighbors then begin coming in. Christians greet each other with a kiss and handshake, a real bond of love. At nine o'clock everyone goes to church in Muscat, which is three miles from the mission home in Matrah. At this service the school children sing carols and recite the gospel message. The two oldest classes recite the prophecies of Christ from the Old Testament and their fulfillment as given in the New Testament. This is an outstanding presentation.

In 1958, the custom which promises to become a tradition began, that of all the Arab Christians visiting each other, thus making a stronger bond in the national church. They sing carols and pray together. After the church service, the missionaries go to one of the mission homes for Christmas dinner and exchange gifts. Throughout the meal, people from the village—merchants, the governor, and others—stop to wish the missionaries a happy holiday and to share a cup of coffee and candy. Later a service is held in the hospital for the patients and their families. All patients who can walk or be moved are brought to the open ward in the upstairs of the hospital. At dusk the annual Christmas supper is held in the home of the minister for the members of the Church of Christ in Muscat. Shoes are left at the door in true Arab fashion. There is a fully trimmed tree (courtesy of Montgomery Ward), a lovely fire in the fireplace, and the Christmas story in flannelgraph on the mantlepiece. A supper is served on trays—sandwiches, tea and cookies and gingerbread men for all the children. Hymns and friendly chatter follow. As the name of each child is called, he excitedly comes to the tree for his gift. The adults have drawn a name of someone in the group, and progressing around the circle, each one must present it in a humorous way. Laughter and warmth abound; brothers and sisters are happy together because Christ has come for all. Christmas in Muscat is a wonderful time of the year.

JAPAN

"Meri Kurisumasu"

CAN YOU IMAGINE December without Christmas? No lighted tree? No gifts hidden away in closets?

You can't imagine such a thing, you who have lived all your lives in a Christian country. But in Japan, schools, banks, and offices are open as usual. Christmas is nothing more than December 25!

Of course, there are plenty of Santa Clauses prominently displayed in the big department stores. Tinsel and lights abound in dance halls, cafés, and pinball parlors, where gay young moderns celebrate Christmas in a manner far from religious.

But among the Japanese Christians, what does Christmas mean? First, it is not a family day, as it is with us, for in Japan there are few families in which every member is a Christian. Next, there is no turkey or plum pudding. Rather, Christmas in Japan is the day in which all Christians try to do something for others, especially for the sick in the hospitals.

Although most of the hospitals in Japan are unattractive and unheated, without suitable rooms for holding meetings, Christian young people decorate whatever space is allowed with a small tree and a "back" (a piece of black cloth upon which are fastened stars, shepherds, and Wise Men cut from cardboard).

The very best students from the Sunday school are chosen to sing Christmas carols for the patients, to recite Bible passages, and put on a short drama or Bible pantomime. And then, of course, there is always a treat of cakes or candies for the Bible class patients; and Christmas tracts for everyone in the hospital—from the superintendent and head surgeon down to the lowliest scrub woman.

Christmas is the happiest day of the year for Sunday school children all over Japan. On Christmas Eve or Christmas night, they give an elaborate program, hours long, on which they have worked for weeks. When they sing, they make the rafters ring! When they recite, everyone can hear them. Eyes shining and cheeks rosy with excitement, they can hardly wait for their turn to perform.

And the dramas! They are so realistic that you can easily imagine yourself back on the plains of Bethlehem two thousand years ago. What if the shepherd's garment is an old blanket, and the angels are wearing white dress shirts from the missionary barrel?

Best of all, at the end of the program come Sunday school

pins for perfect attendance, and simple gifts for the ones who have not missed too many Sundays. There is never enough money for gifts for everyone, but usually each child takes home an orange or a small box of caramels.

Christmas for a missionary in Japan is a wonderful time, lasting generally for a month or more. Here in Gifu we start preparing in November with groups at our home weekly, cutting the pictures from old Christmas cards and pasting them carefully on the front of our printed Christmas tract.

One week the neighborhood women meet here, scissors and tongues equally busy. How they exclaim over the beautiful cards from America! Although most of these women are not yet Christians themselves, they work on this project as if their lives depended on it.

For all of the Bible classes we had candlelight services. Try to picture forty-five earnest young university students holding lighted candles and singing "Joy to the World." Remember that most of these are boys and girls who have never before heard of Bethlehem—or the star—or the Wise Men. Remember that these are the leaders of the Japan-to-be. Remember that unless they realize what Christmas really means, they will never know true joy!

Christmas for Christians in Japan means Christ coming again into their hearts with new power. It means Christ coming for the first time into hearts that have never known him before. Thus it is truly a *Meri Kurisumasu*!

Missionaries' Reports and Letters

Our House on Christmas Day

We wish you could have been at our house on Christmas Day. The simulated stained-glass window, of pressed board and multicolored cellophane, was nailed in place, and the plump little cedar tree sparkled in unaccustomed splendor. Its lower boughs were tinted by the blues, reds, and purples of the stained-glass manger scene. All the flower vases with their gay red berries and white lilies were up high out of reach and all the furniture had been removed into other parts of the house. Two large baskets of oranges were hidden on the back porch, and many bags of candy and cookies were well out of sight. The gift of cookies and candies was a project of Friendship Home Hostel.

Joe had driven over to Friendship Home, our oldest student hostel, and brought the four teachers over for Sunday school (four of the hostel boys, as busy as they are, have organized this Sunday school because they felt that they should do something to demonstrate to God their thankfulness for the privilege of living in a Christian hostel).

The boys had been caroling all night long, so they were quite tired. At three P.M. our gate started bulging and the children started shouting: "Is it time? Is it time yet?"

If three of us hadn't been at the gates when they were opened, perhaps two tiny children would have been trampled to death. Such a stampede and then exclamations of delight as they scampered across the yard and burst into the living room.

The afternoon sun streaming through the cellophane window and falling in a colorful crazy-quilt pattern on the brightly lighted tree was a feast for the black eyes of 153 children as they squeezed together trying to get closer to the front of the room. There were many more children than we had estimated. Yes! 40 new ones.

They sang "Silent Night" in anything but a silent manner, said Bible verses, displayed their notebooks (some were beautifully kept with a Bible verse under each Bible picture, some were *very* poor), sang songs, told stories, played games, and received prizes for attendance, good work, and talent. They received the Christmas story as they pointed to Mary and the baby Jesus, the shepherd and the sheep pictured in the bright window.

Then the new children were told to stand. Each was given an orange and a Christmas tract with a pretty Christmas card pasted on the front to take home. Your old Christmas cards brought delight to many.

After these children were dismissed, the others received candy, cookies, oranges, and a tract.

How empty the house felt after the sounds of their wooden clogs and chirping voices died away!

We want to ask you to pray for these four shining Christian witnesses who, though burdened with university work, give their time to Christ so that these 153 children can learn of a dear Savior who came to save them all. Wilbur is studying mechanical engineering at Taiwan University—he is a senior. Julius is a senior, studying plant pathology. Bryan is a sophomore in the medical department, and Peter is studying chemistry.

Thank you for your lovely Christmas cards, prayers, and letters. May God be gracious to you all. We are enclosing a prayer calendar to remind you of the work over here throughout 1961. Happy, happy New Year!

Sincerely,
Beth and Joe Farlow

Presbyterian Church U.S.
January 13, 1961

A Pre-Christmas Glimpse

I hope our little angels over at school, who are singing "Gloria in excelsis deo" in our Christmas pageant, won't get the giggles as badly as they're doing for rehearsals! But girls do giggle at the age of fourteen or so, and I suppose always will. Zechariah is extremely dignified in the Temple scene, and so is Joseph at the manger. In spite of all I used to say about the innate dramatic ability of the Japanese, I don't believe, after all, that they have it universally any more than we do. In other words, they're just like us! But they are, this generation of Japanese girls, wonderfully ingenious and creative,

I think, and most of them take responsibility very well. After years in a little school where I was the only one to put on a pageant at Christmas, it is wonderful to be in a larger school and find both staff and students eager to help—whether it's making something do in place of a seven-branched candelabra, or finding something for incense that won't remind us too forcibly of similar Buddhist rites, or making artificial lilies, or getting your husband (this is one of the staff) to translate "We Three Kings."

The Commercialization of Christmas

Japan has taken over completely the commercial observation of Christmas. All department stores and even some of the smaller shops are elaborately decorated; newspapers are full of advertisements urging early shopping; carols are broadcast over loud-speakers even on the streets; the crowds of shoppers are tremendous, for they have combined the newer idea of Christmas gifts with the time-honored New Year's celebration.

While I suppose we should rejoice that this nation with less than 500,000 Christians in a population of 85,000,000 is so aware of the day on which we remember the birth of the Child in a Bethlehem stable, yet it saddened me to hear the sweet old carols blared forth as a background for the indifferent confusion of the packed streets and stores.

In a way, the celebration of Christmas and New Year's is just opposite from our American way: here New Year's is celebrated at home, and Christmas is for parties and outside-the-home gaiety. This is partly because the real meaning of Christmas is only vaguely known. There has grown recently some sharp criticism of Christmas celebration, not from the foreigners in Japan or even from the Japanese Christians. But some of the non-Christian Japanese, in the press and letters to the editors, have voiced their uneasiness that a religious holiday, even of a "foreign" religion, should be occasion for only revelry, with no thought of the underlying meanings.

How Missionaries Contribute to
the Christmas Celebration

During the Christmas season, for two weeks our living room was in daily use as we entertained the English teachers, the seminary girls, faculty wives, and Bible classes—one of which trimmed our Christmas tree—the seminary senior class, the neighborhood children, then the seminary students who could not go home because of distance and were lonesome. There were many Christmas celebrations, such as the beautiful pageant and the candlelight service; also festivities in the churches. Carolers came one evening at eleven, another group at midnight, a third around three in the morning, and a fourth at dawn! Each time, we jumped out of bed and, in overcoats, shivered with candle in hand until they greeted us with a "Merry Christmas!" before departing for their next place.

Making Christmas Meaningful to Japanese Girls

I have spent two days of this week answering the Christmas letters received from students, both graduates and those still in school. One wrote, "I never understood what Christmas meant until this year, but this year I was filled with happiness." Another said: "I had been influenced by the Christmas activities of sending greetings and gifts, but I had not understood the spiritual meaning. I have longed for some security. During my two years in college, I have learned faith in God— the chapel talks will always remain in my mind and heart and be my spiritual food in future days." Others wrote of the inspiration received from caroling or from the Christmas play. One first-year girl wrote: "All was calm. On my way home I thought, On such a night Jesus was born! I walked on home, humming 'Holy Night.' I shall never forget that night." One of my former students now studying in America wrote, "At Christmas time I always remember the pageants and plays which you helped us put on." Still another, a new girl this year from a non-Christian background, wrote in appreciation of the message of this year's Christmas play put on by the religious drama class and added that she was praying that she would not forget it.

Christmas Means Singing

The following is a Christmas address by the Rev. Kenneth C. Hendricks, which was broadcast in the Japanese language by shortwave on Christmas Day, 1958, throughout Japan and neighboring areas. This is the only published English translation. Mr. Hendricks is a missionary of the Disciples of Christ.

Late in a chilly December in an early postwar year, I was lying abed with influenza and in a somewhat depressed state of mind, I must confess. There was little in the prevailing situation to buoy up one's spirits.

The people of this land were ill fed and ill clad, and lacking in the common necessities of self-respecting daily living. There was no heat for the classrooms of our school, nor enough glass for the windows. The scarcity of books, paper, ink, pencils, chalk, and even water to clean the premises, was pitiful.

It was almost unbelievable that teachers and students could keep going against such odds.

But one evening the entire tone of things was suddenly transformed for me by what happened outside my sickroom window. Eager young voices of a caroling troupe of our students, proceeding through the campus on their way around the community, were lifting the old heart-warming strains of familiar Christmas hymns.

Glancing out, I could see, by the flickering candlelight thrown upon their sheets of music, the contrast between their enraptured faces and their shabby garments. "It came upon the midnight clear. That glorious song of old . . . ," they sang. And I am sure that the angel voices from the skies over Bethlehem's shepherd fields had no greater power to charm the hearers.

Christmas means singing. Christmas without song is unthinkable. And there is something of magical power in the old well-loved Christmas carols and hymns to cheer the sorrowing, give hope to the despairing, humble the proud, reconcile the quarrelsome, and bring out the finer qualities of human nature that may be hidden beneath the petty materials of everyday life.

Some years ago, on a railway station platform here in Japan, several young Occidentals were behaving in a boisterous manner, doing things that at home, in their own familiar environment, they might have been ashamed to do. An elderly Japanese woman, of a thoughtful, motherly type, watched the young men, thinking of this fact and mentally putting herself in place of their mothers.

Suddenly an inspiration came to her, one that took rare courage for a woman in such a public place, and in the presence of entire strangers. Yet she dared to try the plan. Stepping up to the rollicking young fellows, she managed, out of her limited supply of English, to say, "Boys, let's sing!" Then, as they glanced at the earnest, friendly face of the aged woman, they were startled to hear a well-known tune that aroused sleeping memories, as she began, in her own tongue, the universally loved hymn, "Silent night, holy night. All is calm, all is bright. . . ." After an embarrassed pause, first one, then the others, took up the song with her, and presently the bystanders also, waiting for their train, came under the strange spell both of the incident itself and of the charming music.

This Christmas Day, in every land, in a thousand tongues, that song and others, old and new, are sweeping over the heart-strings of millions, with old-time mystic power, bringing new joy, new peace, new hope, and brotherly love.

Friends, the best thing that we can say to one another, wherever we are, on this another Christmas Day, is "Let's sing!" Let's sing songs of friendship and rejoicing, songs of simple faith, songs of Christmas! A Merry Christmas to you all! Let's sing!

KOREA

Songs, Gifts, and Love

SATURDAY AFTERNOON we had a program including a pageant for the hospital in-patients. This was held in the main ward of our present hospital. The pageant depicted the story of Jesus' birth from the Annunciation through the visit of the Wise Men. The hospital storerooms were well raided to provide costumes—bathrobes, pieces of material for head coverings, cotton for beards, mosquito netting for the angels' draperies, anything which could be adapted for use. The pageant was put on by the permanent-staff nurses and doctors, and we all had to take part.

Saturday evening we had our staff party, with each making a contribution to the entertainment. . . . On the day before Christmas, we had our own dinner and gifts.

Christmas carries the tradition of giving gifts to others. The preparation and wrapping of gifts went on for days before Christmas. The total reached staggering proportions before we were through. It is the kindness and generosity of church people in our homelands which makes this possible. Besides gifts, in connection with our hospital here in Pusan, I packed two large wooden cases early in December to go to the orphanage in the country at Hamyang.

The joy of Christmas has been expressed since earliest days in song, and Christmas carols are sung in every tongue around the world. We have a short chapel service every morning in our main ward before starting the work of the day, and during December the familiar Christmas hymns were sung over and over again. On Christmas Eve at our staff party, before the purely social part, the staff nurses came singing into the darkened room where the rest of us were sitting. Each nurse was dressed in white Korean skirt and jacket and carried a lighted candle. They sang several carols, and never have I heard them sing more beautifully. During Christmas Eve, groups of carolers came and went most of the night. The nurses sang to the in-patients at three A.M. . . . After our own Christmas dinner and festivities on Monday night, we sang Christmas hymns and carols most of the evening—many of the old well-loved ones, but also some recently composed Australian carols.

The birth of Jesus came as God's great gift to man. . . . There was something of special significance to me in assisting at the birth of a baby in the dark hours of Christmas morning.

As people remember the true meaning of Christmas, the spirit of thankfulness to God expresses itself in worship, either in churches or in groups gathered together elsewhere. The Koreans express their Christian faith freely. All our parties began with a brief Christmas worship service—prayer, Christmas hymns, the Christmas story from the Bible. On Christmas morning the nurse on duty at the hospital had a short service for the patients, telling the Christmas story and illustrating it with a flannelgraph. I went to Korean church with Dr. Mackenzie and Dr. Lee. In the afternoon on Christmas Day, we had our foreign church service with a buffet supper and a time of fellowship.

The whole meaning of Christmas is love. "God so loved the world . . ." Christmas as I have experienced it three times in Korea shows that love is present here, and the evidences of love are here. At Christmas, the spirit of love and service shines forth around us even more than at other times.

Christmas at a Hospital

CHRISTMAS is a joyous time for gathering together for fun and social enjoyment. We had a round of parties at the Il Sin Women's Hospital and the Australian Presbyterian Mission. A committee of the hospital staff decorated the big delivery ward in the new building. The room was resplendent with streamers, large Christmas tree with lights, and Santa Claus. Blankets were placed on the floor for the guests to sit on.

On Wednesday before Christmas, the babies who attend our milk station and their mothers were invited to a party. Out of a total of 230 babies about 190 came. The room was filled to overflowing with the babies and at least that many adults. A short worship service explaining the meaning of Christmas was followed by the distribution of gifts—new baby clothes from church women's groups in Australia and America. The mothers themselves had organized and purchased refreshments and also a gift for each of the three members of our staff who carry on the milk station.

The next evening we had a party for the children of our staff. Each family had to stand up as a unit and sing a Christmas song or some other song. Sometimes it was just a mother with one small child in arms, and sometimes a group of six or more. Santa Claus (done very well by the oldest son of our social worker) then produced a gift for each child.

Missionaries' Reports

How to View Christmas

First, we want to thank you for your numerous letters, snapshots, and cards sent to us during the Christmas season. These helped to make us feel closer to you at home and to ease any "homesickness" we may have felt. I wish time permitted a personal letter to *each*.

Christmas here in Korea was different in many ways from our previous celebrations at home. Tuesday evening before Christmas, the children participated in a pageant at the Seoul Union (English) Church. Their "joy" gift consisted of five pounds of rice, each to be distributed to orphanges, needy families, etc.

Christmas Eve, the Korean Christians paraded in the streets in large groups, carrying paper lanterns lighted by candles and decorated with red crosses. They sang Christmas carols as they marched. At ten thirty P.M., they congregated in the various churches for a two-hour worship and carol service. After this service a special supper was served of *Duck Kook* (which is a soup, highly seasoned, and "laced" with duck, or bread, pieces). Also served was *kimchi* rice, rice cakes, fruit, and perhaps benne or ginger candy. We were surprised (and pleased) that the Koreans use a lot of benne seed in their candy and cookies. This reminds us of our Charleston cookery. I made Christmas cookies with South Carolina benne seed brought from home. After this heavy midnight snack, they again caroled until the four thirty A.M. (daily) early prayer service. Usually, another service is held on Christmas morning at eleven o'clock. Homer Rickabaugh, our missionary boarder, attended the Christmas Eve celebration. We, however, listened to the *magnificent* combined Korean choirs singing *The Messiah* in English, broadcast by the Christian Radio Station here in Seoul.

Christmas Eve each Christian home can be "identified" by a paper (cross) lantern, hanging on the gatepost. We followed this custom. Many banks, YWCA, YMCA, churches, schools, businesses of Christians—all were decorated by numerous lanterns, which could be seen for blocks.

Since there are few street lights in Seoul (perhaps due to the shortage of electricity), the lamp light "gave off" an added light which seemed to signify that *Jesus Christ IS THE Light of the World!* Joy to the world! In a heathen culture (less than 5 per cent Christian of 30,000,000 people) this simple custom is a "witness" in itself.

Christmas morning, the Seoul Union Church had an eleven o'clock service. John and Virginia Somerville and their three boys ate Christmas dinner with us. We also invited three American soldiers and a bachelor civilian friend. We had delicious baked ham this year, which is a rare treat in Korea, and a South Carolina fruit cake (a rare treat anywhere)!

Here in Seoul, many Christmas cards and gifts were sold. I fear some of our "commercialism" has spread to Korea. Many non-Christians celebrate Christmas here much as they do at home (but in a much different way from the Christians here).

Koreans, although very poor, are great "gift givers." We were given numerous dolls and brassware this year. I wish there were some way to "graciously refuse" these gifts. We know how little most of these students and Korean friends have—and yet, they would be deeply offended if we refused their gifts and denied them the pleasure of "giving." We were very happy *not* to receive the usual gift of a "live chicken" on foot. (This gift is especially popular for friends departing on planes, trains, etc., I'm told.)

Many of our American servicemen "shared" their Christmas with the thousands of orphans in Korea and Japan. This generous giving to the orphans is a tremendous "witness" and a strong "binder" for friendship for America (which we certainly need in this world of turmoil). Until we came to Korea, I never fully appreciated our UN troops (and especially our Army troops) stationed up in "no man's land"—just along the Thirty-eighth Parallel. They keep a twenty-four-hour vigil —so we, here in South Korea, and you at home, may have peace and security. We certainly owe them a debt of gratitude. Theirs is a lonely, bleak existence—and they didn't come by choice. They certainly need our prayers and letters from home.

Before Christmas, we gave a dinner party for the language class. It was a new experience for the language teacher and Joe's tutor, to eat our American food. They seemed to have special trouble with the tomato juice cocktail but were too proud not to drink it (in spite of our protests). Both men had beautiful voices—we enjoyed singing Christmas carols and listening to records after dinner.

—From a letter by Mrs. Helen Cameron, January 3, 1960 (Presbyterian Church in the U.S.)

Christmas in Taejon

Let me take this opportunity to thank you all for the many cards and letters of Christmas tidings. I know how busy everyone is during this season, but your faithfulness and thoughtful deeds have warmed our hearts during this first Christmas away from home. Then, too, it is always a joy to be reminded of the responsibility we have to represent Christ for you. After enjoying the cards, we cut the pictures out to use in evangelistic work, then we save the rest, including the envelopes, to use for scratch paper in language study. You can see from this how profitable your efforts are for the work in Korea.

This has truly been a glorious Christmas as we celebrate again the coming of our Lord and Savior to earth and renew our hopes as we await his return "in the fullness of glory." I began the season in our mission station in Taejon where our college and new foreign school are located. The Sunday prior to Christmas I arose to find a beautiful snow and as I looked across the area I thrilled with the excitement of recognizing familiar roof tops and the church steeple and felt the warmth of belonging. However, it was with some hesitation that I parted company with my shoes at the church door and took a seat on the bench at the back of the church. There was a little stove in the center, trying hard to get rid of the chill of the subfreezing temperature. The missionary beside me moved

over to make room between us for the splatter of water leak-
ing from the melting snow on the roof and then I noticed the
wide cracks between the boards on the floor where the people
were sitting. As we sang, the vapor froze from our mouths and
I smiled at the rows of nails for the rice bags, which is the way
many Koreans give their offering to the church. But in no
time the worship service was in progress and these differences
were forgotten and we shared the presence of God. Isn't it
wonderful to realize anew that God is the same at all times
and in all places!

—From a letter by Miss Sylvia E. Haley, January 6, 1960
(Presbyterian Church in the U.S.)

MICRONESIA

Christmas at Ponape
in the Caroline Islands

AT THE PASTORS AND TEACHERS TRAINING SCHOOL we
learned how Christmas is celebrated throughout the
islands of Micronesia, because the students come from all the
districts. The greatest thrill for those on the field is to see these
islanders plan, rehearse, and put on some appropriate entertainment pertaining to the season. This is a great accomplish-
ment for people who have been denied opportunity for initia-
tive for so many decades.

Men from the Marshalls put on their "Christmas Tree," as
they call it. A colorful hand-wrought tree is ingeniously hidden inside a large wood cross. During the singing of Christmas
carols and hymns the cross slowly opens and the "tree" rises

from it. The first opening is accompanied by the noise of tiny firecrackers, which the singing group explode as they sing. Then the tree descends again into the cross until the singing of the last carol, when the two sides of the cross part and the tree remains—a Micronesian attempt to symbolize the birth, death, and resurrection of Christ.

Girls of the Oa Christian Training School taught the lesson of the holiday through a tableau narrated by the "Spirit of Christmas," who sought to convince a doubting Thomas that the birth of Christ was an event of everlasting worth.

When Micronesian teen-agers attempt to present the birth of our Savior in pageantry, they mix their culture and tradition with Biblical history. Their unfamiliarity with pastoral scenes of the earlier centuries was apparent from the part taken by the shepherds in the pageant last year. Yet their following of the star was quite effective, for a large "star" lighted by a kerosene lamp was drawn across the long room on an overhead wire.

Christmas Day is a church family day for Protestant Christians of Micronesia. Everyone attends the local church and spends most of the day there. The long worship service includes a message from every minister, lay preacher, and missionary in the area. Another hour or two is spent in hymn and carol singing. If gifts are presented, it is considered proper for each recipient to applaud himself as he goes to receive the two bars of soap he is likely to be given. American Board missionaries often present gifts to mission school students at the annual Christmas parties. Such gifts come from our churches at home.

PALESTINE

In Bethlehem for Christmas

MADELEINE SWEENEY MILLER

IN BETHLEHEM FOR CHRISTMAS! Who has not longed to spend one Nativity season here, where still "the silent stars go by"? Frosty winter skies set Judean stars atremble—celestial tapers lighted for the Feast of Lights. The same stars which startled Judean shepherds as they watched their shaggy flocks down in the Field of Boaz and heard the angelic song which lifted their eyes to Bethlehem, huddling on its hill—cozy outpost of the homes of men, before the lonely desert. Shepherds and angels—the sordid and the ethereal, the practical and the aesthetic! Eternal paradox of the elements which entered into the incarnation of the King of Love.

Even if December skies let down their loads of heavy winter rain on Christmas Eve, rains cannot extinguish the charm of little lights blinking out from the stout stone cubes of Bethlehem homes. For Bethlehem has a glory all its own, which has not departed down the centuries of racial strife and religious feud. In Bethlehem imagination is fired, hearts sing, people leap over barriers of creed and circumstance to join about the cradle of a Child unseen, yet known.

> His light still shines in Bethlehem town
> > Where long-limbed camels stately stalk
> > And matrons virtuously walk
> In ample headdress flowing down
> About their ample-skirted gown.
>
> His light still shines in children's eyes
> That nightly feast on starry skies

And intimately know the sheep
That shepherds on their hillside keep
On nights too heavenly for sleep.

His light still shines above the lamps
Where creeds contend in hostile camps.
For not in incense-stifled air
His presence breathes, but yonder where
The people walk in Bethlehem square.

Following the trail to Bethlehem year after year, we have come to feel deep attachment for this domestic little town on its hilltop of history. Its personality has the simplicity of all eternally abiding things. Its elevation, 2,800 feet above the Mediterranean, satisfies one's expectations for the place where "the Word was made flesh, and dwelt among us." We wish that we might say that from every one of its two thousand flat-roofed homes the lights of Christmas trees blaze forth—for Bethlehem is predominantly a Christian Arab town, with few Jews and only a minority of Moslems. But Bethlehem knows no such extravagance as Christmas trees loaded with strings of lights, peppermint candies, and glittering toys, with a village laid out below. Bethlehem is itself that Christmas village— eternally. Life is real and life is earnest in this romantic little city of narrow streets, outer staircases, crusader arches and vaultings built into homes that have stood century after century with nothing to disturb them but occasional earthquakes. More substantial, these Bethlehem homes, than flimsy suburban houses in quick-building America, each with its Christmas tree, even if whole forests have been cut down in the process.

Yet Bethlehem homes have their own type of Christmas merry-making. It consists in the arrival of kinsfolk from neighboring villages to feast together on homemade cakes and home-pressed grapes from the terraces below the town. Bethlehem citizens have emigrated far and wide, even as did Naomi and her sons. But they never lose the bonds of home. If on Christmas Day they find it possible to return, like Joseph, to be "enrolled" in the house of their fathers, happy they are. And in many a Christian home, denoted by a white cross painted over the door—a square one if the family is Greek Orthodox, a Latin one if it belongs to the Western branch of Christendom—there is a homemade crèche, modeled after the original manger lying under the basilica in their own town. Of toys there are few; *piasters* are too scant in the average Bethlehem purse. The nearest approach to a community Christmas tree is the "eternal light," a star set up by the British on a pole in the open square in front of the Basilica of the Nativity.

Just as Luke's Gospel features Christmas at the manger and the shepherds' Christmas in the fields, so do modern celebrants at Bethlehem center their observance of the day about those two scenes. Foreign consuls, Government dignitaries, and patriarchs of the branches of Christendom, followed by throngs of picturesque villagers and stately citizens of Bethlehem, make Christmas Eve in the Grotto of the Manger at the old Basilica of Constantine a memorable event each year. And down in the Field of the Shepherds the International YMCA of Jerusalem sponsors an informal Protestant service, which is both artistic and soul-satisfying.

The Latin Patriarch starts out from Jerusalem's Jaffa Gate in the afternoon of Christmas Eve by motor—formerly by horse—following his equestrian cross-bearer, whose banner floats proudly between silver olive groves as they near Wise Men's Well—where, tradition says, the lost star was refound, when its reflection was seen in the water while the thirsty camels drank. Reaching the last hilltop before mounting to Bethlehem, the procession of joyous Palestinian Christians, foreign consuls, Government commissioners, and Arab police is seen by Bethlehemites thronging their roof tops. And what roof tops, for star-scapes twinkling with silver beauty; and for entrancing vistas over the valley toward the Jordan and Moab, north to Jerusalem's Mount of Olives, or southeast to queer, truncated Frank's Mountain, where Herod's pleasure palace stood.

"They are coming!" echoes through the deep Judean valley. Bands of orphans from the Franciscan and Salesian Schools play. "Te Deums" are sung by Jerusalem clergy in the company. And in the Latin portion of the historic basilica, the Church of St. Catherine, vespers begin: *"Rex Pacificus magnificatus est"*; and the Canticle of Mary, *"Fecit mihi . . . magna . . . beatam me decent omnes generationes."* One service follows another, with visiting priests from several nations participating. The midnight Mass, of course, brings the climax. It is sung down in the Grotto of the Manger, where the words are chanted, "She wrapped him in swaddling clothes and laid him in a manger."

But even more stately is the procession presided over by the Greek Patriarch of Jerusalem, his bearded face veiled and crowned by the tall black cylindrical hat of his office. His branch of Christendom holds the choicest portions of the Basilica of the Nativity—Constantine's own, begun in the fourth century, improved by Justinian in the sixth century, and today the most-loved church in all the world. Its four rows of massive red monolithic columns with Corinthian capitals, on which Crusader knights carved their crosses, divide the spacious nave into five aisles. When the bells of midnight sound the beginning of Christmas from the towers where mother birds guard their young, the Greek Patriarch enters the basilica from the monastery and begins the exalting service of worship. Elaborate crowns and vestments of the Eastern Church are donned and doffed, the wealth of carved icons on the rood screen and the tremendous Greek cross catch the glint of flickering candles, amid wreaths of rising incense. Balls of red and blue, like Christmas tree ornaments, glitter on the decorative chandeliers. Bethlehem Christian women, in tall tarboosh with floating white veils, look like flocks of great white birds as they bow and rise in the ritual of worship. Thrilling is the moment when the thronging procession of Palestinians and visitors from many lands moves round and round, circumambulating the precious colonnade, behind bishops, priests, nuns, school girls, and acolytes, and then finally descends to the grotto for the climax of the service.

That rocky grotto, cut into the side of the east face of Bethlehem hilltop, is one of a series of caves and was probably used as the stable of the inn when Mary and Joseph were assigned places there by an unsympathetic and unimaginative inn-keeper two thousand years ago. At least Jerome, who in a similar cave nearby translated the Scriptures into Latin in the fourth century, believed it to be so. And in the second century Justin Martyr mentioned this Cave of the Manger. The grotto is only fourteen yards long and four yards wide, its walls hung with incense-stiffened tapestry, and its silver star marking the place "where the young child lay." The arrangement of the fifteen silver lamps of the three Christian bodies having claims there—Greeks, Latins, Armenians—is as delicate a matter as the rites of sweeping the grotto. In fact, a quarrel between the Russians, sponsoring the Greek Orthodox Church, and the French, sponsoring the Latins, sped up the Crimean War—yet out of that war came a Florence Nightingale and the founding of the modern humanitarian profession of nursing. Great are the potential quarrels when annual cleaning day, December 28, comes. About two years ago, a providential snow fell on that nervous day, so that the particularly "delicate" matter of the north cloister windows could not be gone through with. So they were left "*in status quo*." No disorders that year! The slightest change, even to the bringing in of one extra candle, is complained about to the Government and is used to trump up dissatisfaction.

How little the worshiping throngs on Christmas Eve in the vast, impressive basilica are aware of the historic scenes which have taken place there! For example, that Christmas Day in 1101 when Baldwin came to be crowned first Christian King of the Latin Kingdom of Jerusalem, after the noble Crusader leader, Godefroy de Bouillon, had been elected to this high office and declined, preferring to be known only as "Guardian of the Sepulcher of Christ." How little the worshipers know of the priceless treasure under the stones on which they walk —no, not treasure of gold and silver, but more precious treas-ure of archaeological knowledge. For in 1934, during extensive repairs on the basilica, a large extent of the original mosaics laid for Constantine's floor in about A.D. 330 came to light, about eighteen inches below the present floor. Why such beauty was ever covered over by Justinian in the sixth century no one knows! Was it just a whimsical "change in style" that dumped construction rubble over the colorful pomegranates, apricots, grapes, and conventional scrolls of bright yellows, blues, violet, and green? At any rate, the rubbish preserved them for later centuries to see. After the mosaics had been photographed and studied by the Palestine Department of Antiquities, they were again covered with a floor for modern worshipers, with only a few choice portions left on exhibit for visitors to enjoy.

The fact that five Masses are proceeding at one time in the Basilica of the Nativity, and that throngs of worshipers jam it to utmost capacity, with a jealously-guarded "schedule" maintained for rights of the various groups to enter the Manger Grotto with their smoking tapers, makes the Christmas Eve a disappointment to many Westerners, who prefer the informal program of the Jerusalem YMCA in the Field of the Shepherds.

Several years ago, Dr. A. C. Harte, former general secretary of the Jerusalem Young Men's Christian Association, to whom much of the exquisite symbolism of the superb new edifice on Julian Way is due, with its Jesus Tower, its Prayer Chamber, and its Arabic fireplace, had also another vision. It occurred to him that if the YMCA could purchase a portion of the Field of the Shepherds, where rich Boaz tilled the land below Bethlehem, it would be forever an ideal place where Protestant Christians might celebrate the birthday of the Christ. An acreage was bought in that historic place, gleaned once upon a time by Ruth, ancestress of Jesus. Not until sometime later was it discovered that there was a delightful cave on the property—one which apparently had been used for centuries by shepherds for their shelter when storms overtook them as they watched their flocks. Many interesting implements were found in it. But more valuable than these "unconsidered trifles" is the Christmas Eve atmosphere the cave lends to those who "to Bethlehem hasten, to worship the King." Within the past year, the Field enclosure has been surrounded by newly planted trees—a boon to denuded Judea.

About noon on the day before Christmas, a party of "Senior

Leaders" go out from the YMCA, by bus to Bethlehem, and hike down over the stony terraces to Tel-Boaz. There they find that Audeh, the caretaker, has already assembled the makings of a huge bonfire, and Hannah is in the cave preparing the *tabun* (flat loaves) for the feast. After a hearty meal, the Y men set to work increasing the wood supply at the western end of the field, looking up to Bethlehem. At five in the afternoon of Christmas Eve, hundreds of visitors begin to arrive from Jerusalem—members of Protestant churches in the Holy City, travelers from the west and east, and onlooking Palestinians who have come to see what it is all about.

Already athrill with the privilege of spending this Christmas Eve in the Field of the Shepherds, the guests are summoned to partake of the simple feast consisting of mutton roasted on live embers and served in little chunks with the flat coarse bread in little round loaves, similar to those which Jesus ate. By the time the shepherds' open-air meal is over, twilight has fallen and the twinkling lights of Bethlehem mass together like a galaxy of stars. The guests stroll over to the bonfire to drink their fill of lighted Bethlehem windows and of huge, low-leaning Judean stars. Never do the heavens bend so low as above the Field of the Shepherds on Christmas Eve. Huge, trembling, intimate they are, looking as though the very heavens would open and again an angelic chorus would sing of "great joy which shall be to all people." And right through the fields of the celestial spaces, shooting stars fall with thrilling brilliance.

The Christmas Eve service of worship is simple and brief— just the singing of carols; the reading of the Christmas narrative in Arabic and in English: "For unto you is born this day in the city of David a Savior, which is Christ the Lord. . . . Ye shall find the babe. . . lying in a manger"; a short message from a visiting clergyman; and an informal prayer. But what overflowing hearts, each reading into that high experience a wealth of personal memories and everyone feeling himself a part of that original shepherd group who, "as the angels were gone away from them into heaven, . . . said one to another, Let us now go even unto Bethlehem, and see this thing which is come to pass, which the Lord hath made known unto us"!

Each year more people attend this Christmas Eve service—last year about four hundred. And the holy season does not end then. It is continued in Jerusalem in the magnificent new building, the enduring Christmas gift of a American, James Newbigin Jarvie, of Montclair, New Jersey. At the entrance two growing trees are effectively floodlighted for the occasion. Inside the elegant lobby with its Arabic art a real Christmas tree is gay with a Western gaiety unfamiliar to the ancient East. In the auditorium a Christmas pageant is presented, "The Three Wise Men," in which the participating shepherds, seekers from the Orient, Herod, and other participants are so "native" that they look as if they had just strolled in from Jerusalem streets. Palestinians so love drama portraying scenes from their own history that they demand an extra performance of this excellent Nativity play. Such projects are building that brotherhood of the Prince of Peace which he came to establish for all the world.

But even if it is never your good fortune to spend a Christmas Eve in Bethlehem, you may always have Bethlehem come to you, as you seek the Child who came to earth on a Judean hilltop:

HOW FAR TO BETHLEHEM?
"How far is it to Bethlehem Town?"
"Just over Jerusalem hills adown,
Past lovely Rachel's white-domed tomb—
Sweet shrine of motherhood's young doom.

"It isn't far to Bethlehem Town—
Just over the dusty roads adown,
Past Wise Men's Well, still offering

Cool draughts from welcome wayside spring;
Past shepherds with their flutes of reed
That charm the woolly sheep they lead;
Past boys with kites on hilltops flying—
And soon you're there, where Bethlehem's lying,
Sunned white and sweet on olived slopes,
Gold-lighted still with Judah's hopes."

And so we find the Shepherds' Field
And Plain that gave rich Boaz yield;
And look where Herod's villa stood.
We thrill that earthly parenthood
Could foster Christ, who was all-good:
And thrill that Bethlehem Town today
Looks down on Christian homes that pray.
It is not far to Bethlehem Town!
It's anywhere that Christ comes down
And finds in people's friendly face
A welcome and abiding place.
The road to Bethlehem runs right through
The homes of folks like me and you!

PERSIA (IRAN)

In the Land of the Magi

CHRISTMAS IN IRAN is known as the Little Feast, Easter being known as the Great Feast. For the first twenty-five days of December, a great fast is observed, during which no meat, eggs, milk, or cheese is eaten. It is a time of peace and meditation; a time for attending services at the church. But when the fast is over, the feast is begun, for plenty of meat is prepared for the Christmas dinner.

Christmas Eve is the last day of the fast. Almost before dawn on Christmas Day, the people attend Mass to receive Communion, and it is not until they have received this Communion that they are permitted to break fast.

The boys and girls of Iran have never heard of Santa Claus, and gifts are not exchanged at Christmas. But the children are sure to receive a new suit of clothes, which they proudly wear all during the happy Christmas week.

A popular dish for Christmas Day is a kind of chicken stew. It is cooked in large quantities and generally lasts several days.

Iran played an important part in the history of the first Christmas, for it was supposedly from there that the three Wise Men came, the Magi who studied the stars.

THE PHILIPPINES

How the Filipinos Observe Christmas

IN THE PHILIPPINES, Christmas is a season in the real meaning of the word. For twenty-two long, lively days, December 16 to January 6, the devout Filipinos express the spirit of Christmas with a series of Masses, pageants, and festivals to the background of unending music by carolers and brass bands.

Celebrations begin at dawn on December 16, when townspeople are awakened by the pealing of church bells, heralding the first of a novena of dawn Masses. Many services begin at four A.M., thus the name, *Misa de Gallo* (since the Mass presumably starts at the first cock's crow).

Following the service, streets begin to show signs of festivity. People bundled in warm coats pour from the church, stopping at nearby stalls for tea and warm *bibingka* (rice cakes).

They talk with friends, walk leisurely home, or join a group of wandering carolers.

At night, star lanterns and strings of multicolored lights shine over windows and doorways. Lights are everywhere, illuminating the town plaza, public buildings, and trees.

On Christmas Eve, in the town of San Fernando in Pampanga, forty-four miles from Manila, lavishly decorated star lanterns, measuring fifteen to thirty feet, are paraded in a contest to find the most elegant, gigantic, and colorful lantern in the land.

In many Tagalog towns, one of the most impressive pageants in Christendom, *panunuluyan,* is staged each Christmas Eve. Characters dressed as the holy couple re-enact the search for shelter on the night Christ was born. As the pair wander through town, knocking on doors, townspeople follow them. Shortly before midnight, the procession—which has increased to include almost everyone in town—arrives at the church, where they knock and find shelter. There the Nativity story is relived. Goats and lambs nestle in the straw, richly dressed Magi bring gifts, and proud Filipino children in white robes and cellophane wings are angels for one evening.

As Missionaries See Christmas

C HRISTMAS MEANS MANY THINGS to many people, and the Christmas activities start early in December here in the Philippines. Only in late January does the final noise of Christmas die away. There are dozens of groups composed of young and old who go about the city caroling for money. There are usually five or six people in each group, and with the aid of a musical instrument they can be heard singing every night. They serenade until the early hours of the morning. "Jingle

Bells" and "I'm Dreaming of a White Christmas" are the most common numbers. However, they often sing lovely Filipino Christmas carols as well as the traditional carols.

Hanging in the front window of every home is a large crepe-paper star. The Christmas star is the most important part of the decorations. Decorated Christmas trees are not too common, as the right type of tree is rare.

Regular church activities are the usual order of the day on Christmas Day. The children's annual church school program is held early in the morning.

The Christian Youth Fellowship members often hold regular services in the jail every Sunday. The traditional Filipino Christmas dinner of *lechon* (roast pig) is served in the evening.

Christmas cards hanging from red and green ribbons on living room walls lend a festive Christmas air to the homes. The needles on the Christmas pine tree soon turn brown and the holiday decorations then are put away for another year.

THAILAND

Thailand Celebrates Christmas

ESTELLE CARLSON

THE CELEBRATION OF CHRISTMAS in Thailand is an institution of the church. It does not center around the family as it does in America. Decorating the home and preparing home-coming dinners for Christmas is foreign to Thailand. It is the custom here for young and old to gather together for a church-centered celebration.

Last year our Christmas activities lasted about two weeks as Christians went from one church or Christian center to another to help one another celebrate.

On December 19, the young people had a joint dinner and party. On December 21, the Thai church in Nakon Pathom gave a feast which was attended by about one hundred fifty Christians. Besides the local members, visitors came from Sam Yek, Ban Pong, Bangkok, Hua Phai, and Lumphai. Following the feast, Kru Shalot (manager of the Nakon Pathom boys' school and elder in the Thai church) led the special worship service.

The church was beautifully decorated with garlands of crepe paper, full-size manger scene, and a Christmas tree. All these decorations were handmade by the young people from Sam Yek.

After the worship service the Christians joined with four or five hundred non-Christians to see two plays presented on a specially built stage in the yard of the girls' school. The young people of Sam Yek, under the leadership of missionary Richard Carlson, presented the story of the Nativity. The youth group in Nakon Pathom, directed by Frances Sams, presented a pageant about "The Spirit of Christmas."

On Sunday morning, the twenty-second, twelve people were baptized in the Thai church in Nakon Pathom. On Sunday afternoon a bus was rented by the Christians from Nakon Pathom, who wanted to share with worshipers in Ban Pong as their Christmas activities got under way at the street chapel there. In Sam Yek on December 23 and 24, the school, the young people's group, and the Christians joined with visitors in a program which included a pageant, games, and all-night caroling.

A high point in the Christmas activities comes on Christmas Eve as large groups of young people take part in an all-night carol sing. They walk from house to house, honoring Christians and non-Christians alike as they sing the songs of the birth of the Savior.

In the course of the night's activities last year, they called on most of the Christian families. Many of these families had not gone to bed, since they often prepare hot drinks, candy, and cakes for the group of singers.

At midnight, the group called on the newly elected representative to the Senate from this area. He was a former student from our boys' school. He was high in his praise for the school and for what Christianity had done for Thailand.

At three A.M., the party awakened the governor. He came out and wished the church, the mission, and each and every family a happy and prosperous Christmas season and new year.

At four A.M., they called on the manager of the bank. He was not a Christian, but he had prepared cakes and hot tea for the group. He stated that he felt honored that the Christians would come to his home and ask that God's blessing be given to him for the coming year.

By the time the group finished their singing tour at eight thirty A.M. on Christmas Day, many of us who had been with them throughout the night had one big Christmas Day wish— for a long winter nap. Such is the way Christmas is celebrated in Thailand.

EUROPE

AUSTRIA

Christmas in Austria

CHRISTMAS IN AUSTRIA is the time of year when family members get together for hours of quiet and thoughtful celebration. The Christmas tree plays a most important part. Every town sets up its own huge tree on the main square and frequently there will be an extra one, adorned with bread crumbs, for the birds. In families, it is usually the father of the house who selects the tree and decorates it with gold and silver or sometimes colored balls, tinsel, sweets and candy wrapped in tin foil, gilded nuts, etc. Electric Christmas lights are not too popular throughout Austria and in most homes candles are used. Candles are also placed in windows as a symbolic Christmas greeting to those absent from home and in commemoration of deceased family members.

` On Christmas Eve, all the shops close by six P.M. There are no movie or theater performances and no concerts. Bars, restaurants, night clubs are likewise closed and traffic is almost nonexistent. Around seven P.M. on Christmas Eve (December 24), the tree is lighted for the first time and the whole family gathers to sing Christmas carols. "Silent Night, Holy Night," written on December 24, 1818, by Josef Mohr in the Austrian village of Oberndorf, is still the favorite Christmas carol. Presents are placed unwrapped under the tree and young children believe that they were brought to them—as a reward for good behavior—by Knecht Ruprecht or by the Christ-child (Christkind). Knecht Ruprecht closely resembles Santa Claus with his long white beard, red coat, heavy boots, and his reindeer-drawn sleigh. After all gifts have been inspected, the family sits down to the traditional Christmas dinner, consisting of fish soup, carp, and potato salad, as well as Sacher cake for dessert. At midnight it is customary, especially in the country, to attend Christmas Mass.

Christmas Eve is followed by two more Christmas holidays, which are spent in a gayer mood, visiting relatives and friends.

The Song That Went from Austria Around the World

THROUGHOUT NEARLY A CENTURY and a half, scores of legends have been woven around the conception and composition of the world's most simple and beautiful Christmas song, "Silent Night, Holy Night." The story itself hardly needs embellishment. Neither scholarly nor mystic interpretations are necessary, and one need not even ask what impelled the Rev. Josef Mohr to put the words of this song on paper, because he was a priest of implicit faith and childlike trust in the goodness of man. Schoolteacher Franz Gruber, well versed in music and dabbling now and then in composition, was the priest's close friend. Both spoke to the hearts of the people and with this song gave them an anchor of hope and peace, an everlasting spring of good will.

While the song is sung in practically all civilized tongues, not many thoughts are ever given to poet and composer, nor to town and country in which they worked and lived.

It was Christmas Eve, 1818. After the Napoleonic wars, Europe was at peace, and peace also reigned in the streets and homes of Oberndorf, an old settlement of boatmen on the river Salzach, province of Salzburg, Austria. The people prepared for the traditional midnight Mass in the little church of St. Nicola. That year's midnight Mass would be less impressive, they said, because the old organ had finally given out and the service would be without music. Some said the organ had grown tired, but the more realistic pointed out that mice had chewed up the bellows. They knew little that Mohr and his organist Gruber had found a remedy: a brand-new Christmas song of simple melody, designed to touch the heart and please the ear. During the brief winter afternoon of December 23, 1818, Mohr had handed to his friend the text of this song and a few hours later Gruber had set the words to music for two voices and choir. To provide the musical accompaniment Gruber used one of the most worldly of instruments, the guitar. We do not know exactly whether the song was first sung during or after the Mass, but we do know that the song touched the hearts of the little community of worshipers and kindled in them the desire for truth, righteousness, and good will. None even remotely guessed that this song and with it Mohr and Gruber would become immortal.

It was spring again when the organ builder Mauracher came to Oberndorf to repair the old organ. It was he who took text and music along with him to Tyrol. There the brothers Strasser, manufacturers of gloves who visited many markets and trade fairs in Europe, heard the song. Thirteen years later they sang it before a Catholic congregation in Leipzig. The song had started on its long and glorious road around the world. Christian people everywhere accepted it, but no one apparently knew poet or composer. It was not until 1854 that the Royal Chapel in Berlin made inquiries.

On December 30 of that year (1854) Gruber, then organist at the city church of Hallein, wrote a letter to Berlin giving the authentic data of the song and short biographies of the author and composer. From this letter we know that Mohr died as vicar on December 4, 1848, in Wagrein, Salzburg. He passed on, much beloved and highly respected, but so poor that the town had to pay the funeral expenses. Fame came to him posthumously. Franz Gruber had fared a little better, but according to present-day standards both author and composer were as poor as the shepherds on the fields near Bethlehem. Mohr was not a great poet, nor was Gruber to be numbered among the masters of music, but both were men imbued with the lofty spirit of humanity and Christian charity. They were indeed men of good will.

The old church of St. Nicola no longer stands. In its place stands a simple memorial chapel. Today it is a shrine receiving pilgrims from all parts of the world, and its guestbook shows many illustrious names. But one entry is perhaps the most significant:

"Don't forget that this song is Austria's most precious gift—not just to you and me but to the whole world."

BELGIUM

Christmas in Belgium

DECEMBER IS THE CHILDREN'S MONTH, the month of family holidays, banquets, and abundant libations.

The preparations for the approaching Christmas and the New Year's Day réveillon are made long in advance, and St. Nicholas' serves as the children's prelude to the family festivities. It would be interesting to study the evolution of toys throughout the ages, and the sudden changes wrought in them by the coming of the railroad, the automobile, and the airplane. However, these changes are only imaginary, for a toy is, after all, everything except what it is supposed to be, a thing conceived by an adult, a concrete thing so precise and complicated that it does not usually become interesting until the gears are jammed, the wheels broken, and the mechanism ruined. Actually, toys have a soul, breathed into them by the children, and this soul is always the same, whether it be in a doll, a locomotive, or a broom. Thus, the styles are changed in vain, for the child always seeks and finds one thing: the springboard for his dreams, the pretext for creating, just a bit more cleverly, the realm into which no one can penetrate, no one but himself and his brother, the poet, who will go on with the game when the children have grown to men. This, of course, is a fact recognized by the bakers and candymakers who dip their illusory sweets in dream-colored sirups.

In Western Europe, St. Nicholas' Day, December 6, has remained the great day for the children; not even Christmas has been able to replace it. St. Nicholas, a dignified saint who wears a bishop's robe and miter, white gloves, and an enormous bishop's ring on his left hand which bewitches every small soul, brings toys and sweets to fill the little wooden shoes in château and cottage alike. Between St. Nicholas' Day and Christmas there is an interruption which helps to prolong the happiness associated with the white-bearded saint and to anticipate with less impatience the somewhat less spontaneous joy of Christendom's greatest holiday.

The twenty-first, St. Thomas' Day, brings the above-mentioned interruption. In former times, in the Ardennes, the schoolboys would set fire to little paper roosters placed before the door of the school building. This apparently innocent custom is, according to some historians, a survival of the animal sacrifices made at the same time of the year in the pre-Christian era. This seems to be substantiated by the fact that only seventy years ago in certain localities, the schoolteacher used to give the students a rooster or a hen which they were to behead. St. Thomas' is the day when the school children play tricks on their teachers, the chief trick being to entice him to the door of the classroom and lock him up in a little room until he will succumb to the caprices of his young torturers. In Brabant and Limburg, the servants resort to the same strategy with their masters. These innocent pranks are called *buitensteken* and *buitensluiten*. The day of the Holy Innocents, the twenty-eighth, which brings further evidence of childhood's mischievousness, is a. very ancient holiday included in the annals of the church at Carthage at the end of the fifth century. It was established in memory of the young children massacred by Herod to stop the rumors announcing the coming of the Messiah. The legend is of particular significance to Belgians, for popular imagination has it that the bodies of two innocents were buried at the Convent of St. Gérard in the province of Namur. In Antwerp, Brabant, and certain parts of Limburg, the children used to dress up as "grownups," taking advantage of the authority conferred by the cast-off garments of their parents to run around the house making a great racket.

It is unnecessary to enlarge upon the customs, festivals, visits, and receptions connected with the observance of Christmas, for the holiday has become so universal as to be almost the same in all Western lands.

In Flanders, in the past, a delightful pageant called the "Bethlehem" was presented. A young man dressed as an angel, and burdened with two huge wings, would recite the Ave Maria to a girl. She would answer *"Fiat,"* and then he would kiss her. A child concealed in a big pasteboard rooster cried out, imitating the song of a little bird: *"puer natus est nobis"* (a child is born to us); a great ox then interposed a sonorous *"ubi"* (where), while four kids bleated "Bethlehem." Finally, a donkey sounded a *"hihamus"* (for Eamus) and the procession set off, followed by all the animals, while a jester brought up the rear, shaking his bells.

Most characteristic of the magic spirit of the season, collection centers have been set up in the past for contributions of token gifts and candy by the children of Brussels for distribution to orphans and sick youngsters of the city.

Throughout Belgium, open-air re-enactments of manger scenes are charming. The Marionnette Theater in Liège performs special Christmas stories. Christmas midnight Masses are held everywhere.

DENMARK

Christmas in Denmark

WILLY BREINHOLST

THE DANES LOVE CHRISTMAS. It starts as early as October, when the papers bring their first notices about it being high time to send your Christmas mail to Kamchatka, Tasmania, and the Fiji and Aleutian Isles, if you want it to get there in time. This forewarning will invariably make the Dane exclaim in mingled surprise and joyful expectation: "Fancy, only three months till Christmas now!"

The next infallible sign of Christmas drawing nigh is a press notice stating that the Copenhagen theater, Folketeatret, for its Christmas program this year has decided to present "Christmas in Nøddebo Rectory." This has gone on every year since 1888. If they skipped a year, the theater manager would be lynched. No one meddles with the Danish Christmas traditions with impunity.

A few days later the papers publish a reproduction of this year's Christmas stamp. If it doesn't picture a trumpet-blowing cherub, a dove of peace, or a church bell garlanded with fir, it will be received with profound skepticism. In any case people always agree that it was much prettier last year. The Christmas stamp, used in the cause of charity to overstamp Christmas letters in countries all over the world, was invented in 1904 by a Danish postmaster. Nowadays no Dane would dare post a Christmas card before making it unrecognizable by slapping Christmas stamps all over it. If he doesn't, he is regarded as a coldhearted, cynical, anti-Christmas monster, who should by rights be banished to the uttermost darkness.

Next follows a front page picture of a ninety-foot-high fir

tree in Grib Forest, North Zealand. The caption reads: "Yesterday in Grib Forest the chief forest ranger selected the city's tree." By "the city's tree" they mean the stately fir which all through December will stand in the square facing Copenhagen's town hall, decorated with thousands of lamps, and rallying all hearts to the festival.

After these preliminary heats, which all serve to warm up the Dane and get his mind tuned for Christmas, there is nothing further about Christmas for some time. But that doesn't mean to say that the Dane is not thinking about it. He is preparing for it in secret—and then, suddenly on a dark November day, Christmas bursts out in full bloom. All at once, as at the touch of a magic wand, three alluring letters on great, frost-glittered cardboard signs blaze from every shop window in the country: *Jul!* (Christmas!). The Dane knows no word more beautiful than *Jul.* It makes his eyes dreamy and his voice mellow. Even on the tongues of hard-boiled businessmen the word will melt, assuming the same blithe tones as those in which a devoted son by the sickbed breathes the word: "Mother."

But the shops don't just leave it at *Jul* alone. Oh no, they surround every display window in the country with a green frame of fir garlands; they stretch fir garlands from lamppost to lamppost, from one side of the street to the other, decorating them at suitable intervals with large papier-mâché Christmas bells and Christmas stars. And electricians draw long wires through the garlands, equipping them with myriads of little electric light bulbs, and when dusk comes creeping, someone presses a button, and the whole country is bathed in the light from millions of feet of electrified fir garlands. Behind the glass panes in the store windows Christmas gifts are piling up, and everywhere you see little *nisser* peering out. *Nisser* is the plural of *nisse,* a small, jolly, Nordic Christmas creature who is absolutely indispensable for the Danish Christmas. Although, so far, nobody has ever caught as much as a glimpse of a real, live *nisse,* it is common knowledge that they have their natural habitat in the country, more accurately in the lofts of old farmhouses. They are dressed in gray homespun with a red bonnet, long red stockings, and white clogs, and they are kindly disposed toward the farm folk, as long as they are not teased, in which case they may well upset a pail of milk or hide one of the farmer's wooden shoes. On Christmas Eve they gather in the tower of the village church, where they help the sexton toll the advent of Christmas. They are extremely frugal by nature. Only once a year—namely, on Christmas Eve—they have a bowl of rice pudding brought up to them in the loft. They must be fastidious too, for they never touch the stuff.

Every year at Christmas time the *nisser* descend upon the country like a nightmare. You cannot open a paper, a periodical, or a Christmas magazine without seeing them; they turn up in cartoon strips, on Christmas cards, in toy shops; they are sold by the sheet ready to cut out and hang on the Christmas tree; they are hawked on every street corner as jumping jacks or little, fuzzy fellows made of red and white knitting wool. No one can claim to be without them in one form or another. A particularly obtrusive, almost sinister species goes by the name of Creepy *nisser,* and at Christmas time you can see them leering out from behind curtains, wall plants, and chandeliers, riding astride picture frames and knickknacks. When Christmas is over, they come to an ignoble end, being heartlessly crumpled up and thrown in the fire.

But to revert to the Christmas decorations in the shop windows: apart from the little Christmas *nisser,* every single thing in the window is adorned with a little sprig of fir, a paper heart, or a Christmas star, and one's attention is drawn to the fact that this is "the ideal Christmas gift," be it a necktie, a hearing aid, a tractor, a camel-hair cummerbund, or a double-barreled shotgun. Among those Christmas decorations which, according to the experience of the window dressers, hold the power to soften Danish hearts, there is first and foremost the little white village church, made of plaster and placed on a large slab of cotton wool (to give the illusion of snow). Over the cotton wool a generous hand will have sprinkled some dozens of little tobogganing Christmas *nisser* and some glimmery stuff, and the Christmas decoration is complete. You see it everywhere all over the country: at ironmongers' stores the little white church (with a red electric light fitted behind the Gothic windows) is placed among kitchen scales, eggbeaters, and cooky jars; at the grocer's it is slipped in between cereal cartons, date boxes, and canned goods; in the ladies' underwear shop it is stuck among nightgowns, panties, and brassieres; and at the baker's it is given a decorative site midst pastry and cream cakes— the only difference being that here the church is not made of plaster, but of marzipan. Only at the butcher's may you look for it in vain. He prefers to go his own way, and Christmas-decorates his window with a pig's head, a brightly polished red apple wedged between its jaws. To make it even more festive, it may be furnished with a *nisse* bonnet and little Danish flags stuck behind each ear.

Naturally the little white village church is chicken feed to the more imaginative chief decorators of the big department stores. They prefer to exploit the most up-to-date techniques of model craft, and with the aid of surgical cotton and papier-mâché by the ton they conjure up enormous snowscapes that seem to be carved right out of the Danish countryside, with everything from picturesque windmills (their wings tufted with cotton snow) to commemorative, ancient Viking graves, topped with their decorative cairns (and a *nisse* peering out between the stones). Through this peaceful, snow-clad winter landscape plows the invariable electric toy train, crammed full of Christmas gifts and Christmas *nisser*. When the train has run a certain distance, it is imperative that it should disappear into a tunnel—otherwise it wouldn't be a real Christmas train. Although tunnels are simply nonexistent in Denmark, where cliffs are an unknown geographical feature, the public demands that a long, deep, and dark tunnel is built into the snowscapes of big department stores—that's just the exciting part, watching the train come *out* of the tunnel. People will stand fascinated for hours on end, staring at the tunnel opening and getting a big thrill every time the lilliput train pops out. A sigh of rapture sweeps through the crowd on the sidewalk—there it comes! If the current breaks down, and the train stays in there, it will invariably mar the Dane's enjoyment of Christmas; he will feel cheated, and he certainly won't go near that department store for some time.

Toward the end of November whole forests of fir trees start sprouting up all over the sidewalks, wherever there's a little room to spare. This is the country's supply of Christmas trees, but until a few days before Christmas nobody will even deign to look at them, and their vendors (often impecunious students) stand there, frozen stiff and blue, stamping their feet on the pavement, never getting rid of a single tree. This is not because people consider it too early to get hold of their tree; the inclination is there all right, but one happens to know from experience that they are slightly reduced in price just before closing time on Christmas Eve. And so you wait. Two or three days before Christmas you are suddenly struck by a terrible thought: What if they sell out, so there will be no Christmas tree for you this year! That would be a catastrophe. Thereupon you rush out to buy one, even if it means paying top prices, because everyone gets his Christmas tree two or three days before Christmas.

Now the Santa Clauses begin to turn up in the streets too. Disguised beneath vast bolsters of white cotton-wool beard, they curse everything connected with Christmas through teeth chattering with cold, casting un-Christmasy glances at passers-by, and wielding their signboards with *nisser* perched astride "the ideal Christmas gift."

And now the gingerbread stalls appear. Only one hundred years ago gingerbread was a kind of luxurious national food in Denmark. Nowadays you buy it only for something amusing to hang on the Christmas tree, as Danish gingerbread is always made in the shape of peasant men or women, or hearts. To make them appetizing they have been coated with icing sugar, and yet, somehow you never get down to eating them. You may chew an arm or a leg off the peasant; then you've had enough. Gingerbread holds no attraction for the palate of the modern Dane—but do without it, never! It is an integral part of Christmas.

Stalls selling Swedish *julebukke* do a roaring trade all

through Christmas month. A *julebuk* is a billy goat made of plaited straw, and you can get them any size from the tiniest, inexpensive fellow to hang on the Christmas tree to costly super species containing several loads of hay. *Julebukke* have nothing whatever to do with the Danish Christmas—they are a Swedish custom—but one day, several years ago, there was suddenly a man hawking them in a Copenhagen street, and as the Danes at Christmas time are easily lured to spend their money on anything, no matter how useless or devoid of value it may be, he had sold out all his straw billy goats in next to no time. Now the Dane buys a *julebuk* every year, although he hasn't the faintest idea what to do with it.

The only Danish Christmas vendors who have a thin time of it are the people in the jumping jack trade. For centuries it has been the custom for jumping jack salesmen to appear around Christmas, hawking their double-jointed cardboard men in the streets or from door to door. In olden times a sharp jumping jack salesman could support a wife and twelve kids. Not so now. Today no one would dream of buying a jumping jack. When the jumping jack salesman still faithfully turns up every Christmas, it is because he knows that he is part of Christmas, and that in spite of everything one wouldn't like to do without him. So now and then you do drop a penny in his hat, while firmly declining to accept his jumping jacks. There is something impoverished and essentially small-time about jumping jacks, and for that reason they are denied admission to rooms adorned for the Christmas festival.

By the middle of December, letters to Santa Claus start pouring into Denmark by the thousands. For the most part they are written by English and American children and addressed to "Santa Claus, Greenland," and as Greenland is a Danish possession, the letters turn up at the Tourist Association in Copenhagen, where kindly ladies work round the clock answering them (possibly enclosing a little Christmas tale by the great Danish fairy tale writer, Hans Christian Andersen, as a personal greeting from Santa Claus). Danish kids never write to Santa Claus. They know perfectly well that it's Daddy who is Santa Claus. They can tell by his voice, no matter how hard he tries to disguise it. Nor do they ever hang their stockings over the mantelpiece for Santa Claus to come down through the chimney and fill them with presents. For one thing, they know that Santa Claus is much too fat to squeeze through the narrow chimney pipe in one piece, and besides that, Danish kids never, never hang any garments up when they undress. They just drop the lot on the floor and leave it.

As Christmas Eve draws nigh, the problem of Christmas gifts can no longer be ignored. But as everything turns out to be so expensive, the whole population forms a mutual agreement that this year nobody will give each other presents. The kids can have a few trifles, but apart from that, one will buy nothing. This decision is stubbornly stuck to until approximately December 20. By this time the *nisser* have systematically undermined the resistance of Danish men, Christmas fever holds them in its grip, and they rush out to buy presents for the wife—everything she has wished for: pressure cooker, French perfume, coffee set for twelve people, aprons (when you can't think of anything else, there's always aprons), heat-proof glassware, cake dishes, powder compacts, bed jackets, and kitchen towels. Underwear is another sure item on her lists of wishes, but this is one she never gets, for Danish men are too bashful to buy that sort of thing.

Now the Danish woman knows very well that she can't take her husband seriously when he starts mumbling something about "hard times" and "no Christmas presents this year," and his clumsy hiding places (he is, for instance, naïve enough to believe that his wife never looks under the bed) clearly reveal that this is going to be a Christmas-present year after all. Accordingly she hurries out to buy presents for him—half a box of cigars and a necktie. Danish men always get cigars and neckties—never anything else. While Danish women can write a list of their wishes several yards long, Danish men always feel strangely empty-brained when faced with a blank sheet of paper headed "List of Christmas Wishes." Their imaginations fail miserably, and they can get no farther than "tobacco and neckties." Her husband's gifts purchased, the

Danish woman goes on to buy presents for the kids, parents and parents-in-law, uncles, aunts, sisters, brothers, friends, and acquaintances. She knows no peace before her purse is empty, refilled with the family's last reserves, and emptied once again.

During the last eight days before Christmas, the Danish kitchen is a scene of feverish activity. The Danish housewife is now doing her Christmas baking. It wouldn't be a real Christmas without home-baked Christmas cakes. In Denmark there are three kinds of Christmas cakes, baked by the billion every Christmas. First and foremost there is *klejner*. This is a four-inch-long, one-inch-wide cooky made of flour, butter, and sugar, and fried pale-brown in a saucepan of oil. The singular thing about *klejner* is that you tie them in a knot before dropping them into the saucepan. Another indispensable kind of cake in Denmark around Christmas time is *brune kager*. A batter consisting of flour, butter, sirup, and sugar is flattened with a rolling pin to a thin layer covering the entire kitchen table, after which you use a beer glass to cut the batter into little, circular cakes, which you put on a tray and bake in the oven. Half a scalded almond is stuck on top of each cake. Finally the third kind of Danish Christmas pastry: *pebernødder*. They are small, round, pale-brown cookies about the size of a pigeon's egg, and Danish housewives have been baking them for as long as there has been something called Christmas. However, as they don't taste very nice, they are never eaten, but passed straight on to the children to play with.

Christmas Eve is without any doubt the busiest day in the year for the Danish housewife. In the first place she has to roast the goose. All Danes have goose for dinner Christmas Eve (although people who don't like goose may eat duck, and people who don't like duck may have roast pork). No other form of Christmas dinner is known. But besides watching the goose in the oven, she has a thousand other things to do. The Danish husband has a much easier time of it. He merely has to see that a *juleneg* is hung out for the birds. A *juleneg* is a sheaf of corn hung up in a tree, so that the little feathered friends of the garden may know that it's Christmas too. Apart from that he only has to knock up a Christmas tree foot in his workshop. Now you may buy an excellent Christmas tree foot with your Christmas tree for a very small extra charge, but you wouldn't think of doing that. Here at last is an item where you can save money, and therefore the man-about-the-house makes his own Christmas tree foot. Even if it takes him the better part of the day, the finished result will rarely bear comparison with his exertions.

In the afternoon the whole family goes to church. It is handsomely decorated with lots of candles, fragrant fir garlands, and a Christmas tree placed before the altar. And it's packed to the rafters too. Normally Danes are not habitual churchgoers. Apart from the annual Christmas visit, they rarely show up until it's time to be buried. The service starts with the singing of "Silent Night, Holy Night" and then the parson speaks a few words about Christmas. But the housewife hasn't got the peace of mind to listen. She keeps worrying about the goose in the oven at home. Won't do if it gets *too* brown. The kids have an even harder time sitting still in the pew, and Father can't help thinking about all the money Christmas is costing him (nor can he quite forget the unsuccessful Christmas tree foot). The parson is aware of his responsibility—hundreds of golden-brown geese are at stake—and he makes his sermon a short one.

The church is emptied, and through the softly falling Christmas snow people hurry to their homes. An hour later you are summoned to the table to partake of the largest and most festive meal of the year. The table is laid with a white cloth and beautifully decorated with lots of red and white candles, little sprigs of fir with painted, white cones, and a long runner of crepe paper printed with little, merry *nisser* eating rice pudding out of huge earthenware bowls, while a pussy cat laps its milk from the same source.

Christmas dinner starts with this rice pudding, called *risengrød* (rice boiled in milk until it takes on a firm, pudding-like consistency, which is sprinkled with cinnamon and washed down with *juleøl,* a nonalcoholic, dark beer, chiefly distinguished by the label on the bottle picturing a ruddy *nisse* with a red bonnet). As no Dane can stand *risengrød,* and as one is disinclined to ruin one's appetite for the goose by gulping down too much of this indigestible stuff, the Danish housewife is faced with a grave problem: how to get the *risengrød* finished up and thus lighten the impending assault on the goose. There has been an attempt at solving the problem with the so-called "almond prize." A large almond is dropped into the vessel containing the pudding, and the lucky one who gets the almond in his plateful is handed the prize, which as a rule consists of a marzipan pig with a red silk bow around its neck. The more pudding you eat, the greater your chances of winning the marzipan pig will obviously be. When in spite of this the *risengrød* is still never finished up, it is because the housewife cheats and always manages to slip the almond into the portion allotted to the youngest family member to struggle with. Thus the other Christmas dinner participants know beforehand that they have lost, for which reason they make do with a very modest helping.

The *risengrød* goes out, the goose is brought in. The goose is stuffed with prunes and apples, and with it you serve potatoes browned in sugar, jam, and mountains of sweet red cabbage. Christmas Eve is the only time of the year when goose is served in Danish homes, and therefore it is regarded as an occasion of the utmost solemnity, when the door leading to the kitchen swings open and the housewife carries in the great, golden-brown roasted bird. Her husband is so overcome by the situation that he volunteers to carve the goose himself, but as the skill of the Danish male in this exacting respect leaves much to be desired (his daily fare consists of meatballs or hamburgers, which may be carved without the aid of poultry scissors), he usually makes a rotten job of it.

He starts off well enough by stabbing a two-pronged fork into one side of the goose. Then he confidently raises the carving knife, and—amid the breathless silence of the expectant assembly—he aims it at the goose in an effort to sever the drumstick from its body in one clean and elegant cut. He never succeeds the first time. With a grim and determined smile he has another try. Still no result. The trouble is that he

knows too little about the anatomy of the common, farm-bred
goose. He clings to the naïve belief that the only thing con-
necting a drumstick to a goose is the crisply browned skin. The
simple fact—that the bone he will be holding later, when he
sits gnawing the drumstick, forms a jointed connection with
the entire skeleton structure of the goose—will never really
dawn on him. In his eagerness to get results, so that the feast
may begin, he will make one futile assault after the other on
the defenseless bird, while everyone sitting around him starts
offering helpful advice. Furiously he calls for silence, throws
down the carving knife, and makes a desperate bid to rip the
drumstick off the goose with his bare hands. Still without success. At this point the housewife usually interferes and takes
the goose away from him, but there are some Danish husbands
who won't give in before they have clawed the whole wretched
bird apart . . . or before it gives them the slip, landing in the
laps of their mothers-in-law, which obviously doesn't count in
their favor when the Christmas presents are handed out later
in the evening. Having reached this stage, they mostly capitu-
late, but to be quite truthful there have been cases of husbands
who couldn't be dragged away from the goose, before they
had succeeded in blowing it to smithereens with the aid of an
indoor firework. In any case the subject of carving will always
be a grim chapter in the history of the Danish Christmas
goose.

After dinner the candles on the Christmas tree are lighted.
It has been decked with garlands of red-and-white Danish
flags, hearts made of glazed paper and filled with Christmas
candy, crackers and Christmas bells. Thrilled at the sight of
all the many candles, you sing "Silent Night" and "High on
the green top of the tree, Christmas shines in splendor" . . .
and then, at last, the great moment has come when the gifts
are passed around. Father vanishes, and five minutes later
there is a knock on the door. It opens and in comes Santa
Claus wishing everyone "a merry Christmas" in a deep, gruff
voice. He asks if the kids have been good, and they answer,
"Yes, Santa Claus!" And then he asks if they'll promise to be
good all next year too, and again they answer, "Yes, Santa

Claus!" And then he asks if they'll promise always to obey Mummy and Daddy, and the kids lose their patience and say: "Aw, cut out the fooling, Pop, and let's have those presents!" The fact that he is recognized always knocks a little off Father's Christmas spirit. Danish fathers love playing Santa Claus. If they had their way, they would go around dressed as Santa Claus all year.

Now the kids are given their toys—they may include anything from expensive electric trains to building bricks and complete cowboy outfits—Mother gets her French perfume, her aprons, and a hundred other things, and Father gets his half a box of cigars and his necktie.

The excitement subsides. While the kids fight over their toys, Mother spends the rest of the evening in the kitchen washing up, and Father lies down on the couch to have a well-deserved snooze, while his digestion tackles the goose.

Christmas Day is celebrated with a sumptuous Christmas meal. During the day the numerous Christmas cards from family, friends, and acquaintances are looked through. They are in a crystal bowl placed at some conspicuous point in the house, so that anyone who feels inclined can browse through them at leisure. The chief pictorial subject on Danish Christmas cards is, of course, *nisser,* but you don't have to look far either for the little, white village church, dressed in its mantle of Christmas snow.

Boxing Day is spent eating, sleeping, and calling on the family to taste their Christmas baking and see if the other Christmas trees are as prettily decorated as your own. By now the Christmas spirit is slowly fading out, and you pull the candles and the little red-and-white flags off the tree and throw them in the cellar or some remote part of the garden. When Mother has exchanged all her Christmas presents for things she needed more, when the kids have smashed that electric train, and when Father has smoked the last of his Christmas cigars, the Danish Christmas will be irrevocably over. Now no one mentions the word *Jul* before some time in October, when there is a newspaper notice to the effect that it is now high time to send your Christmas mail to Kamchatka,

Tasmania, and the Fiji and Aleutian Isles. Then the Dane will exclaim with shining eyes: Fancy, only three months till Christmas now!

Yep, no getting away from it . . . the Danes love Christmas.

The Danes Love Christmas

THE DANES OBSERVE CHRISTMAS EVE. It's the big event of the year. Work ceases in the afternoon. At five o'clock church bells in town and country begin to "chime," ringing out by beats of the hammer against the bell, to summon people to worship in candlelit churches decorated with green. Home again, families sit down to Christmas dinner. After dinner, the Christmas tree is lighted and gifts are distributed.

On Christmas Eve the children are allowed to "stay up late." Then, their Christmas gifts stacked at the foot end, they are put to bed, a young world transported into pleasant dreams.

Where Santa Claus appears in Denmark he is called the "Yule Man," but the Danes have their own gnomelike *"nisse."* They have two Christmas holidays and usually enjoy a "white Christmas."

Snow-white Christmas

Yes, the Danes hope for a white Christmas and often have it. Time and again you may see snow beginning to fall as soon as church bells begin to *kime* (chime), calling to each other from parish to parish, summoning people to worship.

Snow falls in large flakes white and soft as swan's down. When the sky clears, snow casts blue shadows. On clear, frosty nights its crystals reflect the light of stars.

Now the snow covers the countryside and droops over the eaves of houses like white frosting overflowing on cake. Birds would go hungry were it not for the thoughts which rise spontaneously in the hearts of good people, who then cut slices of bread into small cubes and crumbs and drop them out of windows. No, better clear the snow off the window ledge and leave the bread there lest the crumbs disappear into the soft snow out of the reach of small birds. In Denmark, farmers put out a sheaf of grain stuck on a pole. They have saved it from the harvest to feed the birds at Christmas.

Danish Christmas is steeped in old tradition. Christmas is the oldest of Nordic festivals. Even in heathen times, midwinter festivals were held around the shortest day of the year. Bonfires were made, and offerings, to appease evil powers. But gentleness and gifts and peace belonged to yule even in heathen times. And, to this day, some Christmas customs are not altogether free from the influence of both old heathen and early Christian tradition. Some old folks still remember the times when people made the sign of the cross before the bake oven and the yule dough and cast omens for the coming year.

"Peter's Yule"

A favorite in Danish homes is a book of verse in stiff cover called *Peter's Jul.* J. Krohn wrote it in the days of our grandparents. The drawings are simple and charming and resemble those made by Vilhelm Pedersen for the first illustrated Danish edition of Hans Christian Andersen. Danish mothers still show *Peter's Jul* to their young children and read to them the simple verses, for—as the first verse says—if mother now will read aloud the very simple song, the little verses will take wings upon her Danish tongue—

> For they are true for now and aye
> The old and golden words that say,
>   In following one another:
> Like Father only few are found
>   But never one like *Mother.*

And the verses go on to tell of all the great expectations of children and the final revelation of their Christmas in faith and joy and glory.

"Was I Born to Such Glorious Destiny?"

To Christmas in Denmark in our days belongs first of all the Christmas tree. Hans Christian Andersen in his tale "The Fir Tree" tells how the tree is picked in the woods and brought into the home, where it is decorated with little nets and cones and hearts cut out of colored papers and filled with sweets. And with gilded apples and walnuts hanging from its branches! And with garlands of tinsel, flags, and lights and everything! "Was I really born to such glorious destiny?" the fir tree wondered.

The Christmas tree is a guest in every Danish home, in hospitals, hotels or restaurants, and stores, and is raised in the public squares and tied atop the mast of Danish ships at sea.

But the Christmas tree as a symbol of Christmas is relatively recent in Denmark. It was known in Alsace as early as the sixteenth century. And Goethe in 1774 let his young Werther tell of the Christmas tree he had known in the home of his childhood. He thus established this Christmas custom in Western Europe. In Denmark and in Sweden, the Christmas tree was introduced in the early nineteenth century. So this symbol of Christmas is some one hundred and fifty years old in the north.

In Denmark, the tree is decorated the day before Christmas, but in homes with children colorful paper decorations have already been cut and pasted or woven together during cozy December evenings. Then, when the tree stands dressed in all its glory, the little paper cones and baskets filled with sweets and the lights fastened, the door to the living room is closed and locked. But the children are not allowed to see the tree before Christmas Eve when all are gathered together, the lights lighted, and the doors opened into the radiant tree.

Christmas baking is traditional in Denmark. Cookies of many sorts and shapes belong to a Danish Christmas, and among them are "pepper nuts."

The Christmas Eve church service is of the Danish Christmas observance. The service is in the late afternoon, before dinner. All work ceases, church bells peal, and people flock to churches festively lighted and decorated with fragrant greens.

The traditional Christmas Eve dinner is rice porridge sprinkled with cinnamon, and with a piece of butter in the center, and then comes roast goose stuffed with apples and prunes and served with red cabbage and small caramel-browned potatoes. The dessert is often apple cake—layers of bread crumbs, apple sauce, and jam and topped with whipped cream. Hidden in the rice porridge is an almond, and whoever gets the almond receives a prize.

Now dinner is over and the dishes washed up. Expectations are high. Father and Mother disappear into the locked room, light the tree, and open the door with a key and a smile. Behold the tree in all its glory! A silver star at the top, radiant with lights and tinsel and everything, and around the foot of the tree gifts wrapped in gay papers—

But wait! It's a Danish custom that all take one another by the hand and go around the tree singing some of the old Danish Christmas hymns, and among them is "Merry Christmas, Lovely Christmas," to the tune of "Holy Night."

The gaily wrapped gifts stacked on tables and floor are exchanged about the tree. Sometimes the "Yule Man" enters with gifts in his bag, a member of the family having dressed up as a Santa with long white beard and red cap.

The "Nisse"

But even though the Danish "Yule Man" in the likeness of our American Santa is not so common in Danish homes, Denmark has a similar spirit. He is a sprite and is called *"Nissen."* The *"Nisse"* is much smaller than Santa Claus, which is perhaps not so strange considering that Denmark is so much smaller than America. For the last hundred years the *Nisser* (plural for *Nisse*) have attached to Danish homes. Today they are the lone representatives of the many supernatural beings who in old days played a part in the Danish yuletide. They are all that's left of them now. They are given to all sorts of mischief—even as children at Halloween—but are good little sprites. They keep a friendly eye on cows and horses in the barn and on other domestic animals and are seen most frequently on Danish Christmas cards, often in the company of the house cat. They marry and have children. The old *Nisse* affects a long white beard in the manner of Santa, and all, old or young, wear red caps. They remind folks to pour milk in a saucer for the cat. But people are wont also to put a platter with the rice porridge outside the kitchen door on Christmas Eve for the *Nisse,* and the platter is always licked clean by morning. Only unimaginative people have been known to suggest that the cat must have eaten the porridge.

Is the Danish Christmas *Nisse real?* Certainly, he is just as real as Santa Claus, and everybody knows that there is a Santa Claus.

Denmark is the home of the original Christmas seal. Some fifty years ago Einar Holboll, then a post office clerk, got the idea. Jacob A. Riis brought the idea to America through an article in the magazine called *The Outlook.*

Glaedelig Jul is the Danish way of saying Merry Christmas.

ENGLAND

Christmas at Bracebridge Hall

WASHINGTON IRVING

THE DINNER WAS SERVED up in the great hall, where the squire always held his Christmas banquet. A blazing crackling fire of logs had been heaped on to warm the spacious apartment, and the flame went sparkling and wreathing up the widemouthed chimney. The great picture of the crusader and his white horse had been profusely decorated with greens for the occasion, and holly and ivy had likewise been wreathed around the helmet and weapons on the opposite wall, which

I understood were the arms of the same warrior. I must own, by the by, I had strong doubts about the authenticity of the painting and armor as having belonged to the crusader, they certainly having the stamp of more recent days, but I was told that the painting had been so considered time out of mind; and that as to the armor, it had been found in a lumber room and elevated to its present situation by the squire, who at once determined it to be the armor of the family hero; and as he was absolute authority on all such subjects in his own household, the matter had passed into current acceptation. A sideboard was set out just under this chivalric trophy, on which was a display of plate that might have vied (at least in variety) with Belshazzar's parade of the vessels of the temple: "flagons, cans, cups, beakers, goblets, basins, and ewers," the gorgeous utensils of good companionship that had gradually accumulated through many generations of jovial housekeepers. Before these stood the two yule candles beaming like two stars of the first magnitude; other lights were distributed in branches, and the whole array glittered like a firmament of silver.

We were ushered into this banqueting scene with the sound of minstrelsy, the old harper being seated on a stool beside the fireplace and twanging his instrument with a vast deal more power than melody. Never did Christmas board display a more goodly and gracious assemblage of countenances; those who were not handsome were, at least, happy; and happiness is a rare improver of your hard-favored visage. I always consider an old English family as well worth studying as a collection of Holbein's portraits or Albrecht Dürer prints. There is much antiquarian lore to be acquired, much knowledge of the physiognomies of former times. Perhaps it may be from having continually before their eyes those rows of old family portraits, with which the mansions of this country are stocked; certain it is that the quaint features of antiquity are often most faithfully perpetuated in these ancient lines; and I have traced an old family nose through a whole picture gallery, legitimately handed down from generation to generation, almost from the time of the Conquest. Something of the kind was to be observed in the worthy company around me. Many of their faces had evidently originated in a Gothic age and been merely copied by succeeding generations; and there was one little girl, in particular, of staid demeanor, with a high Roman nose, and an antique vinegar aspect, who was a great favorite of the squire's, being, as he said, a Bracebridge all over, and the very counterpart of one of his ancestors who figured in the court of Henry VIII.

The parson said grace, which was not a short familiar one, such as is commonly addressed to the Deity, in these unceremonious days; but a long, courtly, well-worded one of the ancient school. There was now a pause, as if something was expected, when suddenly the butler entered the hall with some degree of bustle; he was attended by a servant on each side with a large wax light, and bore a silver dish, on which was an enormous pig's head decorated with rosemary, with a lemon in its mouth, which was placed with great formality at the head of the table. The moment this pageant made its appearance, the harper struck up a flourish; at the conclusion of which the young Oxonian, on receiving a hint from the squire, gave, with an air of the most comic gravity, an old carol, the first verse of which was as follows:

> *Caput apri defero*
> *Reddens laudes Domino.*
> The boar's head in hand bring I,
> With garlands gay and rosemary.
> I pray you, all sing merrily
> *Qui estis in convivio.*

Though prepared to witness many of these little eccentricities from being apprised of the peculiar hobby of mine host, yet, I confess, the parade with which so odd a dish was introduced somewhat perplexed me, until I gathered from the conversation of the squire and the parson that it was meant to represent the bringing in of the boar's head—a dish formerly served up with much ceremony, and the sound of minstrelsy and song, at great tables on Christmas Day. "I like the old custom," said the squire, "not merely because it is stately and pleasing in itself, but because it was observed at the college at Oxford, at which I was educated. When I hear the old song chanted, it brings to mind the time when I was young and gamesome—and the noble old college hall—and my fellow students loitering about in their black gowns; many of whom, poor lads, are now in their graves!"

The parson, however, whose mind was not haunted by such associations, and who was always more taken up with the text than the sentiment, objected to the Oxonian's version of the carol, which he affirmed was different from that sung at college. He went on, with the dry perseverance of a commentator, to give the college reading, accompanied by sundry annotations, addressing himself at first to the company at large, but finding their attention gradually diverted to other talk, and other objects, he lowered his tone as his number of auditors diminished, until he concluded his remarks, in an under voice, to a fat-headed old gentleman next him, who was silently engaged in the discussion of a huge plateful of turkey.

The table was literally loaded with good cheer and presented an epitome of country abundance in this season of overflowing larders. A distinguished post was allotted to "ancient sirloin," as mine host termed it; being, as he added, "the standard of old English hospitality, and a joint of goodly presence, and full of expectation." There were several dishes quaintly decorated, and which had evidently something traditionary in their embellishments; but about which, as I did not like to appear overcurious, I asked no questions.

I could not, however, but notice a pie, magnificently decorated with peacock's feathers, in imitation of the tail of that bird, which overshadowed a considerable tract of the table. This the squire confessed, with some little hesitation, was a pheasant pie, though a peacock pie was certainly the most authentical; but there had been such a mortality among the peacocks this season, that he could not prevail upon himself to have one killed.

When the cloth was removed, the butler brought in a huge silver vessel of rare and curious workmanship, which he placed before the squire. Its appearance was hailed with acclamation, being the Wassail Bowl so renowned in Christmas festivity. The contents had been prepared by the squire himself, for it was a beverage in the skillful mixture of which he particularly prided himself, alleging that it was too abstruse and complex for the comprehension of an ordinary servant. It was a potation, indeed, that might well make the heart of a toper leap within him, being composed of the richest and raciest wines, highly spiced and sweetened, with roasted apples bobbing about the surface.

The old gentleman's whole countenance beamed with a serene look of indwelling delight as he stirred this mighty bowl. Having raised it to his lips, with a hearty wish of a merry Christmas to all present, he sent it brimming round the board, for every one to follow his example, according to the primitive style, pronouncing it "the ancient fountain of good feeling, where all hearts met together."

There was much laughing and rallying as the honest emblem of Christmas joviality circulated and was kissed rather coyly by the ladies. When it reached Master Simon he raised it in both hands, and with the air of a boon companion struck up an old Wassail chanson.

Much of the conversation during dinner turned upon family topics, to which I was a stranger. There was, however, a great deal of rallying of Master Simon about some gay widow, with whom he was accused of having a flirtation. This attack was commenced by the ladies, but it was continued throughout the dinner by the fat-headed old gentleman next the parson, with the persevering assiduity of a slow hound; being one of those long-winded jokers, who, though rather dull at starting game, are unrivaled for their talents in hunting it down. At every pause in the general conversation, he renewed his bantering in pretty much the same terms, winking hard at me with both eyes whenever he gave Master Simon what he considered a home thrust. The latter, indeed, seemed fond of being teased on the subject, as old bachelors are apt to be; and he took occasion to inform me, in an undertone, that the lady in question was a prodigiously fine woman and drove her own curricle.

The dinnertime passed away in this flow of innocent hilarity; and, though the old hall may have resounded in its time with many a scene of broader rout and revel, yet I doubt whether it ever witnessed more honest and genuine enjoyment. How easy it is for one benevolent being to diffuse pleasure around him; and how truly is a kind heart a fountain of gladness, making everything in its vicinity to freshen into smiles! The joyous disposition of the worthy squire was perfectly contagious; he was happy himself and disposed to make all the world happy; and the little eccentricities of his humor did but season, in a manner, the sweetness of his philanthropy.

When the ladies had retired, the conversation, as usual, became still more animated; many good things were broached which had been thought of during dinner but which would not exactly do for a lady's ear; and though I cannot positively affirm that there was much wit uttered, yet I have certainly heard many contests of rare wit produce much less laughter.

I found the tide of wine and wassail fast gaining on the dry land of sober judgment. The company grew merrier and louder as their jokes grew duller. Master Simon was in as chirping a humor as a grasshopper filled with dew; his old songs grew of a warmer complexion, and he began to talk maudlin about the widow. He even gave a long song about the wooing of a widow, which he informed me he had gathered from an excellent black-letter work, entitled *Cupid's Solicitor for Love,* containing store of good advice for bachelors, and which he promised to lend me. The first verse was to this effect:

> He that will woo a widow must not dally,
>> He must make hay while the sun doth shine;
> He must not stand with her, shall I, shall I?
>> But boldly say, Widow, thou must be mine.

This song inspired the fat-headed old gentleman, who made several attempts to tell a rather broad story out of Joe Miller, that was pat to the purpose; but he always stuck in the middle, everybody recollecting the latter part excepting himself. The parson, too, began to show the effects of good cheer, having gradually settled down into a doze and his wig sitting most suspiciously on one side. Just at this juncture we were summoned to the drawing room, and, I suspect, at the private instigation of mine host, whose joviality seemed always tempered with a proper love of decorum.

After the dinner table was removed, the hall was given up to the younger members of the family, who, prompted to all kind of noisy mirth by the Oxonian and Master Simon, made its old walls ring with their merriment, as they played at romping games. I delight in witnessing the gambols of children, and particularly at this happy holiday season, and could not help stealing out of the drawing room on hearing one of their peals of laughter. I found them at the game of blindman's buff. Master Simon, who was the leader of their revels and seemed on all occasions to fulfill the office that of ancient potentate, the Lord of Misrule, was blinded in the midst of the hall. The little beings were as busy about him as the mock fairies about Falstaff, pinching him, plucking at the skirts of his coat, and tickling him with straws. One fine blue-eyed girl of about thirteen, with her flaxen hair all in beautiful confusion, her frolic face in a glow, her frock half torn off her shoulders, a complete picture of a romp, was the chief tormentor; and from the slyness with which Master Simon avoided the smaller game, and hemmed this wild little nymph in corners, and obliged her to jump shrieking over chairs, I suspected the rogue of being not a whit more blinded than was convenient.

While we were all attention to the parson's stories, our ears were suddenly assailed by a burst of heterogeneous sounds from the hall, in which was mingled something like the clang of rude minstrelsy, with the uproar of many small voices and girlish laughter. The door suddenly flew open, and a train came trooping into the room, that might almost have been mistaken for the breaking up of the court of Fairy. That indefatigable spirit, Master Simon, in the faithful discharge of his duties as Lord of Misrule, had conceived the idea of a Christmas mummery, or masking; and having called in to his assistance the Oxonian and the young officer, who were equally ripe for anything that should occasion romping and merriment, they had carried it into instant effect. The old housekeeper had been consulted; the antique clothes presses and wardrobes rummaged and made to yield up the relics of finery that had not seen the light for several generations; the younger part of the company had been privately convened from the parlor and hall, and the whole had been bedizened out into a burlesque imitation of an antique mask.

Master Simon led the van, as "Ancient Christmas," quaintly appareled in a ruff, a short cloak, which had very much the aspect of one of the old housekeeper's petticoats, and a hat that might have served for a village steeple and must indubitably have figured in the days of the Covenanters. From under this his nose curved boldly forth, flushed with a frost-bitten bloom that seemed the very trophy of a December blast. He was accompanied by the blue-eyed romp, dished up as "Dame Mince Pie," in the venerable magnificence of faded brocade, long stomacher, peaked hat, and high-heeled shoes. The young officer appeared as Robin Hood, in a sporting dress of Kendal green, and a foraging cap with a gold tassel. The costume, to be sure, did not bear testimony to deep research, and there was an evident eye to the picturesque, natural to a young gallant in the presence of his mistress. The fair Julia hung on his arm in a pretty rustic dress, as Maid Marian. The rest of the train had been metamorphosed in various ways: the girls trussed up in the finery of the ancient belles of the Bracebridge line, and the striplings bewhiskered with burned cork, and gravely clad in broad skirts, hanging sleeves, and full-bottomed wigs, to represent the characters of Roast Beef, Plum Pudding, and other worthies celebrated in ancient maskings. The whole was under the control of the Oxonian, in the appropriate character of Misrule; and I observed that he exercised rather a mischievous sway with his wand over the smaller personages of the pageant.

The irruption of this motley crew, with beat of drum, according to ancient custom, was the consummation of uproar and merriment. Master Simon covered himself with glory by the stateliness with which, as Ancient Christmas, he walked a minuet with the peerless, though giggling, Dame Mince Pie. It was followed by a dance of all the characters, which, from its medley of costumes, seemed as though the old family portraits had skipped down from their frames to join in the sport. Different centuries were figuring at cross hands and right and left; the Dark Ages were cutting pirouettes and rigadoons; and the days of Queen Bess jigging merrily down the middle, through a line of succeeding generations.

The worthy squire contemplated these fantastic sports, and this resurrection of his old wardrobe, with the simple relish of childish delight. He stood chuckling and rubbing his hands, and scarcely hearing a word the parson said, notwithstanding that the latter was discoursing most authentically on the ancient and stately dance of the Paon, or Peacock, from which he conceived the minuet to be derived. For my part, I was in a continual excitement, from the varied scenes of whim and innocent gaiety passing before me. It was inspiring to see wild-eyed frolic and warmhearted hospitality breaking out from among the chills and glooms of winter, and old age throwing off his apathy, and catching once more the freshness of youthful enjoyment. I felt also an interest in the scene, from the consideration that these fleeting customs were passing fast into oblivion, and that this was, perhaps, the only family in England in which the whole of them were still punctiliously observed. There was a quaintness too, mingled with all this revelry, that gave it a peculiar zest; it was suited to the time and place; and as the old Manor House almost reeled with mirth and wassail, it seemed echoing back the joviality of long-departed years.

(THE ISLE OF MAN)

Fiddler, Play Fast—Play Faster

RUTH SAWYER

IT IS A STRANGE ISLAND and an enchanted one—our Isle of Man. It took many a thousand years and more before mankind discovered it, it being well known that the spirits of water, of earth, of air and fire did put on it an enchantment, hiding it with a blue flame of mist, so that it could not be seen by mortal eye. The mist was made out of the heat of a great fire and the salt vapor of the sea, and it covered the island like a bank of clouds. Then one day the fire went out, the sea grew quiet, and lo, the island stood out in all its height of mountains and ruggedness of coast, its green of fens and rushing of waterfalls. Sailors passing saw it. And from that day forth, men came to it and much of its enchantment was lost.

But not all. Let you know that at all seasons of the year there are spirits abroad on the Isle, working their charms and making their mischief. And there is on the coast, overhanging the sea, a great cavern reaching below the earth, out of which the devil comes when it pleases him, to walk where he will upon the Isle. A wise Manxman does not go far without a scrap of iron or a lump of salt in his pocket; and if it is night, likely, he will have stuck in his cap a sprig of rowan and a sprig of wormwood, feather from a seagull's wing and skin from a conger eel. For these keep away evil spirits; and who upon the Isle would meet with evil, or who would give himself foolishly into its power?

So it is that in the south upon the ramparts of Castle Rushen the cannon are mounted on stone crosses above the ramparts; and when a south Manxman knocks at his neighbor's door he does not cry out, "Are you within?" But rather he asks, "Are there any sinners inside?" For evil is a fearsome thing, and who would have traffic with it?

I am long at beginning my tale, but some there may be who know little of our Isle, and a storyteller cannot always bring his listeners by the straightest road to the story he has to tell. This one is of the south, where the mists hang the heaviest, where the huts are built of turf and thatched with broom, where the cattle are small and the goats many, and where a farmer will tell you he has had his herd brought to fold by the fenodyree—a goblin that is half goat, half boy. But that is another tale.

Let me begin with an old Manx saying—it tunes the story well: "When a poor man helps another, God in his heaven laughs with delight." This shows you that the men of Man are kind to one another, and God is not far from them even when the devil walks abroad.

Count a hundred years, and as many more as you like, and you will come to the time of my story. Beyond Castletown in the sheading of Kirk Christ Rushen lived, then, a lump of a lad named Billy Nell Kewley. He could draw as sweet music from the fiddle as any fiddler of Man. When the Christmas time began, he was first abroad with his fiddle. Up the glens and over the fens, fiddling for this neighbor and that as the night ran out, calling the hour and crying the weather, that those snug on their beds of chaff would know before the day broke what kind of day it would be making. Before yule he started his fiddling, playing half out of the night and half into the day, playing this and playing that, carrying with him, carefully in his cap, the sprig of rowan and the sprig of wormwood, with the iron and salt in the pocket of his brown woolen breeches. And there you have Billy Nell Kewley on the Eve of St. Fingan.

Now over Castletown on a high building of cliff rises Castle Rushen. Beyond stands the oldest monastery on the Isle, in ruin these hundreds of years, Rushen Abbey, with its hundred treens of land. It was through the Forest of Rushen Billy Nell was coming on St. Thomas' Eve, down the Glen to the Quiggan hut, playing the tune "Andisop" and whistling a running of notes to go with it. He broke the whistle, ready to call the hour: "Two of the morning," and the weather: "Cold—with a mist over all," when he heard the running of feet behind him in the dark.

Quick as a falcon he reached for the sprig in his cap. It was gone; the pushing through the green boughs of the forest had torn it. He quickened his own feet. Could it be a buggan after him—an ugly, evil one, a fiend of Man who cursed mortals and bore malice against them, who would bring a body to perdition and then laugh at him? Billy Nell's feet went fast—went faster.

But his ear, dropping behind him, picked up the sound of other feet; they were going fast—and faster. Could it be the fenodyree—the hairy one? That would be not so terrible. The fenodyree played pranks, but he, having once loved a human maid, did not bring evil to humans. And he lived, if the ancient ones could be believed, in Glen Rushen.

And then a voice spoke out of the blackness. "Stop, I command!"

What power lay in that voice! It brought the feet of Billy Nell to a stop—for all he wanted them to go on, expected them to keep running. Afterward he was remembering the salt and iron in his pocket he might have thrown between himself and what followed so closely after him out of the mist. But he did nothing but stop—stop and say to himself: "Billy Nell Kewley, could it be the Noid ny Hanmey who commands—the Enemy of the Soul? And he stood stock still in the darkness, too frightened to shiver, for it was the devil himself he was thinking of.

He who spoke appeared, carrying with him a kind of reddish light that came from everywhere and nowhere, a light the color of fever, or heat lightning, or of the very pit of hell. But when Billy Nell looked he saw as fine a gentleman as ever had come to Man—fine and tall, grave and stern, well clothed in knee breeches and silver buckles and lace and such finery. He spoke with grace and grimness: "Billy Nell Kewley of Castletown, I have heard you are a monstrous good fiddler. No one better, so they say."

"I play fair, sir," said Billy Nell modestly.

"I would have you play for me. Look!" He dipped into a pocket of his breeches, and drawing out a hand so white, so tapering, it might have been a lady's, he showed Billy Nell gold pieces. And in the reddish light that came from everywhere and nowhere Billy saw the strange marking on them. "You shall have as many of these as you can carry away with you if you will fiddle for me and my company three nights from tonight," said the fine one.

"And where shall I fiddle?" asked Billy Nell Kewley.

"I will send a messenger for you, Billy Nell; halfway up the Glen he will meet you. This side of midnight he will meet you."

"I will come," said the fiddler, for he had never heard of so much gold—to be his for a night's fiddling. And being not half so fearful he began to shiver. At that moment a cock crew far away, a bough brushed his eyes, the mist hung about him like a cloak, and he was alone. Then he ran, ran to Quiggan's hut, calling the hour: "Three of the clock," crying the weather: "Cold, with a heavy mist."

The next day he counted, did Billy Nell Kewley, counted the days up to three and found that the night he was to fiddle for all the gold he could carry with him was Christmas Eve. A kind of terror took hold of him. What manner of spirit was the Enemy of the Soul? Could he be anything he chose to be—a devil in hell or a fine gentleman on earth? He ran about asking everyone, and everyone gave him a different answer. He went to the monks of the abbey and found them working in their gardens, their black cowls thrown back from their faces, their bare feet treading the brown earth.

The abbott came, and dour enough he looked. "Shall I go, your reverence? Shall I fiddle for one I know not? Is it good gold he is giving me?" asked Billy Nell.

"I cannot answer any one of those questions," said the abbott. "That night alone can give the answers: Is the gold good or cursed? Is the man noble or is he the devil? But go.

Carry salt, carry iron and bollan bane. Play a dance and watch. Play another—and watch. Then play a Christmas hymn and see!"

This side of midnight, Christmas Eve, Billy Nell Kewley climbed the Glen, his fiddle wrapped in a lamb's fleece to keep out the wet. Mist, now blue, now red, hung over the blackness, so thick he had to feel his way along the track with his feet, stumbling.

He passed where Castle Rushen should have stood. He passed on, was caught up and carried as by the mist and in it. He felt his feet leave the track, he felt them gain it again. And then the mist rolled back like clouds after a storm and before him he saw such a splendid sight as no lump of a lad had ever beheld before. A castle, with courtyard and corridors, with piazzas and high roofings, spread before him all aglowing with light. Windows wide and doorways wide, and streaming with the light came laughter. And there was his host more splendid than all, with velvet and satin, silver and jewels. About him moved what Billy Nell took to be highborn lords and ladies, come from overseas no doubt, for never had he seen their like on Man.

In the middle of the great hall he stood, unwrapping his fiddle, sweetening the strings, rosining the bow, limbering his fingers. The laughter died. His host shouted:

"Fiddler, play fast—play faster!"

In all his life and never again did Billy Nell play as he played that night. The music of his fiddle made the music of a hundred fiddles. About him whirled the dancers like crazy rainbows: blue and orange, purple and yellow, green and red all mixed together until his head swam with the color. And yet the sound of the dancers' feet was the sound of the grass growing or the corn ripening or the holly reddening—which is to say no sound at all. Only there was the sound of his playing, and above that the sound of his host shouting, always shouting:

"Fiddler, play fast—play faster!"

Ever faster--ever faster! It was as with a mighty wind Billy Nell played now, drawing the wild, mad music from his fiddle. He played tunes he had never heard before, tunes which cried and shrieked and howled and sighed and sobbed and cried out in pain.

"Play fast—play faster!"

He saw one standing by the door—a monk in a black cowl, barefooted, a monk who looked at him with deep, sad eyes and held two fingers of his hand to his lips as if to hush the music.

Then, and not till then, did Billy Nell Kewley remember what the abbott had told him. But the monk—how came he here? And then he remembered that too. A tale so old it had grown ragged with the telling, so that only a scrap here and there was left: how long ago, on the blessed Christmas Eve, a monk had slept through the midnight Mass to the Virgin and to the newborn Child, and how, at complin on Christmas Day, he was missing and never seen again. The ancient ones said that the devil had taken him away, that Enemy of All Souls, had stolen his soul because he had slept over Mass.

Terror left Billy Nell. He swept his bow so fast over the strings of his fiddle that his eyes could not follow it.

"Fiddler, play fast—play faster!"

"Master, I play faster and faster!" He moved his own body to the mad music, moved it across the hall to the door where stood the monk. He crashed out the last notes; on the floor at the feet of the monk he dropped iron, salt, and bollan bane. Then out of the silence he drew the notes of a Christmas carol—softly, sweetly it rose on the air:

> Adeste, fideles, laeti, triumphantes,
> Venite, venite in Bethlehem:
> Natum videte, Regem angelorum:
> Venite, adoremus, venite, adoremus,
> Venite, adoremus Dominum.

Racked were the ears of Billy Nell at the sounds which surged above the music, groans and wailing, the agony of souls damned. Racked were his eyes with the sights he saw: the servants turned to fleshless skeletons, the lords and ladies to howling demons. And the monk with the black cowl and bare feet sifted down to the grass beneath the vanishing castle—a heap of gray dust. But in the dust shone one small spark of holy light—a monk's soul, freed. And Billy Nell took it in his hand and tossed it high in the wind as one tosses a falcon to the sky for free passage. And he watched it go its skimming way until the sky gathered it in.

Billy Nell Kewley played his way down the Glen, stopping to call the hour: "Three of this blessed Christmas morning," stopping to cry the weather: "The sky is clear . . . the Christ is born."

FINLAND

A Christmas Broadcast from the Trenches, 1939

WILLIAM L. WHITE

WILLIAM L. WHITE, speaking to you on this Christmas night from Finland, the country where our legend of Santa Claus and his reindeers first began. Reindeer still pull sleighs in the north of Finland tonight, carrying supplies to the little nation's army which is fighting to press back the great army which would come in. But if part of our Christmas story began in Finland, it, Finland, is also the country where Christmas ends, for beyond the line of its armies lies that great land where there is no Christmas any more, and where the memory of its stories is dimming fast.

And this is why, since I have come from a front-line post of command of this Finnish army, I can tell you tonight about the last Christmas tree. And although you have many finer ones in America tonight, tall trees gay with tinsel, proud with sparkling colored balls and rich with presents underneath wrapped in pretty papers and tied with silver cords, I think you would like these even better when you know about that brave and sad last little Christmas tree at the very edge of the land where Christmas ends.

Even without our guide we might have found the last Christmas tree by following the sound of big guns from far off. Presently, when they were close, we left our cars and followed a trail in the deep snow which wound toward the guns through a tall spruce forest, the snow on the branches glistening in the moonlight. The trail led past the second-line dugouts on through the woods toward the guns, and sometimes we stepped aside to let pass a horse-drawn sleigh, fitted to carry warm boilers of steaming hot soup up to the men ahead.

We were told to walk quietly now. Talking in whispers, we passed places where the white snow had been gashed deep by shell craters, and at last we came to the front-line post-of-command. The officer here greeted us in a tired voice, saying we should go no further, as this forest had only yesterday been retaken from the Russians, whose lines were a few hundred yards ahead, and his men had not had time to dig safe trenches. Beyond us was no real front line, but only machine-gun nests, dugouts, and a few shallow trenches, a place where it was not safe for any man to crawl who had not first seen the country by clear light of day. But perhaps we would like to go down into his front-line command post dugout, talk to his men, and see their Christmas tree.

The dugout was deep beneath snow and earth and warmed from the zero weather by a tiny stove. Tired men were lying on the straw-strewn floor and when they rose to greet us we could see by the light of the shaded lantern that their faces were weary and unshaven. The officer explained this, saying fighting had been very hard, the enemy had greatly outnumbered them, so when there was no fighting there was time for little but sleep.

We asked him what the men would have for Christmas dinner and he told us their mess kits would be filled with thick warm pea soup, rich with pieces of mutton and pork, with plenty of bread spread thick with butter and for dessert porridge with sugar. And then, because it was Christmas, the army had sent up four Christmas hams, which would be sliced and eaten with bread.

He said we should remember that several sledges had come laden with Christmas presents for the men—warm sweaters and socks knitted by their wives or Christmas cookies and tarts baked by them—and there would be something for each man.

We asked when the men up ahead in the last machine-gun posts and dugouts would get their presents and he said not until tomorrow, but they would not mind, because each man knew why he must be there and what must be done and not one would wish himself in any other place, and because the people of this country love Christmas so much, each one could carry it with him in his heart.

Then we asked if, at our own risk, we might not crawl up and give them some of the cigarettes and sweets and tobacco we had brought. He shook his head, saying that if we made a noise and attracted Russian artillery there might be losses among his men, and this was not good to happen on Christmas night in any land.

But tomorrow those men would get their presents in this dugout, and also the Christmas tree would be saved for them to see. The tiny tree was standing near the stove. Little red and white wax candles had been tied by men's clumsy fingers to its branches. The officers said the candles could not be lighted, because this might be seen by bombers through the dugout's canvas roof. Also tied to the green spruce twigs were a few gumdrops—the kind you buy twisted in colored wax papers. At the very top was tied, not a sparkling glass star, but a cheap cardboard image of Santa Claus—and this was all. No strips of tinsel, no shining balls, no winking electric lights. . . . You can be very glad that the Christmas tree in your home tonight is so much finer. We asked the officer who sent these ornaments, and he smiled kindly and said that they came from a very small girl whose father was out on the last line tonight, and with them a note from her mother explaining that the child was very young, and could not understand why he could not come back to them even on Christmas, and had cried bitterly until they let her send him these little things so that at least he could have his own Christmas tree. So the tree would be kept as it was in the dugout until he came back from his outpost tomorrow.

So when you take your last look at your own fine tree tonight before turning out its lights, I think you will like it even better since you know about the last sad little Christmas tree of all, which could not even have its poor candles lighted because it faces the land where there is no Christmas.

Christmas in Finland

IN THE FINNISH HOME the Christmas tree is set up on Christmas Eve. Apples and other fruits, candies, paper flags, cotton, and tinsel are used as decorations, and candles are used for lighting it.

The Christmas festivities are usually preceded by a visit to the famous steam baths, after which everyone dresses in clean clothes in preparation for the Christmas dinner, which is generally served from five to seven in the evening.

Christmas gifts may be given out before or after the dinner. The children do not hang up stockings, but Santa Claus comes in person, often accompanied by as many as half a dozen Christmas elves (in brown costumes, knee-length pants, red stockings, and red elves' caps) to distribute the presents.

The main dish of the dinner is boiled codfish served snowy white and fluffy, with allspice, boiled potatoes, and cream sauce. The dried cod has been soaked for a week in a lye solution, then in clear water to soften it to the right texture. Also on the menu are roast suckling pig or a roasted fresh ham, mashed potatoes, and vegetables.

After dinner the children go to bed, their elders staying up to chat with visitors and drink coffee until about midnight.

Christmas Day services in the churches begin at six in the

morning. It is a day also for family visits and reunions. In some parts of the country the Star Boys tour the countryside singing Christmas songs. During all these days the people keep wishing each other a "Merry Yule."

FRANCE

Christmas in Provence

HELEN HILL AND VIOLET MAXWELL

LITTLE TONINO AND HIS SISTER lived in Nouvilo in the South of France. They lived with Papo, their father; Mamo, their mother; and Mameto, who was their grandmother. There were many pets in the household. Little Tonino had a donkey all his own, a donkey named Tintourlet.

Tonino loved to model in clay. One day, not long before Christmas, he made a model of Tintourlet and of Lavanda, the goat. Then he had an idea. He said to his little sister: "Nanou, we won't show anything that I have made this afternoon to anybody. We will keep it a big secret, and next week when the figures are dry we will paint them and then we will set them up with all Mameto's little *santons* for the crèche at Christmas. And won't they all be surprised!"

Now I must explain exactly what a *santon* is. In the land of Provence, where Tonino and Nanou lived, it has been the custom for hundreds and hundreds of years for every family, at Christmas time, to make a crèche (you pronounce this, kresh), which is a model of the stable in Bethlehem where Christ was born. All the churches have a crèche in a side aisle at Christmas time, and this is sometimes very elaborate and wonderful. In Provence every family makes one all for itself too and sets it up in the corner of the kitchen or living room.

Besides the figures of the holy family and the shepherds and the kings and the Wise Men bringing their gifts, the people of Provence have in their crèches any number of other little figures bringing gifts to the Christ-child. There are peasants with loads of hay on their backs, women carrying water jars, hunters with their little guns, fishermen fishing in the brook, little schoolboys and little schoolgirls, old ladies with their sticks and young ones with spinning wheels—in fact, I could not begin to tell you one quarter of all the fascinating little figures that the Provençal people set up in their crèches. These little clay figures are called *santons,* and, of course, no family could have them all; some are very old and they are seen only at Christmas time and then packed very carefully away. But if any do get broken, one can buy new ones at Christmas time, for in every village a peddler comes around and sets up his booth in the market place, filled with hundreds of little *santons.*

Tonino's grandmother had a box full of *santons;* in fact I think that the crèche that she made at Christmas had more *santons* than any other in the village. Some of her *santons* were very old; they had been given to her by her grandmother and her grandmother had given them to her, and very likely her grandmother had passed them on to her! Some of Mameto's *santons* were more than a hundred years old, yet only one had ever been broken, and that was the black king!

It had happened only the Christmas before. What made it especially sad was that when Tonino's grandmother went to the peddler's booth to buy a new black king, there were not any more left. So this Christmas Eve there would be no black king with scarlet mantle, bringing gifts to the Christ-child.

It was of this that Nanou suddenly thought when she saw the beautiful figures that Tonino could make out of his big lump of clay. She said: "Oh, Tonino, let me have a little piece of clay and see if I can make a black king for the crèche to replace the one that was broken last year. Wouldn't that surprise them all?"

So she took a piece of clay and she pinched and smoothed and rolled it; but alas and alack, Nanou did not have the potter's touch, and try as she would she could not make her piece of clay look like a king or indeed anything at all. Then she said, "Oh, Tonino, I can't do it at all. You try."

But Tonino said: "I don't think I could do it either without looking at the figures of the other kings. I'll tell you what I'll do; I'll ask Mameto to lend me the *santon* of the king with the golden crown, and I'll make the black king exactly like him, only we'll paint his cloak scarlet instead of purple and I'll make him a turban as well as a crown."

Then he looked out of the window and said: "Why, there are Papo and Mamo and Mameto coming toward the house, and it's beginning to get dark! I didn't think we had been working so long. Let's find a hiding place for Tintourlet and Lavanda where they will get dry and where Papo and Mamo and Mameto won't find them."

Nanou found a beautiful hiding place, on a little shelf above the window that neither she nor Tonino had known was there before. She climbed onto a chair and put the little figures of Tintourlet and Lavanda very carefully side by side on the shelf. They only had time to pull the chair away and rush to the other side of the room and pretend to be examining a spot on the wall, when their father and mother and grandmother came in all ready to admire the beautiful things that Tonino had been making with his lump of clay.

The next morning was Sunday, and Papo and Mamo went to church. When they had gone Tonino begged Mameto to lend him the *santon* of the king with the golden crown. He promised to be ever so careful of it. He did not tell Mameto why he wanted it and she did not ask him any questions, but went to her wedding chest, where she kept all her treasures, unlocked it, and handed Tonino the little *santon*. Tonino took the king back to the kitchen and got out a little lump of clay and tried to make a little figure just like it.

Instead of the crown he planned to make a turban, as the Moorish king always wears a turban. He found it was more difficult than he had expected. He had to squeeze up the clay and try again and again before he was satisfied. But at last he made a little figure that pleased him very much, which looked exactly like a tiny man in a long cloak with a turban on his head.

Already he had a new idea. He took a little lump of clay and the green water pitcher and he ran up to his mother's room, where there was a looking glass. He climbed up on a chair so that he could see himself from head to foot in the looking glass, and he put the water pitcher on his head and held it there with one hand, and looked at himself very hard. Then he put the pitcher down and he molded the clay and made a little figure of a boy carrying a water pitcher on his head. Of course it was the figure of the little water carrier in the story about Citronella.

He had just finished when he heard Nanou running up the stairs; and when she saw what Tonino had done she was astonished. She could not believe that he had made them all by himself. Suzetto had promised to let them use her paints one day soon, but the figures, she had told Nanou, must be quite dry before they could be painted. They must wait for several days.

Tonino and Nanou thought the time would never come. At last all the little clay figures were dry, and one afternoon at the end of the week they climbed the staircase that led to Suzetto's kitchen. They found her putting the finishing touches to a bowl she was decorating with a little white house with a red roof and a pine tree growing beside it.

Suzetto's table was drawn up close to the window and her saucers of paint were in a row in front of her, white paint and red and blue and yellow and green and a lovely shade of purple. On a shelf, beside the window and easy to reach from her table, were the cups and saucers and bowls and salt cellars that she had finished painting that day. Some of them were painted only with a coat of white, which must dry before Suzetto could paint the little flowers and garlands around it.

Tonino and Nanou admired them all, but the one that Tonino liked best was the bowl with the little house and green trees painted on it. He was afraid that he would never be able to paint as beautifully as that. But, when Tonino and Nanou opened their package, it was Suzetto's turn to admire and she was amazed at the little figures that Tonino had made. Of course, Suzetto would have loved to paint them herself, but she knew that it was Tonino's right, as he had made them.

So Tonino sat down in Suzetto's chair and filled his brush with gray paint and proceeded to paint Tintourlet gray; he painted him all gray except for his nose, which he painted white, and then he tried to put in his eyes. But alas and alack, he could not get Tintourlet's eyes in the right place; the first time he tried he put one eye up near Tintourlet's ear and the other close to his nose! So he painted them out and tried again, but with no better success.

All this time Nanou had been watching and longing to get the paint brush in her hands, and now she said: "Oh, Tonino, do let me try. I'd like to help to earn the money to keep Tintourlet, and I know that I could paint his eyes beautifully. I painted a picture of a donkey last week in school and the teacher said mine was the best of all. Please let me try, Tonino!"

So Tonino did let her try and Nanou sat down and filled a very fine brush with brown paint, and she put out her tongue a little way and gave one tiny dab with the brush, and then another and behold, Tintourlet had two beautiful brown eyes in exactly the right place. Then, after washing her brush clean, she took some red paint and painted his red bridle; and, when she had painted the grass he was standing on a bright green, the figure of Tintourlet was complete.

Tonino was delighted. He was so delighted that he allowed Nanou to paint the water carrier; and she was just as successful with the water carrier. She painted his pitcher and the grass green and she gave him a red cap and a red sash, and made his shirt white and his hair and breeches black. His hands and face, of course, were pink. Last of all she put two little black dots for his eyes and a little red dot for his mouth.

Then Suzetto was allowed to paint Lavanda and, of course, she did it beautifully. She painted her white, just like Lavanda, with black spots and dear little black hoofs. Last of all Tonino painted the black king. He painted his coat with the beautiful purple paint, his turban white, his face a dark brown, but it was Nanou who painted his eyes and his black beard.

Now all the figures were painted and Suzetto suggested that they put them on her shelf with all her other pottery to dry. Tonino and Nanou thought this a very good plan, especially when Nanou said: "Let's leave them there till Christmas Eve, if Suzetto will let us, and not say a word to anyone at home. Then when the crèche is all ready Tonino can run over and get the figures and we'll slip them in among the other *santons* and see how surprised they'll all be when they notice that there is a new black king and three other new *santons!*"

Not so very long after that it was Christmas Eve. Mamo and Mameto had been growing corn and grass seed in flat dishes to decorate the crèche and to make a grassy meadow for it. After dinner Tonino's father brought up a big packing case, and placed it in the corner between the window and the fireplace. Mamo got a green cloth and covered the box so that the folds fell over the sides of the packing case to the floor. Then Mameto went to her wedding chest and brought out the *santons*. She also brought out the little stable, which was made of wood and which had a roof made of corrugated cardboard painted red to look like the tiled roofs in Nouvilo, only the tiled roofs in Nouvilo have all turned gray with age.

In front of the stable she put the green meadow, and at the side of the dish with the tall blades of corn; then she arranged the moss and the stones that Tonino and Nanou had collected, so that the sides of the tin and the dish were quite hidden. At the back of the stable she arranged all the tiny trees with more rocks and moss, so that it looked as if the stable were built on the edge of a wooded cliff with a green meadow in front.

When Mameto had finished arranging all the *santons* you have no idea how beautiful it looked. In the stable she put the holy family, with the Christ-child lying in his manger and a donkey and two cows near him. Then on the grassy meadow she arranged the shepherd *santon* with his sheep, the hunter, and the woodcutter and the gypsy lass, and the washerwoman and others coming through the corn fields.

There were the knife grinder and the spinner and the gardener and so many peasant *santons,* some carrying baskets of fruit on their heads or bundles of firewood or casks of olive oil. Even the fisherman was not forgotten; there he sat beside a pool at the edge of the wood with his fishing line, and the pool was made of a little round mirror that belonged to Nanou.

On the highest tree behind the stable Mameto pinned a golden star, and in front of the crèche she arranged four candles in pottery candlesticks. Now all the *santons* were in their place except for the kings, but these would not arrive until the Feast of Kings, which is on the sixth of January. So Mameto put them at the very edge of the table right by the candlesticks, and she would move them forward a little every day until on the Feast of Kings they would be standing near the stable to present their gifts.

As Mameto looked at them she said: "It is too bad that the Moorish King is broken. I have never seen a crèche where there were only two kings. If it had been another king I might have put another *santon* in his place, but the Moorish King is the only one that has a brown face."

Tonino and Nanou looked at each other and found it difficult not to laugh, for they had the new *santons* that Tonino had made all ready in their pockets. At last Papo said, "Well, I must be going to milk Lavanda." Mamo said, "I will put on a pretty dress in honor of the crèche." Mameto began to prepare the vegetables for supper. The very moment that her back was turned Tonino slipped over to the table and put Tintourlet and Lavanda and the water carrier beside the shepherd in the grassy meadow. As for the Moorish King he put him beside the other two kings on the edge of the table and only just in time, for Mameto turned around and told him not to meddle with the crèche.

But she did not notice anything, though she passed quite close to the table when she went to get the butter from the window cupboard. After supper, however, when the candles in front of the crèche were lighted, Mameto suddenly said: "Who moved the donkey from the stable and put it among the shepherds—and who put the goat among the sheep? And where did this figure of a little water carrier come from?" Then at last she saw the Moorish King and she said: "Why, it is a miracle! Here are three kings where I put only two, and one is like the Moorish King that was broken last year!"

She looked at Tonino and Nanou—and the secret was out! You may believe that their Papo and Mamo were delighted to know that Tonino had made such beautiful figures with his lump of clay and that Nanou had painted them so beautifully.

Then Tonino and Nanou recited the little prayer that all Provençal children learn to say in front of the crèche at Christmas:

> Teach us, Holy Child, we ask,
> Cheerfully to do our task.
> Make us love to delve and toil
> Like the tiller of the soil,
> Like the oxen, strong and steady,
> Like the watchman, ever ready.
> Make us like the shepherd, wise
> To know the warnings in the skies.
> Make us patient as the ass,
> Merry as the gypsy lass,
> Like the potter at his wheel
> For his handcraft full of zeal.

There are more verses than we can print, and Tonino and Nanou did not know them all either, as there is one for every figure in the crèche and it would need another book to print them all. But Tonino never forgot to say the verse about the potter.

Before they went to bed, instead of hanging up their stockings, they left their shoes on the hearthstone for Papo Noël to fill with presents. The next morning, when Tonino and Nanou came tiptoeing down to see their presents they found their shoes full of little toys and candy and nuts. Beside their old shoes they each found a pair of straw sabots lined with rabbit fur.

Christmas Festivities in France

CHRISTMAS CUSTOMS, originating in the Orient, were introduced into France by the Romans. Rheims, which had known Rome's *triumphs*, was the scene of the first French Christmas celebration when, in 496, Clovis and his three thousand warriors were baptized. Bishop Rémi had purposely chosen the day of the Nativity for this ceremony. Then other important events took place on Christmas Day in the following years. Charlemagne "crowned by God, the Great and Pacific Emperor," received the crown from the hands of Pope Leo III on Christmas Day in 800. In 1100, Godefroy de Bouillon's successor, his brother Baudouin, was crowned in the Basilica of Saint Marie of Bethlehem. Later King Jean-le-Bon founded the Order of the Star in honor of the "manger"; it remained in existence until 1352. In 1389 the crowd shouted Noël! Noël! in welcoming Queen Isabeau of Bavaria to the capital.

Thus, gradually, Christmas became a religious and secular celebration which, in fact, until the end of the Middle Ages, was confused with the celebration of the coming of the year, now held on "New Year's Day."

Today Christmas in France is a family holiday, a religious celebration, and, for the children, an occasion for merrymaking. New Year's Day is a more strictly adult festival, where gifts are exchanged and calls are made.

Christmas Trees

The fir tree was first presented as the holy tree of Christmas in the city of Strasbourg in 1605. It was "decorated with artificial colored roses, apples, sugar, and painted hosts," and symbolized the tree in the Garden of Eden.

In France, Christmas trees are rarely seen in public places, but the shop windows of big department stores, principally in

Paris, compete with one another in fabulous displays of animated figures; a day spent visiting and comparing the exhibits is practically a must for parents.

Family celebrations begin with decoration of the Christmas tree a few days before Christmas; candles and lights, tinsel and many-colored stars are attached to it. On Christmas Eve, when the children are asleep, little toys, candies, and fruits are hung on the branches of the tree as a supplement to the gifts that "Santa Claus" has left in the shoes before the fireplace.

The Manger

Another custom is that of the manger, *la crèche,* originating in twelfth-century France in the form of liturgical drama. At first the manger itself resembled an altar and was placed either inside the church or before the portal, as it was at the Abbey of Saint-Benoit-sur-Loire. Antique mangers can be seen in churches at Chartres, Chaource, Nogent-le-Rotrou, Sainte-Marie d'Oloron and in the museums at Marseilles and Orleans.

The popular manger was introduced in Avignon by the family of St. Francis of Assisi between 1316 and 1334, but it was not until the sixteenth century that the making of crèches or *grebbes,* as they were called in old French, became a widespread custom.

Today, the family arranges a manger on a small stage in a prominent part of the house. In Provence, children bring rocks, branches, and moss to make a setting for the manger. Little terra-cotta figures, known as *"santons"* or "little saints" are grouped around the manger to represent the holy family, the other characters of the story of the Nativity, and the people of the village: the mayor, the priest, the policeman, the butcher, the baker, the miller, the farmer. In the stable is a reproduction of the legendary manger of Bethlehem, with the ox and the donkey placed close to Jesus, and Mary and Joseph in the foreground welcoming the visitors: shepherds, weavers, etc.

Since 1803 a special fair for the sale of the *"santons"* has been held in Marseilles during the month of December, but the true capital of the world of *santons* is the little town of Aubagne.

The Midnight Mass and the "Réveillon"

At midnight everyone attends the three Christmas Masses. Churches and cathedrals, large and small, are magnificently lighted and echo the joyful melodies of carols, bells, and carillons. Many churches have a "crèche." Formerly, in certain regions, a real infant was placed on the hay of the manger during the Mass, but this custom is no longer observed.

When the family returns home after midnight Mass, there is a late supper known as *"le réveillon."* The meal varies according to the region of France. In Alsace, for example, the traditional goose is brought in on a platter and given the place of honor on the table. The Bretons serve buckwheat cakes with sour cream. Turkey and chestnuts are served in Burgundy. The favorite dishes of Paris and the Île-de-France region are oysters, *foie gras,* and the traditional cake in the form of a yule log, which reminds one of the *bûche de Noël* which used to burn on the hearth on Christmas Eve. Wines are generally muscatel, Anjou, sauternes, and champagne.

In Paris, Christmas is more worldly. For some people, instead of a religious festival, it is a time for dancing, champagne, and dining in style.

The Children and Christmas

Ordinarily, young children do not attend midnight Mass with their parents, but go to bed early to dream of the miracle of their Christmas gifts. Before going to bed, they put their shoes by the fireside for a gift from *le père Noël* or *le petit Jésus.* Formerly, peasants' wooden shoes, called *sabots,* were very popular at Christmas time, but today shoes of any kind are set before the fireplace or around the tree. However, the *sabots* are not forgotten—chocolate wooden shoes are made by pastry shops and filled with candies.

Christmas Carols and "Mystères"

Christmas carols were at first part of the liturgical drama and of popular origin; they appeared in the fifteenth century. Collections of these songs with rustic themes were numerous as early as the sixteenth century and were presented as Christmas bibles. They often included couplets with a secular significance. Some well-known musicians like Costeley composed new airs from old themes.

Quite burlesque and full of verve at the beginning of the eighteenth century, Christmas songs came to include gavottes and minuets at the end of the century. The nineteenth-century carols have a rather pompous character; the most famous is *"Minuit, chrétiens"* by Placide Cappeau.

From the combination of the first "mangers" and of the earliest carols came the liturgical drama, given in the cathedral squares at Christmas. These dramas, in fact, gave rise to the French theater.

The fourteenth and fifteenth centuries performed only Biblical scenes connected with the story of Christ's birth. These *mystères* were presented with stage settings and evolved into real plays. In our time, companies of young actors still perform miracle plays generally known as *Mystères de la Nativité;* one of the most famous was written by Marguerite, Queen of Navarre, at the beginning of the sixteenth century.

Puppet shows are also given every year at Christmas, principally in Paris and in Lyons. One of the well-known Christmas puppet plays written by Mr. de Marynbourg is called "Bethlehem 1933" and is a masterpiece of popular art.

Local Customs and Legends

Traditional legends and beliefs associated with Christmas are numerous in France. It is undoubtedly in Provence that the Christmas holiday is celebrated with the greatest community spirit and the most exuberant joy. In some towns, shepherds offer a lamb on Christmas Eve while in others, the *"réveillon"* is held in the snowy mountains or a song fest precedes the midnight Mass. In the small village of Solliesville, the whole population gathers in order to take bread. Twelve children are selected, each one to receive an *obol* of bread, meat, and candies as a symbol of the apostles. Then a supper is offered to the important townsmen and their guests. During the Mass, the characters of the manger are portrayed by people from the village.

The magic of Christmas is the magic of the Orient. During the Middle Ages, minstrels wandered through villages and towns, telling *"merveilles qui advinrent en la sainte nuit,"* the legend of the flight into Egypt, or the legend of the sower who, when asked which way the holy family had gone, deceived King Herod. Legends told around the fire on Christmas Eve are nearly all forgotten; but some of them have been transformed into fairy tales or fantasies. Such a story is that of the dancers condemned to dance throughout the year because their movements had turned the priest's thoughts during the midnight Mass. Another such tale is the pathetic and charming story of the little homeless matchmonger who, sitting in the snow on the sidewalk, struck all her matches in order to imagine Christmas in a house; but Christmas is the time of miracles and at the striking of the last match, the little girl was conveyed to Paradise by shining golden angels.

HOLLAND

The Festival of Saint Nicholas

MARY MAPES DODGE

W E ALL KNOW HOW, before the Christmas tree began to flourish in the home life of our country, a certain "right jolly old elf," with "eight tiny reindeer," used to drive his sleigh load of toys up to our house tops, and then bound down the chimney to fill the stockings so hopefully hung by the fireplace. His friends called him Santa Claus, and those who were most intimate ventured to say "Old Knick." It is said that he originally came from Holland. Doubtless he did; but, if so, he certainly, like many other foreigners, changed his ways very much after landing upon our shores. In Holland, St. Nicholas is a veritable saint, and often appears in full costume, with his embroidered robes, glittering with gems and gold, his miter, his crozier, and his jeweled gloves. Here Santa Claus comes rollicking along, on the twenty-fifth of December, our holy Christmas morn. But in Holland, St. Nicholas visits earth on the fifth, a time especially appropriated to him. Early on the morning of the sixth he distributes his candies, toys, and treasures, then vanishes for a year.

Christmas Day is devoted by the Hollanders to church rites and pleasant family visiting. It is on St. Nicholas' Eve that their young people become half wild with joy and expectation. To some of them it is a sorry time, for the saint is very candid, and if any of them have been bad during the past year, he is quite sure to tell them so. Sometimes he carries a birch rod under his arm and advises the parents to give them scoldings in place of confections, and floggings instead of toys.

It was well that the boys hastened to their abodes on that

bright winter evening, for in less than an hour afterward the saint made his appearance in half the homes of Holland. He visited the king's palace, and in the selfsame moment appeared in Annie Bouman's comfortable home. Probably one of our silver half dollars would have purchased all that his saintship left at the peasant Bouman's; but a half dollar's worth will sometimes do for the poor what hundreds of dollars may fail to do for the rich; it makes them happy and grateful, fills them with new peace and love.

Hilda Van Gleck's little brothers and sisters were in a high state of excitement that night. They had been admitted into the grand parlor; they were dressed in their best and had been given two cakes apiece at supper. Hilda was as joyous as any. Why not? Saint Nicholas would never cross a girl of fourteen from his list just because she was tall and looked almost like a woman. On the contrary, he would probably exert himself to do honor to such an august-looking damsel. Who could tell? So she sported and laughed and danced as gaily as the youngest and was the soul of all their merry games. Father, mother, and grandmother looked on approvingly; so did grandfather, before he spread his large red handkerchief over his face, leaving only the top of his skull cap visible. This kerchief was his ensign of sleep.

Earlier in the evening all had joined in the fun. In the general hilarity there had seemed to be a difference only in bulk between grandfather and the baby. Indeed a shade of solemn expectation now and then flitting across the faces of the younger members had made them seem rather more thoughtful than their elders.

Now the spirit of fun reigned supreme. The very flames danced and capered in the polished grate. A pair of prim candles that had been staring at the Astral lamp began to wink at other candles far away in the mirrors. There was a long bell rope suspended from the ceiling in the corner, made of glass beads netted over a cord nearly as thick as your wrist. It generally hung in the shadow and made no sign; but tonight it twinkled from end to end. Its handle of crimson glass sent reckless dashes of red at the papered wall, turning its dainty blue stripes into purple. Passers-by halted to catch the merry laughter floating through curtain and sash into the street, then skipped on their way with a startled consciousness that the village was wide awake. At last matters grew so up-roarious that the grandsire's red kerchief came down from his face with a jerk. What decent old gentleman could sleep in such a racket! Mynheer Van Gleck regarded his children with astonishment. The baby even showed symptoms of hysterics. It was high time to attend to business. Madame suggested that if they wished to see the good St. Nicholas, they should sing the same loving invitation that had brought him the year be-fore.

The baby stared and thrust his fist into his mouth as Myn-heer put him down upon the floor. Soon he sat erect and looked with a sweet scowl at the company. With his lace and embroideries, and his crown of blue ribbon and whalebone (for he was not quite past the tumbling age) he looked like the king of babies.

The other children, each holding a pretty willow basket, formed at once in a ring, and moved slowly around the little fellow, lifting their eyes, meanwhile, for the saint to whom they were about to address themselves was yet in mysterious quarters.

Madame commenced playing softly upon the piano; soon the voices rose—gentle, youthful voices—rendered all the sweeter for their tremor:

> Welcome, friend! Saint Nicholas, welcome!
>   Bring no rod for us, tonight!
> While our voices bid thee, welcome,
>   Every heart with joy is light!
>
>   Tell us every fault and failing
>   We will bear thy keenest railing,
>   So we sing—so we sing—
>   Thou shalt tell us everything!
>
> Welcome, friend! Saint Nicholas, welcome!
>   Welcome to this merry band!

Happy children, greet thee, welcome!
Thou art glad'ning all the land!

Fill each empty hand and basket,
'Tis thy little ones who ask it,
So we sing—so we sing—
Thou wilt bring us everything!

During the chorus, sundry glances, half in eagerness, half in dread, had been cast toward the polished folding doors. Now a loud knocking was heard. The circle was broken in an instant. Some of the little ones, with a strange mixture of fear and delight, pressed against the mother's knee. Grandfather bent forward, with his chin resting upon his hand; grandmother lifted her spectacles; Mynheer Van Gleck, seated by the fireplace, slowly drew his meerschaum from his mouth, while Hilda and the other children settled themselves beside him in an expectant group.

The knocking was heard again.

"Come in," said Madame softly.

The door slowly opened, and St. Nicholas, in full array, stood before them. You could have heard a pin drop! Soon he spoke. What a mysterious majesty in his voice! what kindliness in his tones!

"Karel Van Gleck, I am pleased to greet thee, and thy honored vrouw Kathrine, and thy son and his good vrouw Annie!

"Children, I greet ye all! Hendrick, Hilda, Broom, Katy, Huygens, and Lucretia! And thy cousins, Wolfert, Diedrich, Mayken, Voost, and Katrina! Good children ye have been, in the main, since I last accosted ye. Diedrich was rude at the Haarlem fair last fall, but he has tried to atone for it since. Mayken has failed of late in her lessons, and too many sweets and trifles have gone to her lips, and too few stivers to her charity box. Diedrich, I trust, will be a polite, manly boy for the future, and Mayken will endeavor to shine as a student. Let her remember, too, that economy and thrift are needed in the foundation of a worthy and generous life. Little Katy has been cruel to the cat more than once. St. Nicholas can hear the cat cry when its tail is pulled. I will forgive her if she will remember from this hour that the smallest dumb creatures have feelings and must not be abused."

As Katy burst into a frightened cry, the saint graciously remained silent until she was soothed.

"Master Broom," he resumed, "I warn thee that boys who are in the habit of putting snuff upon the foot stove of the schoolmistress may one day be discovered and receive a flogging—"

(Master Broom colored and stared in great astonishment.)

"But thou art such an excellent scholar, I shall make thee no further reproof.

"Thou, Hendrick, didst distinguish thyself in the archery match last spring, and hit the *Doel,* though the bird was swung before it to unsteady thine eye. I give thee credit for excelling in manly sport and exercise, though I must not unduly countenance thy boat racing since it leaves thee too little time for thy proper studies.

"Lucretia and Hilda shall have a blessed sleep tonight. The consciousness of kindness to the poor, devotion in their souls, and cheerful, hearty obedience to household rule will render them happy.

"With one and all I avow myself well content. Goodness, industry, benevolence, and thrift have prevailed in your midst. Therefore, my blessing upon you—and may the New Year find all treading the paths of obedience, wisdom, and love. Tomorrow you shall find more substantial proofs that I have been in your midst. Farewell!"

With these words came a great shower of sugar plums, upon a linen sheet spread out in front of the doors. A gentle scramble followed. The children fairly tumbled over each other in their eagerness to fill their baskets. Madame cautiously held the baby down in their midst till the chubby little fists were filled. Then the bravest of the youngsters sprang up and burst open the closed doors—in vain they peered into the mysterious apartment—St. Nicholas was nowhere to be seen.

Soon there was a general rush to another room, where stood a table covered with the finest and whitest of linen damask.

Each child, in a flutter of excitement, laid a shoe upon it. The door was then carefully locked, and its key hidden in the mother's bedroom. Next followed good-night kisses, a grand family procession to the upper floor, merry farewells at bedroom doors—and silence, at last, reigned in the Van Gleck mansion.

Early the next morning the door was solemnly unlocked and opened in the presence of the assembled household, when lo! a sight appeared proving St. Nicholas to be a saint of his word!

Every shoe was filled to overflowing, and beside each stood many a colored pile. The table was heavy with its load of presents—candies, toys, trinkets, books, and other articles. Everyone had gifts, from grandfather down to the baby.

Little Katy clapped her hands with glee, and vowed, inwardly, that the cat should never know another moment's grief.

Hendrick capered about the room, flourishing a superb bow and arrows over his head. Hilda laughed with delight as she opened a crimson box and drew forth its glittering contents. The rest chuckled and said "Oh!" and "Ah!" over their treasures, very much as we did here in America on last Christmas Day.

With her glittering necklace in her hands, and a pile of books in her arms, Hilda stole toward her parents and held up her beaming face for a kiss. There was such an earnest, tender look in her bright eyes that her mother breathed a blessing as she leaned over her.

"I am delighted with this book, thank you, Father," she said, touching the top one with her chin. "I shall read it all day long."

"Aye, sweetheart," said Mynheer, "you cannot do better. There is no one like Father Cats. If my daughter learns his 'Moral Emblems' by heart, the mother and I may keep silent. The work you have there is the 'Emblems'—his best work. You will find it enriched with rare engravings from Van de Venne."

(Considering that the back of the book was turned away, Mynheer certainly showed a surprising familiarity with an unopened volume, presented by St. Nicholas. It was strange, too, that the saint should have found certain things made by the elder children and had actually placed them upon the table, labeled with parents' and grandparents' names. But all were too much absorbed in happiness to notice slight inconsistencies. Hilda saw, on her father's face, the rapt expression he always wore when he spoke of Jacob Cats, so she put her armful of books upon the table and resigned herself to listen.)

"Old Father Cats, my child, was a great poet, not a writer of plays like the Englishman, Shakespeare, who lived in his time. I have read them in the German and very good they are —very, very good—but not like Father Cats. Cats sees no daggers in the air; he has no white women falling in love with dusky Moors; no young fools sighing to be a lady's glove; no crazy princes mistaking respectable old gentlemen for rats. No, no. He writes only sense. It is great wisdom in little bundles, a bundle for every day of your life. You can guide a state with Cats's poems, and you can put a little baby to sleep with his pretty songs. He was one of the greatest men of Holland. When I take you to The Hague I will show you the *Kloosterkerk* where he lies buried. *There* was a man for you to study, my sons! he was good through and through. What did he say?

> Oh, Lord, let me obtain this from thee:
> To live with patience, and to die with pleasure!

"Did patience mean folding his hands? No, he was a lawyer, statesman, ambassador, farmer, philosopher, historian, and poet. He was keeper of the Great Seal of Holland! He was a— bah! there is too much noise here, I cannot talk"—and Mynheer, looking with astonishment into the bowl of his meerschaum—for it had "gone out," nodded to his *vrouw*, and left the apartment in great haste.

The fact is, his discourse had been accompanied throughout with a subdued chorus of barking dogs, squeaking cats, and bleating lambs, to say nothing of a noisy ivory cricket that the baby was whirling with infinite delight. At the last, little Huygens, taking advantage of the increasing loudness of Mynheer's tones, had ventured a blast on his new trumpet, and Wolfert had hastily attempted an accompaniment on the drum. This had brought matters to a crisis, and well for the little creatures that it had. The saint had left no ticket for them to attend a lecture on Jacob Cats. It was not an appointed part of the ceremonies. Therefore when the youngsters saw that the mother looked neither frightened nor offended, they gathered new courage. The grand chorus rose triumphant, and frolic and joy reigned supreme.

Good St. Nicholas! For the sake of the young Hollanders, I for one, am willing to acknowledge him, and defend his reality against all unbelievers.

ICELAND

Where Few Trees Grow

THERE ARE VERY FEW TREES IN ICELAND. When Christmas time approaches, these ingenious people make their own decorative tree. On a pole serving as the center shorter ones are fastened as branches.

Should the snow thaw, armloads of shrubs with foliage like our cedars are brought in and fastened to the framework. With its homemade colored-paper ornaments and old-fashioned candles, this artificial tree assumes a genuinely festive air. Prune cake and a thin bread patterned like a leaf and fried in mutton tallow are seasonal delicacies.

Since the population is largely Lutheran, the religious observance of the season is much like that in the Scandinavian countries.

IRELAND

Christmas Folklore

IRISH FOLKLORE IS FULL OF CUSTOMS which originated in medieval or even pagan times. Singing and dancing were an integral part of ancient rites, and it is quite natural that they should have survived in modern festivals, so that until recently Christmas time was celebrated in Ireland by groups of singers and dancers who would go from door to door, their songs and jigs being a degeneration of the medieval mummers' plays. One favorite ballad described a wren which had betrayed St. Stephen to the Roman soldiers, and originally the group carried a wren in a cage and pretended that it was asking for alms. Although such groups are seldom seen today, the wren song is still widely known.

Christmas in southern Ireland—called *Nodlaic,* from the Latin *natalica* meaning "birthday"—is celebrated from Christmas Eve to Twelfth-night.

Most of the inhabitants are Catholic, and Christmas Day itself is celebrated almost entirely as a religious festival. All the people go to church, where they find the building beautifully decorated and a crèche, or manger scene, before the altar.

The next eleven days, however, are given over to gay parties and a great deal of visiting.

Houses in Ireland, except in the larger cities, tend to be rather conservative, with things handed down from one generation to another. There are shutters and lace curtains at the windows, religious pictures on the walls, a fireplace with a marble facing, and, inevitably, a tea table, for the Irish are as fond of tea as the English. Fireplaces often furnish the only heat, and many homes are still lighted with kerosene lamps.

At Christmas the houses are lavishly decorated with holly, especially in the south, where holly grows wild.

A distinctive feature of the decoration is a very large candle, which is placed near a front window and lighted on Christmas Eve. Tradition says that it should be lighted by the youngest member of the family and snuffed only by someone named Mary.

This light is supposed to welcome Mary, Joseph, and the infant Jesus, but candle-lighting at this time of the year can be traced back into antiquity, to the time when the ancient Romans lighted candles at their midwinter festival to signify the return of the sun's light after the winter solstice.

Christmas trees and cards have never been common in Ireland. Their use in the cities in recent years is the result of commercial pressure.

To the Irish people, full of humor, social, emotional, but at the same time deeply religious, true descendants of their Celtic ancestors, Christmas seems a beautiful and happy time, a time for prayer and a time for gaiety, and their attitude is well exemplified in this old carolers' song:

> God bless the master of this house,
>   Likewise the mistress too.
> May their barns be filled with wheat and corn,
>   And their hearts be always true.
>
> A merry Christmas is our wish
>   Where'er we do appear,
> To you a well-filled purse, a well-filled dish,
>   And a happy bright New Year!

The Wren

MARY R. WALSH

O NCE, LONG AGO AND FAR AWAY, there was a boy. It was in Ireland it was. And his name was Tim. It's outdoors he liked to be, and to be singing like the birds.

Sure, when it was Christmas, that was a fine day for Tim! But ah! the day after Christmas, that was the best day of all. For then he'd go singing with other boys. From house to house they'd go, and people would be calling them in and giving them good things for to eat and drink. It's St. Stephen's Day it was, and a great day in Ireland.

They'd catch a wren, they would, a little brown bird, and into a cage they'd put it, and they'd carry it with them, and this is what they'd sing:

> The wren, the wren!
> The king of all birds!
> On St. Stephen's day,
> He was caught in the furze.

It's fine it was on St. Stephen's Day. But other days it's lonely Tim was. In the glen where he lived there was no other child, not one. It's a fine white house he lived in with a big yard to it, and a wall around it. In the yard were hens and pigs and dogs and a goat. But no other child. 'Twas lonely it was for Tim, and everyone too busy to talk with him. So he asked God for a sister. "Just a little one," he said when he prayed to God.

"It's happy I'd be with one small sister," says he. "And I don't care how small she'd be," says he.

And what happened? It was a wonderful thing, let me tell you. One fine day along comes a man, and he is a cousin to Tim's father. And he brings with him a small girl. And it's brown curls she has, and she looks up at Tim with eyes as dark and bright as a bird's. And doesn't the cousin leave her with them!

"This is Maggie Ann, your little sister," says his father.

Tim is so happy he hasn't a word in his mouth.

"You're to take good care of her always," says his father.

Tim takes her hand then and they go out to the yard together. He shows her the hens and the pigs and the dogs and the goat. And she claps her hands and it's laughing and singing they are all day.

" 'Tis like a bit of a bird you are, Maggie Ann," says Tim. " 'Tis as if you flew from heaven itself," says he, "to make our Christmas merry." And he tells her about Christmas, how the night before they'd have a candle in the window. As big as her arm it would be.

And when she went to the bog with him to get turf, he'd say: "What a grand big fire 'twill be that we'll have for Christmas. All night 'twill be burning bright," says he. And when they saw the holly in the fields he'd tell her how they would be putting it all about the window on Christmas Eve.

Sure then Tim had to go to school. And he took Maggie Ann too, he did. Not like any other school it was, for 'twas in a field, with a bit of a fire burning nearby. And in a corner of a hedge they stayed. So they wouldn't be seen by the police that was. For their country had no freedom and it was a rule that no one could teach them to read and write.

But Tim took Maggie Ann by the hand, and to school they went. And they learned to read and write. And the schoolmaster taught them songs too. It's a great singer he was, with all the old songs. And it's glad they were learning and singing out under the blue sky.

Ah, but a day came when it was not far to Christmas time, and didn't they see the police coming over the hill. And the schoolmaster had to throw their books and papers in the fire. And he went away. So there were no books, no schoolmaster, and no school. And that wasn't the worst of it. In a little while there was no Maggie Ann.

Tim left her in the yard in the morning, whilst he went to the bog. With the pony and cart he went to get turf. And he looks back and sees her playing and singing with the hens and the pigs and the dogs and the goat. But when he comes

again—late in the day it is—she is not there at all. A man
came for her, they said, and took her to Listowel town.

"It's sad I am," says Tim every day. And he sang no more.
He'd pay no attention to anything, not even to the goat.
'Twas his pet the goat was, and Tim was to keep him away
from the house. But Tim cared for nothing at all now. And
he didn't watch the goat. So it's onto the house the goat
climbed, high up on the roof, and he eating the green things
that grew there.

"Sure it's no good you're getting to be at all," says Tim's
father to him. The father had to get the goat down from the
roof, he did, and it's no pleasure it was to him nor to the goat.

"It's no good I am," says Tim, "without Maggie Ann."

So he thinks to himself he'll find her wherever she is.

" 'Tis what I'll do," says he, "or Christmas will be no good
either."

So off he goes in the early morning the day before Christmas. Carrying his shoes he is to wear when he'll come to
Listowel. It's to the town she was taken, with no school any
more for her. And who did he meet on the road but the schoolmaster himself.

"It's coming back I am on St. Stephen's Day," says the
schoolmaster. "And you're to come and learn some more,"
says he, "and bring Maggie Ann with you."

"If I can," says Tim. He doesn't know can he find her. And
if he can't, what good will be school or Christmas either?

So he goes on, with the shoes on him now. And he goes
to house after house in the town, and he looks at every small
girl. But there is no Maggie Ann anywhere at all. At last at
the far end, he comes to a small dark house with a cross
woman in it. And she says: "Go along with you. What would
you be wanting with a bad child like that?" And Tim knows
that Maggie Ann is there.

"If she is bad, why for do you keep her?" says he.

"For the money that is paid, why else?" says she. "She's a
great trouble to me," says she. "And do I know will the
money be sent now, with the cousin gone to a far country?
If not, it's to the poorhouse I'll send her then," says she, "and

good riddance to her. Out with you now, and no more questions. Out of my house."

So Tim goes. But a little way off he sits on a stone to think. And across from him sitting in front of her house is an old lady with red cheeks. It's five petticoats she has on and they spread out all around her. Like a pincushion she looks. It makes Tim laugh and he feels better. Soon it's back he goes to the small dark house and he finds the wall at the back of the yard to it. Up and over the wall he goes. And there is Maggie Ann!

"Whist now," says Tim, "not a word out of you." He puts her up on the top of the wall, and climbs up. Then down they jump, the two of them, and off they go. But the woman looks out and she runs from her gate as it's turning the corner they are.

There is the old lady sitting in the sun still with her petticoats spread out around her. Quick as a wink they run to her. And doesn't Tim put Maggie Ann under the petticoats. So when the cross woman comes running up, not a sign of Maggie Ann is there—not in the whole street, nor anywhere at all.

Only Tim can see her once in a while when she takes a little look out. The old lady sits there and she smiling and her cheeks redder than ever.

"Where is that bad child?" says the cross woman. "I'll whip her when I find her," says she. "Did she go up or down?" says she to the old lady.

"I think it's down she went," says the old lady. So the cross woman goes down to the town, and until she is out of sight the old lady stays with her skirts spread out.

"Now then," says the old lady. "There's only one thing to be done. And that's to take Maggie Ann to the farm where she'll be well and good. It's there she must be, and it's myself will write to the cousin to tell him so. It's a blessing you came," says she to Tim.

Out comes Maggie Ann like a bird from a cage, and they run. When they are out of the town, Tim takes off his shoes, and over the hills they go to his father's house.

The sun is down when they come to it. And it is Christmas Eve, and in the window the big candle to light their way. When they come in, everyone gives a big shout of gladness. Tim and Maggie Ann take holly leaves then and string them on a thread and put them all about the window, whilst Tim's father builds a beehive of pieces of turf in the fireplace. And Maggie Ann's eyes are as bright as stars.

All the house has been cleaned and scrubbed and painted, and it is filled with the smell of good things to eat. They have currant bread for their supper with butter to it and jam. And all night long the fire is burning bright.

Then, when the sun comes up, it is Christmas. So they go to church, and when they come home they have a feast with Christmas pudding and cake with fruit in it. And doesn't the goat get up on the roof again! But they say: "Sure, 'tis the blessed day when our Lord came to the earth. All must be happy, even the goat." And they let him stay there till he decides to come down for himself.

And the next day is St. Stephen's Day. You know what they do then? They catch a wren in the bushes, and they put it in a little cage they make from willow branches. And Tim and Maggie Ann go out to sing at all the houses:

> The wren, wren!
>   The king of all birds!
> On St. Stephen's Day,
>   He was caught in the furze.

But after a while they meet the schoolmaster. And they tell him Maggie Ann is free again. And he says, "Please God, one day all will be free."

"Do you think now," he says, "that the little wild bird is happy in the cage? Will he sing there?" says he.

They open up the cage then, and out goes the little wren. And they stand together and they singing happy songs. Ah, but do you know who else was singing, like the angels at Christmas time?

'Twas a small bird sitting on a bush not far away—the little wren.

ITALY

Christmas Worshiping and Feasting

L IKE ALL CUSTOMS AND TRADITIONS in Italy, Christmas celebrations vary greatly in the different regions along the
peninsula. Though each locality—often down to the tiniest
village—has its own firmly rooted customs, a rough division
into northern, southern, and central Italy may be drawn con-
cerning some of the major characteristics and symbols of the
Christmas holidays. Thus in northern Italy, where fir trees
from the Alps are more readily accessible, the Christmas tree
prevails over the holiday scene, while the south sticks pretty
much to the traditional Italian *presepio,* or Crib of the Nativity
(introduced by St. Francis of Assisi in the thirteenth century).
In some parts of the country, particularly in Tuscany, the
burning of a huge log, the *ceppo,* is still an essential feature
of the yule time ceremonies.

A few days before Christmas, the city scene in southern
and central Italy is enlivened by the appearance of the
zampognari—bagpipers—who come down from the mountains to play their characteristic tunes. These are not to be
compared with the American Christmas carols but are,
rather, elaborate variations of simple shepherd tunes. Except
for a few church songs sung at midnight Mass, there are no
popular carols known throughout Italy, nor is group singing
practiced as it is in this country. (This applies to the general
custom, but exceptions of local character must also be kept
in mind).

Christmas, as a rule, is a family affair. Social gatherings,
too, are limited to very close friends and are kept in a spirit

of quiet serenity. Parties with drinking and dancing, particularly on Christmas Eve, are not considered in good taste. Theaters, movies, etc., are closed on Christmas Eve, while on Christmas Day public entertainment is limited to children's shows and special programs in keeping with the holiday spirit. Special dinners and traditional foods are, of course, an important part of the general merrymaking.

Gifts, also limited to the family circle, are brought by *Gesù Bambino,* the Christ-child, and not by Santa Claus. There is, however, a *Babbo Natale* too—a kind old man with a white beard who does resemble Santa without enjoying the popularity of his American counterpart. (Nor is he seen "in person" at every street corner: he lives mostly in a child's dreams, to make one appearance, perhaps, on Christmas morning.)

(Incidentally, the actual season for a large-scale exchange of gifts is not Christmas but the day of Epiphany [January 6], when the *Befana,* a benevolent old witch, comes down the chimney to fill children's shoes with goodies, plus, in retribution for some inevitable misdeed, a few pieces of charcoal. On Befana Day, even policemen are remembered by their patrons who, as they pass their usual routes, drop a package at the feet of their favorite traffic cop.)

On Christmas Eve, Italian children like to "surprise" their parents with the traditional "Christmas Letter"—written on ornate stationery—in which they promise to be good and obedient and wish Mamma and Papà a happy holiday. These letters are surreptitiously slipped under Papà's dinner plate and are then read by the latter amidst the general emotion and edification of the whole family.

Public manifestations at Christmas time are characterized by the usual festive illuminations, decorations, and window displays, but many cities and villages have their own additional feature to the holiday scene. Typical among these is Rome's historic Piazza Navona with its huge *presepio,* its innumerable stands selling crib figurines, or *pastori,* as well as Christmas sweets, the continuous movement of shopper and strollers, the shouts of the vendors and the tunes of the *zampognari* mingling in a carnival of merriment.

All churches, at Christmas time, vie in exhibiting the biggest or most artistic *presepio* in town. Most famous is the Ara Coeli Church, also in Rome, whose crib has long been venerated as a miraculous shrine. (It is said that the Christ-child, having been stolen by thieves, returned that same night knocking at the church door, to be admitted by the monks not without a warning to be better taken care of in the future.) From a high platform erected in front of the *presepio,* Roman children like to deliver little sermons, recite poems, and tell the story of the Nativity to glorify *Gesù Bambino.*

Christmas in Italy is truly a holy day—as well as a holiday—on which cheers and rejoicing have not lost their original meaning: to celebrate the birth of Christ.

The Christmas
Table in Italy

FROM THE SNOW-HOODED HUTS under Mt. Blanc to the whitewashed *trulli* of Alberobello in Puglie, Italian housewives, as Christian housewives everywhere, will soon be shooing everyone out of their kitchen to clear the deck for the readying of Christmas dinners.

Food will vary along the thousand-mile stretch of the land, but it will fall neatly into two categories: the *pranzo della vigilia*—the Christmas Eve supper which will be strictly meatless—and the Christmas Day dinner itself.

Capitone, the big female eel (roasted, but also baked or fried), will figure largely on Christmas Eve not only in Naples and the south, where it is a "must," but as far north as Chioggi, where most *capitoni* are bred. The Christmas Eve supper will also feature *sott'aceti*—an infinite variety of vegetables, mushrooms, fruit rinds, etc., preserved in vinegar and sometimes served with oil and anchovy sauce. *Pasta* in many varieties of shape and size, with *vongole* (small clams), will be popular on Christmas Eve tables. No cheese will be allowed to kill the salty tang of the *vongole*.

The actual Christmas dinner will start practically everywhere with *tortellini in brodo* (broth). *Tortellini*—a smaller variety of ravioli but still, basically, a little cushion of *pasta* stuffed with meat and condiments—are handmade, and what goes into them is generally an individual housewife's or chef's secret. *Tortelli* (without broth) stuffed with pumpkin paste are also used in the north (Venetian country, mostly) on meatless Christmas Eve.

On Christmas Day, capons by the millions will cluck their last, to be served with stuffing. Chestnuts, still plentiful in Italy where the tree has not been blighted, will go along with them. Only in Sicily is turkey considered a Christmas fowl. There it is often stuffed with half-cooked maccheroni, meat, livers, and giblets, and then baked in an oven (often old giant outdoor ovens heated first with a bonfire of twigs and kindling wood). In the north—particularly in Milan—the Christmas capon is often discarded in favor of a mixed boiled dinner of many meats with caper sauce. Also in the north and central Italy *zampone,* a fresh pork sausage packed in a pig's leg, will figure, smothered in lentils.

The Christmas sweets vary from one locality to another— even more widely than the rest of the meal. However, the Milanese *panettone* has in recent years crept down the peninsula, especially since modern packaging has made its fresh delivery possible everywhere. *Panettone* is an extremely light, brown-crusted, domelike golden cake filled with candied fruit. Homemade *panettone* takes twenty-four hours in the making. This is the only cake that is better when mass-produced by giant mechanical mixers—as even housewives admit. In central Italy, especially in Umbria, *pinocchiate* and other cakes filled with the delicate little white nut of the pine cone are in evidence. Siena's *panforte* and a variety of *torroni* and *mandorlate* (hard cakes based on figs, almonds, and nuts) run the *pinocchiate* a close second. As one moves south, figs, almonds, chestnuts, and honey assume increasing popularity in cakes (*rococo* and *mostaccioli* in Naples, *cuccidati* in Sicily . . .). Everywhere they alternate with *strufoli* and *frappe,* ribbons and bows of sweet paste deep-fried in olive oil, which should be so light as to almost blow away. They are sprinkled with powdered sugar and eaten with one's fingers—dipped in very liquid honey, rum, or *alchermes* (a sweet liqueur).

In Sicily the *cassata*—an angel-cake crust filled with frozen whipped cream, currants, and candied fruit—is a Christmas standby. The winter variety of *cassata* often has *ricotta* (a creamy, almost tasteless cottage cheese) in place of the whipped cream.

A Social Worker in Naples Reports

PLEASANTLY INTIMATE have been our little Christmas celebrations which each group of our Center has particularly prepared. It was very nice to see all our social workers gathered in our office, where Miss Stettler had prepared a nice little Christmas tree with old-fashioned candlelight. Also the tailoring and pattern-drafting class under the guidance of the teacher organized an hour of happy and joyful sociability. The same thing occurred the next evening, this time directed by our teen-agers group, which is our athletic class.

Of course, our refugee friends have not been less honored than our own people here at Casa Mia. For the first time, this year it has been possible to organize Christmas celebrations where the religious inspiration was combined with the cheerful participation of all the child population of the camps. Together with our chaplain, Pastor Peyronel, and our Orthodox priest, Padre Arakin, we have brought to the various camps a simple message of Christian solidarity with the hope that in this new year the solution of this terrible problem will be brought nearer and nearer to a final and good end.

Christmas has brought its usual joy to our children and their families. All of them participated in bringing the Christmas message of love and hope to those near and dear to them. Our American friends here in Naples have not forgotten Casa Mia, giving us financial help as well as inviting many of our children to special Christmas parties. How thrilled were the youngsters who were invited to the airport to see Santa Claus arrive in a helicopter!—a truly bountiful Santa, for he brought not only sweets and toys, but also a warm sweater and a pair of shoes for each one who was there! We were pleased to hear from those families who felt moved to come to Casa Mia to express their appreciation. The attitudes of our folk are changing for the better, and with God's continued help things will continue for the good of all.

NORWAY

Old and New Christmas Traditions

As elsewhere in the north, the Christmas celebration in Norway follows close upon the shortest and darkest day of the year. But in a land like Norway, where midday shadows are long already in September, the "turning of the sun" on December 21 gave rise to solstice celebrations long before the introduction of Christianity in the eleventh century. Heathen superstition, associated with the return of the dead at the darkest time of the year, as well as apprehensions regarding the year to come, tended to add an eerie touch to the rejoicing over the impending return of lighter days. Fertility and the worship of the goddess Freia were also a part of the heathen festivities. So, when Catholic priests set up the cross of Christendom against the mark of Thor's hammer they were at once confronted with the problems of joining the old with the new—a task which they evidently approached quite realistically. For even today, yuletide festivities in Norway are in reality a fascinating combination of Christian ritual, shot through with scores of quaint and unique customs that in many cases can be traced back to pagan times—some legitimatized by the church, others persisting on their own. Any description of Christmas in Norway, therefore, must of necessity be something more than a recounting of present custom and practice. Equally fascinating is the tracing back, where possible—which may throw light on why, for example, a marzipan pig, or a game called "Christmas buck," or preparation of the "brownie's porridge," are part of the otherwise Christian festival.

Customs vary from district to district, though it is most often in the rural tracts of Norway that interesting holdovers from a bygone day add color to the yuletide festivities. Common to all regions, however, is the thorough house cleaning and the near-orgy of cooking and baking which precede the Christmas feast. On the farms, fall slaughtering is delayed until just before yule. The Christmas pig, whose growth throughout the year has been carefully watched by all members of the family, plays an important part in the yule ritual. Every part of the animal is used for some traditional holiday dish, several kinds of sausage, hams, cutlets, fat and trimmings, right down to the feet, which are pickled in brine. There are other chores too. Wood has to be chopped for the first three days of yule, the farmyard has to be swept and made ready for the arrival on Christmas Eve night of the *Julesvenn*, the sleds and wagons have to be put neatly in place, and the animals must have an extra portion of feed. On Christmas Eve, all work must be finished by four o'clock in the afternoon, when the village church bell rings in the period of "Christmas peace," a term recalling the more violent days in Norway, long ago when the sound of the bell heralded in a period during which all "bloody encounter" was forbidden.

Indoors, the women have been scrubbing and baking for weeks, and the last day before yule is one of feverish activity. In many districts, it is still a "must" to have fourteen different kinds of cookies baked and on hand—a different kind for each day of the extended yuletide celebration. Meanwhile, the menfolk tend to the important job of brewing the yule ale—still a matter of pride and great competition in most rural districts. For days before yule it is customary to make the rounds of nearby farms to sample the neighbors' brew.

At four P.M., however, all work must cease. The largest sheaf of grain from the year's harvest has been hung high on a pole or on the gable as a treat for winter birds. This practice, common today, goes right back to old heathen rites in which the last scythe swing of grain from the harvest was offered up to the pagan god of growth and fertility. But today, the custom has lost its old significance, although youngsters in many rural districts maintain it is possible to predict the next year's harvest by noting what kinds of birds are first attracted by the grain. Every animal on the farm is remembered. Horses and cows get a generous portion of the finest oats or barley, usually with a time-honored remark such as: "It's Christmas Eve, good friend. Eat well."

In bygone days, this matter of making sure that everyone and everything on the farm was happy and satisfied on this particular evening was often carried to extremes. Superstition had it that there were other than earthly creatures abroad that night. Until a few generations ago, there were farms in Norway where such inanimate things as old trees also were remembered on Christmas Eve. In some districts, at least, a mug of ale, a piece of meat, and a bowl of porridge were placed before a venerable oak standing in the farmyard. In later years, the practice was continued simply as a part of cherished yule ceremonies. Even today there are those who put a bowl of Christmas porridge in the hayloft as a special treat for the family's "barn brownie" who is said to claim the barn, loft and stable, as his own particular domain. With tongue in cheek, farmers will tell their youngsters that should the brownie be overlooked, it might have dire consequences during the coming year. A harness strap might break just as the heavy sled begins to move, a cow might kick over a nearly full bucket of milk, or any one of a number of things might happen just at the wrong time. A farmer may still be heard to say—without blinking—that it's best to be on the safe side of the "brownie."

A good scrubbing from top to toe is also part of the yuletide preparations. This custom—like many others—stems from the days when folk believed that the new year began with Christmas Day.

Folk in city and country still follow the old custom—a good bath and a complete change of clothes for every member of the household in the afternoon of Christmas Eve. On farms, which had a bathhouse in which steam was produced by pouring water over red-hot slabs, it was customary in times past for the last man out of the bathhouse to fire up well before he left; there might be others abroad that night who wished to use it.

Indoors, all is in readiness for the Christmas Eve celebration. The table is set and the fare is traditional, though it may vary from district to district. In most regions, however, it includes a bowl of rice porridge, if rice is available at the store. In one of the bowls, Mother has hidden an almond, which spells an extra something nice for the finder. This dish may be followed by *lutefisk,* or pork cutlets and sausage, or yet again, boiled codfish—depending on the part of the country. The dish known as *lutefisk* is made of dried codfish softened in a lye solution, then rinsed and boiled. Inclusion of the porridge, incidentally, dates back to the days when the whole family ate from the same huge common bowl placed in the center of the table. After this relatively simple dinner, the head of the family often reads the Lord's Prayer, followed by the Christmas story.

Next, the scene moves to the living room, where the Christ-mas tree stands, brightly trimmed with colored paper tinsel, small Norwegian flags, and a variety of decorations. The Christmas tree tradition is of relatively recent origin. First introduced from Germany about 1830, the Christmas tree did not become widely used until the 1860's. Nowadays, the tree is a "must" for the celebration of a Norwegian Christmas. To wit, during the recent German occupation of Norway, every year one of the Norwegian Navy MTB boats stationed in England was dispatched to bring back a Norway spruce to be presented as a gift to King Haakon, who spent the war years in England. This practice of bringing a Norwegian tree to England has been continued since the war, and each Christ-mas a huge Norwegian spruce stands in London's Trafalgar Square, a gift from the Norwegian people.

Before the introduction of the Christmas tree, the center of attraction was the yule log, actually a whole tree dragged into the room with the butt resting in the fireplace. It gen-erally burned and smoldered during the entire holiday sea-son. Lighted candles have long been a part of Norwegian yule, both on the table and on the Christmas tree. In times gone by, there was often a candle for each member of the family; each light was thought to have particular powers over any person or object on which it shone. Centuries ago, farmers used to carry a lighted Christmas candle through the barn, and into the stable—singeing the sign of the cross in the hair of the cattle for good fortune during the coming year. In northern Norway, the use of the lighted candle in the Christmas festival probably stems from the old light rituals attached to the return of the sun.

Until recently, Norway had no Santa Claus tradition. Christmas gifts were generally handed out by the head of the family, or placed under the Christmas tree for distribution by one or several of the children. During recent years, however, the popularity of St. Nicholas in England and Santa Claus in the United States has led to the resurrection of an ancient Norse figure in the form of the gift-bringing *Julesvenn* or *Julenisse*. In ancient times, he was one of the mythical visitors who, on Christmas Eve, would hide a tuft of lucky barley stalks in the house to be discovered Christmas morning. Now he is called on to bring gifts on Christmas Eve—much to the delight of the younger generation. Incidentally, there may be a connection between the *Julesvenn* and his lucky barley stalks and the attractive little straw dolls and figures which are so common in Norway during the Christmas season. The use of straw in these articles may go back to old rites and customs in which this particular material played a most important part. In days when the floors of Norwegian homes were made of stamped earth, it was the custom to spread them with fresh straw preparatory to the Christmas celebrations. Lying on the floor throughout the season's festivities in the mystical candlelight, the straw was believed to acquire certain holy properties of its own. On Christmas Eve—when according to superstition, it was dangerous to sleep alone—the whole family, including servants and hired hands, slept together on the floor in the Christmas straw, well protected against the evil forces which were abroad. On this one night of the year, master and servant were equals. After the Christmas season, the straw was gathered up and strewn on the fields as an offering for good harvest in the coming year.

Christmas Eve in Norway belongs to the children. After the family is finished with the eating and the opening of the presents, usually placed under the Christmas tree, young and old join hands and move about the decorated tree singing the old familiar Christmas carols, recalling the birth of the Savior. Among the colorful decorations are often found a little marzipan pig, which has an interesting background explaining its particular form. The pig was part and parcel of yuletide ceremonies in the north, long before a Christmas carol was ever heard there. It was one of the symbols representative of the Norse goddess Freia, who ten centuries ago was worshiped in Norway at yuletide.

On "First Christmas Day," December 25, it's early rising to be in time for morning church services. The peal of church bells sounds far and wide, and in the countryside long lines of sleds—and nowadays cars—head toward the shrines of

worship. In many coastal districts it may involve many miles
of rowing, providing the fiord is ice free. After church service
there is a general shaking of hands and innumerable exchanges of season's greetings: *Gledelig Jul* or *God Jul*. And
then it's home again to tables laden with the best of food and
drink that can be had in a country where such things as
oranges, nuts, and raisins still are scarce.

While the first two days of Christmas are largely family affairs, December 26 heralds in the season of hospitality. Children's parties begin in midafternoon, with the grownups
taking over in the early evening and carrying through until
the next morning. In the cities, clubs and civic organizations
hold parties for their members, and business firms and factor-
ies for their employees. It's a great time for visiting, especially
in the rural districts. Great pride is taken in the quality of the
food placed before guests at a time like this. In some districts,
the tradition persists that passers-by—rich or poor, old or
young—must visit every farm along their way. In the old days,
this practice was carried to ludicrous extremes. Then, the object of the visitor was to be as reticent as possible, holding
back and making all sorts of excuses for not being able to
come in and taste the yule fare. It was the height of good man-
ners to be so demure that at last the host and hostess were
forced to come out and literally carry the guest into the house.
Once indoors, etiquette demanded his eating as little as possible and being able to say "no" in innumerable polite ways.

On dark afternoons and early evenings, Norwegian youngsters dress up in outlandish costumes and go from door to
door in small groups, asking for handouts of goodies, very
much like American children do on Halloween. This particular tradition is known in Norway as *Julebukk*, or "Christmas
buck." To explain why a goat appears at this point, it is necessary to delve far back into the Viking times, when the pagan
worship of Thor included his goat. In those days a person clad
in a goat skin and carrying a goat's head would burst in upon
a party of singing and reveling celebrants. During the evening
orgy of dancing and singing the "goat" would pretend to die
and then return to life. This pagan yule game persisted into the

Christian era, when it began to take on a different form. The intruder then appeared dressed as the devil and as of yore his entry was the signal for boisterous revelry. By the end of the Middle Ages the *Julebukk* custom was forbidden both by the church and state but persisted under cover to emerge in more recent times as a rather tame offshoot of the earlier tradition.

Parties, visits, and general celebration continue for eight days, until New Year's Day. For a long time this day was of little significance, but eventually New Year's Day became a festive occasion, and for a rather curious reason. As hired hands and persons employed by the year generally received their year's pay on the last day of December, the first day with a year's pay in their pockets became a day of festivity— regardless of the day of the week on which it might fall.

The thirteenth day of Christmas, January 6, was until a few generations ago regarded as the "Day of the Three Wise Men." On that evening it was customary for young students to move through the streets singing ancient carols, led by one of their number carrying a lighted "star." In Bergen, this practice persisted right up until the middle of the last century.

Christmas—even in Norway—comes to an end usually after fourteen days. True, in the rural districts the tree may be kept until the last needle has dropped—and that may be as late as the end of January.

POLAND

The Holiday Season in Poland

IN POLAND, the Christmas and New Year holiday season has a festive family character. They are holidays of joy and brotherly feeling expressed in the atmosphere of the rich traditions of many years. For the older folk, Christmas is the preliminary to the greeting of the new year and is combined with many customs handed down from generation to generation. For the children, it is the colorful Christmas tree decorated with bright, sparkling ornaments and gifts.

The focal point of the Christmas holiday is the festive Christmas Eve supper served as soon as the first star in the sky appears. The table is covered with a white cloth and the whole family partakes of varied dishes specially prepared for this feast. First come the soups—mushroom, fish, beet, or pea soup. Then the fish—pike with saffron, carp with raisins and honey, herring. This is followed by noodles with poppy seeds, buckwheat groats, peas, dumplings filled with sauerkraut and mushrooms, *bigos* without meat, a special Christmas Eve dish called *kucia,* poppy-seed wafers, and finally dessert of *kisiel* (a kind of jelly), *bakalja* (a kind of cooky), pears and dried fruits, nuts, and cakes such as the poppy-seed loaf and gingerbread.

According to tradition, there must always be an odd number of dishes—five, seven, nine, or even thirteen. However, the number of persons at the supper must be just the opposite, even-numbered or paired. Places at the table are always set for the absent members of the family—and, of course, there are always places for unexpected guests.

At the very start of the Christmas Eve supper, the whole

family exchanges felicitations. The order of exchanging them begins with the oldest, the heads of the family, and ends with the youngest. After supper the lights on the tree are lighted, Christmas carols are sung, and gifts are distributed.

In the countryside, the animals are fed with the leftovers from the supper, and the holy wafers are shared with them because, so the legend goes, this night they regain their speech and therefore must be treated as equals of the family.

At midnight, all get ready for church, for the holy Mass called *Pasterka.*

The Christmas and New Year season in Poland is, above all, one of peace, love, and friendship.

POLAND

(As Reflected in the United States)

Aniela's Birthday and Christmas

MARGUERITE DE ANGELI

BELLS! BELLS! RINGING! RINGING! Bells! Caroling! Caroling! Bells! Chiming! Chiming!

Aniela woke with a start and jumped out of bed and ran to the window. Christmas! It was Christmas! It was her birthday too!

Aniela could almost see the angels fluttering around the bell tower, singing, as the happy music rang out! Perhaps they were real angels like the Angel Gabriel! Perhaps they were baby angels like the ones in the painting in the chapel.

Aniela hurried down the stairs, where she heard Mother calling.

"Tadek! Aniela! It is time to go to church, to the Shepherd's Mass, the *Pasterka. Wesolych Swigt!* Happy holiday! Don't you know it is Christmas?" Aniela ran down the dark enclosed stairway, and Tad woke from the chair where he had fallen asleep. Father was already at the church, of course, because he had to play the organ.

Out of the corner of her eye Aniela could see the Christmas tree standing in the light from the window. She could even see the glint of the "angel's hair," but knew she must not look yet. After church was the time for that.

Tad yawned as he put on his jacket. He hadn't been asleep for long. He and Stas had kept up their caroling until almost midnight. Tad thought he would stay awake until the bells began to ring, but the warmth of the stove was too much for him, and he had fallen asleep, even with Mamma there putting the last touches on the tree. Tad was a grown boy of fourteen, big enough to drive the mine mules, so it was all right for him to see that it was Mamusia's patient hands that trimmed the little tree, to see her put the packages under it, then stand for a moment looking to see if all was arranged as it should be.

"Come, Tad, wake up!" Mamusia tousled his head, then smoothed the hair in place. His eyes were only half open. He couldn't find the buttons of his jacket, and when Mamusia clapped his cap on his head, he walked in a daze after Aniela, who hurried down the snowy path and around the corner, looking up to the bell tower, hoping she might really see the angels. Tadek woke up in the frosty air, and he too stopped for a moment.

"Look! Aniela!" he said. "Look! It is like a Christmas card! See how all the church steeples stand against the sky! Look how blue it is!" He shut his eyes for a moment and made strange motions through the air with his mittened hand. Aniela knew that he was trying to put down in his memory what he saw.

The church was filled with the smell of pine boughs, with

smoky incense, and with the odor of burning candles. Every nook and corner held their flickering light, and it gave movement to the figures painted on the wall spaces. At one side the wall was bare and waiting for the picture that Father said was to be painted there after Christmas.

Tadek whispered to Aniela as he sat down and pointed to the wall: "If only I could be the one to paint it!"

But he knew, and Aniela did too, that the day after Christmas he would be back in the mine again and would be saying: "Gee! Haw! Get along there, Rosie!" to the mule who spent her life down deep in the mine. Tadek loved Rosie, but he longed to be up in the light and have time to draw and paint.

By the time the service was over and the family was back in the little parlor, everyone was ready for the coffee Mamma had made. Stan had brought an enormous box of candy. Aniela had never seen such a box!

Then the packages must be opened. There were warm woolen socks for Tadek to wear inside his rubber boots, and a new shirt for Stan that Mamusia had made. For Aniela, a white flannel petticoat, with what she called "sewings" around the hem, and a new guimpe to wear with the jumper dress Mamusia had made over from the rose cashmere, whose sleeves had worn out.

All day long, on Christmas Day, Aniela and Tad went with other boys and girls of the neighborhood to sing carols. Stas and Sue went too, and Cecilia and Michael. They went from house to house and sometimes were invited to come in. They were given cake to eat and sometimes a gift of money for the "Freedom Fund" that the teacher of the Saturday school had started. The boys and girls knew it was to help those in Poland who were trying to keep alive the spirit of liberty such as we have in America.

Christmas Day ended all too soon. It was the end of Aniela's birthday too, but though it was gone, it left her one year older. Now she was ten!

"Old enough," said Mamma, "to have the fire well started, the beds made, the rooms in order, and the supper well begun when I get home from the factory."

Aniela looked ashamed. She knew that sometimes she forgot to smooth Tad's cot at all. She knew that Mamusia worked hard to keep her looking nice for school. Four days a week she went to work in a shirt factory. Father got very little for playing the organ in church, and of late there seemed to be few weddings where he could earn a bit extra. He had several pupils whom he taught, and sometimes there was a dance in the big hall, when he played for hours while the young people had a good time. But it was not enough.

Tad earned five dollars a week driving the mule, but there was rent to pay, coal and food to buy for the family. Besides, there was Stan just finishing his course at the university. He helped to earn his way by doing many things at the college: waiting on table, translating articles for the Polish newspaper, and tutoring students in Latin.

During Christmas week there was the entertainment by the Saturday school. Aniela was one of the angels, and Tadek was King Herod. He had helped one or two evenings making scenery too, and Aniela was very proud of him. Anything Tad did was just right for Aniela.

Father played the piano when they sang the carols. All the fathers and mothers were there, and a strange man who sat with Father Witkowski, the pastor. He sang with the others and seemed to enjoy the party a great deal, and Aniela wondered who he was.

Most of the children whose parents had come from Poland went to the Saturday school. There they were taught the history of Poland and how for a thousand years the people of Poland had loved liberty and the right to speak freely as they chose. They spoke in the Polish language and were taught the grammar and the old songs of Poland.

"Let us keep the language fresh in our minds," said Mr. Kubiak, who was head of the school. "It is a beautiful one. It is pleasant too, for those who are older, to hear the language they know, so let us remember it."

Aniela liked to go to Saturday school. It was fun to sing the songs, and Miss Sadowska was teaching her fancywork. She had tried to finish her embroidered table cover for Mamma for Christmas, but it was slow work, and when she tried to do it at home, she made so many mistakes that she had to take it all out again. So it wasn't finished. But more than the songs, or the embroidery, Aniela loved the folk dances Miss Sadowska taught them.

Sometimes Tad went to the Saturday school too. The teacher had noticed that he liked to draw and tried to help him.

"Of course, I know nothing of drawing," the teacher said, "except this. Draw what you see around you, instead of trying to do things you have never seen. Everything is interesting if you make it so. If you draw what you see and know, it will tell a story."

So Tadek saw pictures in everything: in the soot-covered houses that stood near the mines, in the wheels that turned at the top of the shaft, in Babcia feeding her geese. Father thought Tadek was wasting time on drawing, but he thought the Saturday school a fine thing. Much as he wanted Tadek and Aniela to speak good English, he wanted them to remember their native tongue, and to be thankful that they were free to speak it in America.

"You know," he said, "where I went to school in Poland, we were not allowed to speak our own language, so we kept it alive in secret. When the schoolmaster thought it safe, we were taught the old songs of Poland, the long history of splendid things that had been done by the Poles, and we spoke in our own language. A boy was put on guard to give warning if an inspector should appear, and when the warning came, what a scurry there was! Every Polish book was hidden in a secret place and the other books came out. When the inspector came into the room, we were very busy doing whatever we were supposed to do. The smartest child was called upon to recite, and the inspector went away pleased. When he was well away and out of hearing, how we did shout and sing! And all this is why we have Saturday school in this free country."

Though it was Christmas week, Mamma went each day to the factory. Aniela hurried to get through the work she was expected to do. Sometimes she remembered that she was ten

and did her work more carefully. Then she went coasting with
Sue down the twisting street, or she went down into the town
with Cecilia, where they picked out the things in the store windows they would like to have.

SCOTLAND

Homes Open to the Wanderers

A WAXING MOON is more favorable for the celebration of
Christmas in Scotland than is a waning one. No housewife must leave a piece of work unfinished at this season.

No one retires before midnight on Christmas Eve, since it is
"Open House" for wayfarers. No one is turned away empty-
handed, but all who happen by are served.

The fire should not be allowed to go out at night, for bad
elves will come down the chimney to dance in the cold ashes.
A bonfire, dancing, and music precede the Christmas feast.

On New Year's Eve it is lucky to have a dark-haired person
enter one's home first after midnight. Whoever does this "first-
footing" must bear a gift. Refreshments are served, including
an especially rich pastry known as black bun.

SPAIN

The "Good Night" in Spain

FERNAN CABALLERO

WHO IS HE that has seen a Nativity and has not felt it? Who has not found himself in his own home, in his own domain, there in that fantastic world of cork and gummed paper, with its shadowy caves, where a saintly anchorite prays before a crucifix—sweet and simple anachronism, like that of the hunter who in a thicket of rosemary shrubs aims his gun at a partridge large as a stork perched on the tower of a hermitage, or that of the smuggler with his Spanish cloak and slouch hat, who with a load of tobacco hides behind a paper rock to give free passage to the three kings journeying in all their glory along the lofty summits of those cork Alps? Who does not feel an inexplicable pleasure at seeing that little donkey, laden with firewood, passing over a proud bridge of paper stone? And that meadow of milled green baize in which feed so tranquilly those little white lambs! Does not that hoarfrost so well imitated with steel filings turn you cold? Do you not take comfort in the heat of that ruddy bonfire which the shepherds are kindling to warm the holy Child? Who is not startled to discover, under the strips of glass which represent so well a frozen river, the fish, the tortoises, the crabs, reposing with all ease upon a bed of golden sand and swollen to dimensions unknown to naturalists? Here is a crab under whose claws can pass an eel, his neighbor, as under the arch of a bridge. Here is a colossal rat regarding, with a bullying air, a diminutive and peaceful kitten. Over yonder a donkey is disputing with a rabbit about the respective magnificence of their ears, which are, in fact, of the same size, and a bull is holding a similar discussion, on the subject of horns, with a snail, while a stout duck refuses to yield the honors to a rickety swan. And these birds of all colors, gladdening that profound forest of little evergreens which forms the background of this enchanting scene—would you not think that they had gathered here from the four quarters of the earth? Does it not make you happy to see the shepherds dance? and, above all, do you not adore with tender reverence the Divine Mystery contained in that humble porch with its thatch of straw and, in its depths, a halo or glory of light?

I say it frankly—on that holy and merry Christmas Eve, all these things seem to me to live and feel; these little figures of clay, shaped by clumsy hands, placed there with such faith and such devotion, seem to me to receive breath and being from the joy and enthusiasm that reign. The star which guides the Magi, tinsel and glass though it is, seems to me to shine and shoot forth rays. The aureole surrounding the manger where the holy Child is lying seems to glow not as a transparency with candles placed behind it but with a reflection of celestial light. The tambourines and drums and songs give out melodies as simple and as pleasing as if they were echoes of those heard by the shepherds on that first blest Christmas Eve.

Could there be a festival more joyous, more natural, more tender in appeal and at the same time more exalted in significance—the birth of the Child in the rude stable, with only shepherds to wish Him joy; innocence, poverty, simplicity, the very foundations of the magnificient structure of Christianity? Well may children and the poor keep a merry Christmas. They bring to God the gifts which please him best—purity, faith, and love. O night, well called in Spain "The Good Night," blither than the carnival and holy as Holy Week itself!

Christmas Fiestas in Spain

MRS. HERBERT MEZA

IN SPAIN, Christmas is a very happy and special season of the year. Many of its "fiestas" and observances are like those we enjoy in America; yet there are others which are different and original. Even those customs adopted from other countries are given a "Spanish touch."

It is rare indeed to find a home in which there is not a crèche. Even the very humble homes have the familiar characters of the Christmas story modeled out of clay. At the center is the Babe of Bethlehem with his devoted parents watching over him. A gray donkey and the typical Spanish bull always look on from the nearby stall. The shepherds and the angel are there, too, on the hillside. Also included is the home of Herod, placed at a distance, and the Wise Men from the East bearing their precious gifts.

Every Spanish manger scene includes a small stream where women kneel as they tend to the family laundry, so typical of the scene one may find anywhere in Spain. In addition to the innkeeper and numerous animals, there are sometimes figures of well-known *torreros* (bullfighters) and politicians.

Once the crèche is on the table or mantel it is time to prepare for the special family dinner to be enjoyed the night before Christmas, called *cena de Nochebuena*. It is the counterpart of our turkey dinner on Christmas Day. Even in such places as Ybor City in Tampa, Florida, the *Nochebuena* dinner is still enjoyed by large numbers of American families of Spanish descent.

In addition to roast lamb or pork or fowl there is baked red cabbage stuffed with fried onions and peppers, almond and milk soup, baked pumpkin, and sweet potato. Almonds and marzipan from Toledo are never missing. Also the *turrón* from Valencia or Alicante, a candy loaf of roasted almonds in caramel sirup.

Grandparents, parents, brothers and sisters, aunts and uncles and cousins have assembled for the *Nochebuena* dinner,
never eaten until after midnight.

Following the feast the family gathers around the Christmas
tree which is, perhaps more than any other Christmas custom,
typically Protestant, although the idea is rapidly spreading
throughout Spain. There they sing the great hymns of Christendom and the Christmas carols so beloved to Christians the
world over. The following morning the churches have their
services of worship.

Santa Claus as such does not visit the little Spanish youngsters, but tradition has it that the three Wise Men never fail to
arrive in Spain during the night of the sixth of January, bringing gifts just as they did when they visited Bethlehem many
centuries ago. Children place their shoes on the balcony so that
the Wise Men will know where to leave their gifts, along with
hay or *cebada* for the tired camels who must carry their riders
through a busy night. Amazingly enough, the children awaken
early in the morning to find their shoes overflowing with toys
and fruit.

SWEDEN

The Swedes Love Christmas

MARIE MALMIN MEYER

IN SWEDEN, the celebration begins on December 13, St. Lucia's day. The foreigner in Stockholm on the morning of
that day might be surprised to see as his fellow passengers on
an early streetcar young men and women in long white robes,

the women carrying candles, the young men carrying silver stars and wearing tall hats of silver paper. These are the "Lucia brides" and "Star boys" who on St. Lucia's day serenade their friends with a "Lucia" song and offer them refreshments. Since December 13 was earlier supposed to be the darkest day of the year, the many lights were intended to drive away the darkness.

The Lucia celebration has become quite generally a community affair in the cities of Sweden today, but originally it was a family festival and is still so observed in many Swedish homes. The eldest daughter is the Lucia bride. Early in the morning, she clothes herself in white and places on her head a wreath of whortleberries on which burn seven candles. Thus attired she visits the bedrooms of all the family, serving coffee and Lucia buns (or Lucia "cats," as they are called because they are shaped like a cat's head), and gingerbread cakes made in the shape of goats, in honor of the sacred goats of the pagan god Thor.

The next event of importance is "Dipping Day," which comes on Christmas Eve. This custom is unique among Christmas customs of the world, stemming from a famine winter many years ago in Sweden when on Christmas Eve the only food available was black bread and thin broth. Today as "Dipping Day" is observed, the whole family—servants and all—gather in the kitchen with its rows of bright copper utensils and its gay-colored friezes on the walls. On the stove stands a large kettle in which simmer the Christmas *korv* or sausages, traditional fare for a Swedish Christmas. Each person solemnly dips his slice of *vort* bread into the steaming broth and eats it to insure good luck in the coming year.

The Swedish household seems to specialize in fancy breads for Christmas—saffron bread, *Vortlimpor,* fennel bread, caraway bread. One loaf is to be shaped like a boar's head, decorated, and allowed to remain on the dining room table throughout the holiday. This is regarded as a prayer for next year's harvest. The *vort* bread seems the most important of these many varieties.

VORTLIMPOR

1 cup rich milk	1 cup molasses
2 cups white flour	1 teaspoon salt
1 teaspoon sugar	4 oz. orange peel
1 cake of yeast	(fresh or candied)
2 tablespoons malt in	rye flour
1 cup of hot water	

Set a sponge in the evening, using the scalded milk, the white flour, sugar, and one-half cake of yeast. Let this rise in a warm place over night. In the morning, add the other half cake of yeast dissolved in the lukewarm malt mixture. Then add the salt and enough rye flour to make a stiff dough. Let this rise until light. Mix the molasses and the chopped orange peel and heat to lukewarm. Add this to the dough, kneading well, and adding rye flour to give a very firm consistency. Let it rise again, and then turn it out on a board and knead it until it is firm and elastic. Divide into three or four loaves. Place these on a floured cloth to rise again, keeping the loaves separated from one another. When they are light, you turn them upside down in bread pans and score each of them two or three times down the center. Place in a moderate oven (350°) for ten minutes, and then raise the temperature (375°) for another thirty-five minutes. Toward the end of the baking, brush the tops of the loaves two or three times with hot water.

Christmas Eve is the family day. In the evening the household gathers in the living room in holiday attire. There stands the Christmas tree—the real symbol of Christmas in Scandinavia. Prominent among the trimmings are dozens of tiny gaily wrapped parcels. All through the year one saves pretty bits of paper in colors, in gold and silver. These are used to wrap homemade caramels, an essential for a Swedish Christmas. The wrapping is done in all sorts of novel ways, but there must always be ruffled fringes at either end. The *Juletomte,* first cousin to the *Nisse,* brings the Christmas gifts, deposits them on the floor, and departs. When they have been distributed and opened, the family join hands and weave in and out of every room in the house singing the Christmas welcome.

The Christmas Eve supper is always very elaborate. It begins with as fancy a smörgasbord as the family purse will allow. For the main meal, *lutefisk* is the *pièce de résistance*. This is served with boiled potatoes and white sauce. Rice porridge is also included, served usually before the fish. Before anyone may eat his rice, he must make up a rhyme or a jingle. The rice contains a single blanched almond or sometimes a gold ring instead. If an unwed member of the family gets the prize, he will be the first to be married during the next year.

The family needs to get to rest at a reasonable hour on Christmas Eve, for by four the next morning it must again be stirring. Candles are lighted in every window, to "light the Christ-child on his way." Coffee is served, and then the family is off to church. Services are held at five o'clock in all churches. People in earlier days always carried lighted torches with them to church on that morning or attached them to their sleighs. The church is a sea of light, with candles on the altar, at the end of the pews, and in the wide arches of the windows. No other light is used for that early service.

Christmas Day is a quiet day in Sweden—or has been traditionally. On that day it was not considered in good taste to make visits. But beginning with "Second Christmas Day" the social life of the community swells to great proportions and continues until St. Knut's Day, January 13:

"Tjugonde dag Knut
kör julen ut"

And so ends Christmas in Sweden.

TURKEY

Throwing a Cross Into the Sea

I N CONSTANTINOPLE, the baptism of Christ is celebrated at Christmas. The head of the church throws a wooden cross out into the Bosporus and three boys swim out after it. The boy who gets the cross is blessed by the priest and given a present. He takes the cross from door to door and receives many gifts which the people give him in gratitude for being permitted to see this sacred object.

Most of the people of Turkey are Mohammedans and, of course, do not celebrate Christmas at all. But among the Christian Turks the feast lasts for three days as a rule. There is much visiting and entertaining during that time.

The Turks are famous coffee drinkers and doubly so in Christmas week. They are exceptionally hospitable and everyone who comes to the house is given coffee, sweetmeats, and fruit, and sometimes meat and sour milk, of which they are very fond.

WALES

The Eisteddfod and the Plum Pudding

THE WELSH have two accomplishments that are linked especially with Christmas. They can sing and they can make plum pudding, which would keep for years if it were not so irresistible.

The deeply religious and musical nature of the Welsh people is expressed in their annual Eisteddfoddes. The whole town gathers in the market place to sing carols—thousands of voices led by dozens of trained caroling choirs. Contests are held to find the best music for the words of a song. The song will be sung that year by the carol chorus of which the writer is a member. If it is good, it will be adopted by the people and will be sung the next year by the older carolers, thus gradually becoming a part of the musical heritage of the country.

NORTH AMERICA
CANADA (LABRADOR)

Christmas with Dr. Grenfell

RETURNING AFOOT from the bedside of Long John Wise at Run-by-Guess—and from many a bedside and wretched hearth by the way—the doctor and I strapped our packs aback and heartily set out from the Hudson's Bay Company's post at Bread-and-Water Bay in the dawn of the day before Christmas, being then three weeks gone from our harbor, and thinking to reach it next day. We were to chance hospitality for the night; and this must be (they told us) at the cottage of a man of the name of Jonas Jutt, which is at Topmast Tickle. There was a lusty old wind scampering down the coast, with many a sportive whirl and whoop, flinging the snow about in vast delight—a big, rollicking winter's wind, blowing straight out of the north, at the pitch of half a gale. With this abeam we made brave progress; but yet 'twas late at night when we floundered down the gully called Long-an'-Deep, where the drifts were overhead and each must rescue the other from sudden misfortune: a warm glimmer of light in Jonas Jutt's kitchen window to guide and hearten us.

The doctor beat the door with his fist. "Open, open!" cried he, still furiously knocking. "Good Lord! will you never open?"

So gruff was the voice, so big and commanding—and so sudden was the outcry—and so late was the night and wild the wind and far away the little cottage—that the three little Jutts, who then (as it turned out) sat expectant at the kitchen fire, must all at once have huddled close; and I fancy that Sammy blinked no longer at the crack in the stove but slipped from his chair and limped to his sister, whose hand he clutched.

"We'll freeze, I tell you!" shouted the doctor. "Open the— Ha! Thank you," in a mollified way, as Skipper Jonas opened the door; and then, most engagingly, "May we come in?"

"An' welcome, zur," said the hearty Jonas, "whoever you be! 'Tis gettin' t' be a wild night."

"Thank you. Yes—a wild night. Glad to catch sight of your light from the top of the hill. We'll leave the racquets here. Straight ahead? Thank you. I see the glow of a fire."

We entered.

"Hello!" cried the doctor, stopping short. "What's this? Kids? Good! Three of them. Ha! How are you?"

The manner of asking the question was most indignant, not to say threatening; and a gasp and heavy frown accompanied it. By this I knew that the doctor was about to make sport for Martha and Jimmie and Sammy Jutt (as their names turned out to be): which often he did for children by pretending to be in a great rage; and invariably they found it delicious entertainment, for however fiercely he blustered, his eyes twinkled most merrily all the time, so that one was irresistibly moved to chuckle with delight at the sight of them, no matter how suddenly or how terribly he drew down his brows.

"I like kids," said he, with a smack of the lips. "I eat 'em!"

Gurgles of delight escaped from the little Jutts—and each turned to the other: the eyes of all dancing.

"And how are *you?*" the doctor demanded.

His fierce little glance was indubitably directed at little Sammy, as though, God save us! the lad had no right to be anything *but* well, and ought to be, and should be, birched on the instant if he had the temerity to admit the smallest ache or pain from the crown of his head to the soles of his feet. But Sammy looked frankly into the flashing eyes, grinned, chuckled audibly, and lisped that he was better.

"Better?" growled the doctor, searching Sammy's white face and skinny body as though for evidence to the contrary. "I'll attend to *you!*"

Thereupon Skipper Jonas took us to the shed, where we laid

off our packs and were brushed clean of snow; and by that time Matilda Jutt, the mother of Martha and Jimmie and Sammy, had spread the table with the best she had—little enough, God knows! being but bread and tea—and was smiling beyond. Presently there was nothing left of the bread and tea; and then we drew up to the fire, where the little Jutts still sat, regarding us with great interest. And I observed that Martha Jutt held a letter in her hand: whereupon I divined precisely what our arrival had interrupted, for I was Labrador born, and knew well enough what went on in the kitchens of our land of a Christmas Eve.

"And now, my girl," said the doctor, "what's what?"

By this extraordinary question—delivered, as it was, in a manner that called imperatively for an answer—Martha Jutt was quite nonplussed: as the doctor had intended she should be.

"What's what?" repeated the doctor.

Quite startled, Martha lifted the letter from her lap. "He's not comin', zur," she gasped, for lack of something better.

"You're disappointed, I see," said the doctor. "So he's not coming?"

"No, zur—not this year."

"That's too bad. But you mustn't mind it, you know—not for an instant. What's the matter with him?

"He've broke his leg, zur."

"What!" cried the doctor, restored of a sudden to his natural manner. "Poor fellow! How did he come to do that?"

"Catchin' one o' they wild deer, zur."

"Catching a deer!" the doctor exclaimed. "A most extraordinary thing. He was a fool to try it. How long ago?"

"Sure, it can't be more than half an hour; for he've—"

The doctor jumped up. "Where is he?" he demanded, with professional eagerness. "It can't be far. Davy, I must get to him at once. I must attend to that leg. Where is he?"

"Narth Pole, zur," whispered Sammy.

"Oh-h-h!" cried the doctor, and he sat down again, and pursed his lips, and winked at Sammy in a way most peculiar. "I *see!*"

"Ay, zur," Jimmy rattled eagerly. "We're fair disappointed that he's not—"

"Ha!" the doctor interrupted. "I see. Hum! Well now!" And having thus incoherently exclaimed for a little, the light in his eyes growing merrier all the time, he most unaccountably worked himself into a great rage: whereby I knew that the little Jutts were in some way to be mightily amused. "The lazy rascal!" he shouted, jumping out of his chair, and beginning to stamp the room, frowning terribly. "The fat, idle, blundering dunderhead! Did they send you that message? Did they, now? Tell me, did they? Give me that letter!" He snatched the letter from Martha's lap. "Sammy," he demanded, "where did this letter come from?"

"Narth Pole, zur!"

Jonas Jutt blushed—and Matilda threw her apron over her head to hide her confusion.

"And *how* did it come?"

"Out o' the stove, zur."

The doctor opened the letter, and paused to slap it angrily, from time to time, as he read it.

North poll

Deer Martha

    few lines is to let you know on accounts of havin broke me leg cotchin the deer Im sory im in a stat of helth not bein able so as to be out in hevy wether, hopin you is all wel as it leves me

yrs respectful
Sandy Claws

Fish was poor and it would not be much this yere anyways. tell little Sammy.

"Ha!" shouted the doctor, as he crushed the letter to a little ball and flung it under the table. "Ha! That's the kind of thing that happens when one's away from home. There you have it! Discipline gone to the dogs. Everything gone to the dogs. Now, what do you think of that?"

He scowled, and gritted his teeth, and puffed, and said "Ha!" in a fashion so threatening that one must needs have fled the room had there not been a curiously reassuring twinkle in his eyes.

"What do you think of that?" he repeated, fiercely, at last. "A countermanded order! I'll attend to *him!*" he burst out. "I'll fix that fellow! The lazy dunderhead, I'll soon fix him! Give me pen and ink. Where's the paper? Never mind. I've some in my pack. One moment, and I'll—"

He rushed to the shed, to the great surprise and alarm of the little Jutts, and loudly called back for a candle, which Skipper Jonas carried to him; and when he had been gone a long time, he returned with a letter in his hand, still ejaculating in a great rage.

"See that?" said he to the three little Jutts. "Well, *that's* for Santa Claus's clerk. That'll fix *him.* That'll blister the stupid fellow."

"Please, zur!" whispered Martha Jutt.

"Well?" snapped the doctor, stopping short in a rush to the stove.

"Please, zur," said Martha, taking courage, and laying a timid hand on his arm. "Sure, I don't know what 'tis all about. I don't know what blunder he've made. But I'm thinkin', zur, you'll be sorry if you acts in haste. 'Tis wise t' count a hundred. Don't be too hard on un, zur. 'Tis like the blunder may be mended. 'Tis like he'll do better next time. Don't be hard—"

"*Hard* on him?" the doctor interrupted. "Hard on *him!* Hard on that—"

"Ay, zur," she pleaded, looking fearlessly up. "Won't you count a hundred?"

"Count it," said he grimly.

Martha counted. I observed that the numbers fell slower—and yet more slowly—from her lips, until (and she was keenly on the watch) a gentler look overspread the doctor's face; and then she rattled them off, as though she feared he might change his mind once more.

"—an' a hundred!" she concluded, breathless.

"Well," the doctor drawled, rubbing his nose, "I'll modify

it," whereupon Martha smiled, "just to 'blige *you*," whereupon she blushed.

So he scratched a deal of the letter out; then he sealed it; strode to the stove, opened the door, flung the letter into the flames, slammed the door, and turned with a wondrously sweet smile to the amazed little Jutts.

"There!" he sighed. "I think that will do the trick. We'll soon know, at any rate."

We waited, all very still, all with eyes wide open, all gazing fixedly at the door of the stove. Then, all at once—and in the very deepest of the silence—the doctor uttered a startling "Ha!" leaped from his chair with such violence that he over-turned it, awkwardly upset Jimmie Jutt's stool and sent the lad tumbling head over heels (for which he did not stop to apolo-gize); and there was great confusion: in the midst of which the doctor jerked the stove door open, thrust in his arm, and snatched a blazing letter straight from the flames—all before Jimmie and Martha and Sammy Jutt had time to recover from the daze into which the sudden uproar had thrown them.

"There!" cried the doctor, when he had managed to extin-guish the blaze. "We'll just see what's in this. Better news, I'll warrant."

You may be sure that the little Jutts were blinking amaze-ment. There could be no doubt about the authenticity of *that* communication. And the doctor seemed to know it: for he calmly tore the envelope open, glanced the contents over, and turned to Martha, the broadest of grins wrinkling his face.

"Martha Jutt," said he, "will you *please* be good enough to read *that?*"

And Martha read:

North Pole, Dec. 24, 10:18 P.M.

To Captain Blizzard,
    Jonas Jutt's Cottage, Topmast Tickle, Labrador Coast

Respected Sir:
    Regret erroneous report. Mistake of a clerk in the Bureau of In-formation. Santa Claus got away at 9:36. Wind blowing due south, strong and fresh.   Snow, Chief Clerk

Then there was a great outburst of glee. It was the doctor who raised the first cheer. Three times three and a tiger! And what a tiger it was! What with the treble of Sammy, which was of the thinnest description, and the treble of Martha, which was full and sure, and the treble of Jimmie, which dangerously bordered on a cracked bass, and what with Matilda's cackle and Skipper Jonas's croak and my own hoorays and the doctor's guttural uproar (which might have been mistaken for a very double bass)—what with all this, as you may be sure, the shout of the wind was nowhere. Then we joined hands—it was the doctor who began it by catching Martha and Matilda—and danced the table round, shaking our feet and tossing our arms, the glee ever more uproarious—danced until we were breathless, every one, save little Sammy, who was not asked to join the gambol, but sat still in his chair, and seemed to expect no invitation.

"Wind blowing due south, strong and fresh," gasped Jimmie, when at last we sat down. "He'll be down in a hurry, with they swift deer. My! but he'll just *whizz* in this gale!"

"But 'tis sad 'tis too late t' get word to un," said Martha, the smile gone from her face.

"Sad, is it?" cried the doctor. "Sad! What's the word you want to send?"

" 'Tis something for Sammy, zur."

Sammy gave Martha a quick dig in the ribs. " 'N' mamma," he lisped reproachfully.

"Ay, zur; we're wantin' it bad. An' does you think us could get word to un? For Sammy, zur?"

" 'N' mamma," Sammy insisted.

"We can try, at any rate," the doctor answered doubtfully. "Maybe we can catch him on the way down. Where's that pen? Here we are. Now!"

He scribbled rapidly, folded the letter in great haste, and dispatched it to Santa Claus's clerk by the simple process of throwing it in the fire. As before, he went to his pack in the shed, taking the candle with him—the errand appeared to be really most trivial—and stayed so long that the little Jutts, who now loved him very much (as I could see), wished that the need would not arise again. But, all in good time, he returned, and sat to watch for the reply, intent as any of them; and, presently, he snatched the stove door open, creating great confusion in the act, as before; and before the little Jutts could recover from the sudden surprise, he held up a smoking letter. Then he read aloud:

"Try Hamilton Inlet. Touches there 10:48. Time of arrival at Topmast Tickle uncertain. No use waiting up.
                                                   Snow, Clerk."

"By Jove!" exclaimed the doctor. "That's jolly! Touches Hamilton Inlet at 10:48." He consulted his watch. "It's now 10:43 and a half. We've just four and a half minutes. I'll get a message off at once. Where's that confounded pen? Ha! Here we are. Now—what is it you want for Sammy and mamma?"

The three little Jutts were suddenly thrown into a fearful state of excitement. They tried to talk all at once; but not one of them could frame a coherent sentence. It was most distressful to see.

"The Exterminator!" Martha managed to jerk out, at last.

"Oh, ay!" cried Jimmie Jutt. "Quick, zur! Write un down. Pine's Prompt Pain Exterminator. Warranted to cure. Please, zur, make haste!"

The doctor stared at Jimmie.

"Oh, zur," groaned Martha, "don't be starin' like that! Write, zur! 'Twas all in the paper the prospector left last summer. Pine's Prompt Pain Exterminator. Cures boils, rheumatism, pains in the back an' chest, sore throat, an' all they things, an' warts on the hands by a simple application with brown paper. We wants it for the rheumatiz, zur. Oh, zur—"

"None genuine without the label," Jimmie put in, in an excited rattle. "Money refunded if no cure. Get a bottle with the label."

The doctor laughed—laughed aloud, and laughed again. "By Jove!" he roared, "you'll get it. It's odd, but—ha, ha!—by Jove, he has it in stock!"

The laughter and repeated assurance seemed vastly to encourage Jimmie and Martha—the doctor wrote like mad while he talked—but not little Sammy. All that he lisped, all that he shouted, all that he screamed, had gone unheeded. As though unable to put up with the neglect any longer, he limped over the floor to Martha, and tugged her sleeve, and pulled at Jimmie's coattail, and jogged the doctor's arm, until, at last, he attracted a measure of attention. Notwithstanding his mother's protests—notwithstanding her giggles and waving hands—notwithstanding that she blushed as red as ink (until, as I perceived, her freckles were all lost to sight)—notwithstanding that she threw her apron over her head and rushed headlong from the room, to the imminent danger of the doorposts—little Sammy insisted that his mother's gift should be named in the letter of request.

"Quick!" cried the doctor. "What is it? We've but half a minute left."

Sammy began to stutter.

"Make haste, b'y!" cried Jimmie.

"One — bottle — of—the — Magic — Egyptian—Beautifier," said Sammy, quite distinctly for the first time in his life.

The doctor looked blank; but he doggedly nodded his head, nevertheless, and wrote it down and off went the letter at precisely 10:47.45, as the doctor said.

Later—when the excitement had all subsided and we sat dreaming in the warmth and glow—the doctor took little Sammy in his lap, and told him he was a very good boy, and looked deep in his eyes, and stroked his hair, and, at last, very tenderly bared his knee. Sammy flinched at that; and he said "Ouch!" once, and screwed up his face, when the doctor—his gruffness all gone, his eyes gentle and sad, his hand as light as a mother's—worked the joint, and felt the kneecap and socket with the tips of his fingers.

"And is this the rheumatiz the Prompt Exterminator is to cure, Sammy?" he asked.

"Ith, zur."

"Ah, is *that* where it hurts you? Right on the point of the bone, there?"

"Ith, zur."

"And was there no fall on the rock, at all? Oh, there *was* a fall? And the bruise was just there—where it hurts so much? And it's very hard to bear, isn't it?"

Sammy shook his head.

"No? But it hurts a good deal, sometimes, does it not? That's too bad. That's very sad, indeed. But, perhaps—perhaps, Sammy—I can cure it for you, if you are brave. And are you brave? No? Oh, I think you are. And you'll try to be, at any rate, won't you? Of course! That's a good boy."

And so, with his sharp little knives, the doctor cured Sammy Jutt's knee, while the lad lay white and still on the kitchen table. And 'twas not hard to do; but had not the doctor chanced that way, Sammy Jutt would have been a cripple all his life.

"Doctor, zur," said Matilda Jutt, when the children were put to bed, with Martha to watch by Sammy, who was still very sick, "is you really got a bottle o' Pine's Prompt?"

The doctor laughed. "An empty bottle," said he. "I picked it up at Poverty Cove. Thought it might come useful. I'll put Sammy's medicine in that. They'll not know the difference. And you'll treat the knee with it as I've told you. That's all. We must turn in at once; for we must be gone before the children wake in the morning."

"Oh, ay, zur; an'—" she began; but hesitated, much embarrassed.

"Well?" the doctor asked, with a smile.

"Would you mind puttin' some queer lookin' stuff in one o' they bottles o' yours?"

"Not in the least," in surprise.

"An' writin' something on a bit o' paper," she went on, pulling at her apron, and looking down, "an' gluin' it t' the bottle?"

"Not at all. But what shall I write?"

She flushed. "'Magic Egyptian Beautifier,' zur," she answered; "for I'm thinkin' 'twould please little Sammy t' think that Sandy Claws left something—for me—too."

If you think that the three little Jutts found nothing but bottles of medicine in their stockings, when they got downstairs on Christmas morning, you are very much mistaken. Indeed, there was much more than that—a great deal more than that. I will not tell you what it was; for you might sniff, and say, "Huh! That's little enough!" But there *was* more than medicine. No man—rich man, poor man, beggarman nor thief, doctor, lawyer, nor merchant chief—ever yet left a Hudson's Bay Company's post, under such circumstances, without putting something more than medicine in his pack. I chance to know, at any rate, that upon this occasion Doctor Luke did not. And I know too—you may be interested to learn it—that as we floundered through the deep snow, homeward bound, soon after dawn, the next day, he was glad enough that he hadn't. No merry shouts came over the white miles from the cottage of Jonas Jutt, though I am sure that they rang there most heartily; but the doctor did not care: he shouted merrily enough for himself, for he was very happy. And that's the way *you'd* feel, too, if you spent *your* days hunting good deeds to do.

GREENLAND

Christmas Upon a Greenland Iceberg

ONE HOT JUNE DAY in 1869 there was a great stir in the new harbor of Bremerhaven in Germany. At its entrance lay two stout ships, the *Germania* and the *Hansa,* fully fitted out for Arctic exploration. Visitors and messengers were going back and forth. The King of Prussia himself, with many of his nobles, the Grand Duke of Mecklenburg-Schwerin, Count Bismarck, and General von Moltke among them, had come from Berlin to say Godspeed to the commander and the scientists who were braving unknown dangers, and certain privations and hardships "for the honor of the German navy and of German science," as his Majesty expressed it.

The last of the cases of stores hoisted on board the *Hansa* were stowed away with a peculiar laughing tenderness. They were stout chests cased in lead in which friends of these explorers had placed such friendly little trifles as are inseparable from the celebration of Christmas wherever the Germans may be.

Slowly they made their voyage up beyond the ice line. In July, by some misunderstanding of signals, the two ships separated, never to meet again. In September, the *Hansa* was caught in a great field of floating ice and was carried for two hundred days thereafter in the drift of the floe. An October storm so racked the ship that her captain and crew were forced to abandon her and carry everything out upon the ice. The great coalbin of the ship was taken out and turned into a store hut. All the supplies were taken there, the ship's three boats were carefully secured, everything was taken from the *Hansa* which could be used for fuel, and at last the ship was cut away from the ice lest in sinking she destroy them.

Then began a frightful period of drifting. Storm after storm put them in danger of sudden death, which may have seemed more desirable than waiting for the winds and currents to carry them slowly into a warmer sea and toward the natural breaking up of the ice floe. Hope of rescue in those lonely waters was faint.

But they lived bravely and worked steadily, constructing around the main hut, from the timbers saved from the *Hansa,* small black shelters in which, all but buried in the snow, the men lived. And that they kept Christmas in true German fashion the log of the vessel tells:

"The tree was erected in the afternoon, while the greater part of the crew took a walk; and the lonely hut shone with wonderful brightness amid the snow. Christmas upon a Greenland iceberg! The tree was artistically put together of firwood and raveled matweed (hemp?), and Dr. Laube had saved a twist of wax taper for the illumination. Chains of colored paper and newly baked cakes were not wanting, and the men had made a knapsack and a revolver case as a present for the captain. We opened the leaden chests of presents from Professor Hochstetter and the Geological Society and were much amused by their contents. Each man had a glass of port wine; and we then turned over the old newspapers which we found in the chests, and drew lots for the presents, which consisted of small musical instruments, such as fifes, jews' harps, trumpets, and the like, with draughts and other games, puppets, crackers, etc. In the evening we feasted on chocolate and gingerbread."

"We observed the day very quietly," wrote Dr. Laube in his diary. "If this Christmas be the last we are to see, it was at least a cheerful one; but should a happy return home be decreed for us, the next will, we trust, be a far brighter. May God so grant!"

And he did so grant.

GUATEMALA

Christmas and Three Kings' Day

DELIA GOETZ
Guatemala City, Guatemala

Dear Billy:

Christmas was very different from ours at home. I never thought that I would like one without presents, but there were so many things to do and see that I didn't mind. In Guatemala, people don't give presents on Christmas. The children get their toys on Three Kings' Day, which is January 6. Mother and Daddy knew this and so they kept the presents they had for me until then, when Alfredo would get his presents.

There are other ways, too, in which Christmas is different

from ours at home. In every house at Christmas time they have what they call a *nacimiento*. At one end of the living room they have a small platform. On the floor of it are little figures of men and women around a cradle with a child in it to represent the Christ-child. Some figures are standing and some are kneeling. There are little figures of animals, too—sheep and donkeys and dogs and cows. The platform is decorated with pine branches. Blue-and-yellow and red-and-green toy birds sit all around on them. The one we had looked very bright and pretty.

In the evening, people came from all the other plantations around here. The trees in the yard were lighted with Chinese lanterns. The Indians came dressed in their bright clothes, and it looked like the costume party we had at school last year.

There was a big table all crowded with good things. There were tamales and piles of little cakes with almonds on them, candy and fruit and ice cream and many other things. But the one thing that was just like our Christmas at home was that Mother said she was afraid I would be sick from eating too much.

Alfredo and I stayed up as late as everyone else. We had fireworks, too, at night.

But that was only part of the Christmas holiday. The rest, and almost the best, came when we got back to Guatemala City for Three Kings' Day. The night before, I went downtown with Mother and Daddy.

All the stores that sold toys were open and were crowded and very noisy. Music boxes were playing and children were blowing horns and beating the drums and trying out everything that made noise. Even grown people were winding up the things that moved to see what they would do.

Most of the things in the store were like the toys we have at home. Daddy said he thought it would be much more fun to buy some toys that were really made in Guatemala. So we walked down to the park in front of the cathedral. The band was playing and everything was very gay.

Women were sitting on the sidewalk in front of the park, baking *tortillas* and beans and lots of other things over charcoal fires. Everything smelled very good. Other women were selling little cakes and brightly painted wooden boxes full of candy. An old lady who sold peanuts had them piled in little mounds before her. Mother bought a basket and the old lady filled it with peanuts. Paper is very expensive in Guatemala, and that was why she didn't have any bags for the peanuts.

Then we went to the little booths where people were selling dolls dressed just like the Indians. Some of the women dolls had tiny little baskets on their heads and in the baskets were white beans to look like eggs. Other women had little dolls, no bigger than the end of your finger, tucked in their shawls. The men had big loads of wood or pottery on their backs.

What I liked best of all were the funny little animals made of clay and painted many different colors. Daddy liked them too, and we bought ever so many. There were mother pigs with six or seven little pigs tagging behind. The last one was so small that it was hardly bigger than a bean. But even that one had a little curly tail. There were turtle families and dogs and goats and wise-looking little owls with big eyes. But best of all the clay figures was the family of squirrels—a mother and four little ones.

The park was still filled with people when Mother said it was time to go home because we would want to get up early to look at our presents that had been waiting since before Christmas.

Next morning was just like Christmas Day at home. I had hardly finished looking at the things I got when César and Arturo came. We had a good time playing with the airplane and electric trucks I got. They thought the books were fine, because they had so many pictures. I went home with them to look at their presents, and we spent most of the day going back and forth. In the afternoon we had a *piñata*. I'll tell you what that is another time. But you can see that it's very nice to be in Guatemala for Christmas.

Your friend,
Dick

MEXICO

Juanito and Maria's Christmas

MRS. CLARENCE BASSETT

IT WAS THE LAST DAY OF NOVEMBER and the last day of school. After supper Juanito and Maria and their brothers and sisters were talking about things to do during their school vacation. "I wish we could have a vacation Bible school like we did two years ago," Maria said. "We would hurry with our chores so as to have time to go."

"Wouldn't that be wonderful!" Anita chimed in. "We had so much fun making things and we learned so many pretty hymns."

"I liked the Bible stories and the way we acted them out," Pablo added.

"We had a Christmas program out here, too, that year," Juanito said thoughtfully. "I remember I was a shepherd and I even had our little dog with me on the stage. But I guess there isn't much chance of our having one again soon. Miss Reyes told us that the girls who hold vacation Bible schools and Christmas programs have so many places to go they can't go to the same place two years in succession."

"I wonder when it will be our turn again," Maria sighed.

Several days later Maria and Anita were playing with their small brother David and little sister Elizabeth out in front of the house. The children liked to see the donkeys go by and guess what they were carrying in the sacks or baskets on their backs. Sometimes the afternoon bus would stop for someone to get on or off.

"There comes the bus now," Anita called.

"Oh, let's see if someone gets off today," Pablo said, running from behind the house where he had been feeding the chickens.

"Look, it is slowing down in front of Petra's house. And a young woman is getting off. She has a big suitcase. I wonder who she is. We have not seen her here before."

"Look," Maria clapped her hands, "she is going inside Petra's house. Let's go find out who she is."

Maria picked up her little brother and with Pablo ran to Petra's house. Anita came on behind, holding Elizabeth by the hand. They peered in the door. There was Petra watching the visitor unpack her suitcase. "Oh, come on in, Maria," she invited when she saw them. "This is Miss Martinez. She has come to stay with us till after Christmas. Isn't that wonderful?"

Miss Martinez smiled at the children. They crowded around her.

"Will you have a school for us? Will you teach us some new songs and games? Will you tell us stories? Can we have a Christmas program of our own out here?"

"So many questions," Miss Martinez laughed. "Yes, we will try to do all that. Now let us see, what are your names?" "Maria, Anita, Pablo, Elizabeth, and David."

"We have an older brother, Juanito, too," Pablo added. "He is working in the fields with Father."

Elizabeth was trying to feel into the suitcase, as small children will do. "You would like to see?" Miss Martinez smiled. "I have brought a new Bible storybook which you can look at and read. And a new hymnbook for children that you will especially like. One of our teachers in the Bible school gave me some pretty colored pictures. Friends of hers in the United States sent them for you. We have some pretty cards we will cut up to make picture books too," she added.

"Oh, when will we start?" the children all asked in chorus.

"Monday!" Miss Martinez said.

For the next two weeks the children got up earlier than ever and hurried with their chores so as to get to Bible school by the time the sun reached the top of the houses. They did not want to miss a single thing. So many beautiful stories from the Bible! So many lovely hymns!

They made Christmas books showing the manger scene, the shepherds, the Wise Men, lovely flowers, bells, and candles.

Then they made decorations for their Christmas program.

Long pine needles were brought from the woods and twisted between strands of string to make green garlands to hang across the church. For now that there was to be a Christmas program the men were working extra hard to get the church finished. They fixed little paper Japanese lanterns, baskets, bells, and chains to decorate the Christmas tree. Juanito, as the oldest boy, made the silver star to go on top, as he would do it most carefully.

In the afternoons the children would meet again for a little while to practice for the Christmas program. Petra was going to be Mary. She was practicing hard so that she would say correctly, "My soul doth magnify the Lord, And my spirit hath rejoiced in God my Saviour." Maria, as the Angel Gabriel, was practicing, "Hail, thou . . . highly favored, the Lord is with thee." Juanito's friend Samuel was going to be Joseph, and Juanito a Wise Man. The smaller children were all angels, and sang together, "Glory to God in the highest, And on earth peace, Good will toward men."

It was the twenty-second of December. The children were already getting excited about their Christmas program. They did not know anything about hanging up stockings on Christmas Eve, for they put their shoes out on the eve of the sixth of January for the Wise Men to leave them gifts on their way to Bethlehem. But there would be a *piñata,* their special Christmas game, and the program at the church.

Miss Martinez was going to town that day with Maria's and Petra's mothers to get the things for the *piñata* and the final things needed for the Christmas program. They would use some of the money in the church treasury to get them.

The men were busy putting the last tiles on the roof, but Samuel's father took off long enough to go into town to get the gasoline lantern. Juanito and Samuel went with him. They wanted to help, since the children were buying the lantern with their offering money. Maria and Petra cooked dinner and looked after the smaller children, and then went outside to wait for the afternoon bus.

"What have you, Mother? What have you?" they called as Miss Martinez and Doña Virginia and Doña Elvira got off.

"Here is the clay jug which we will decorate in the morning for our *piñata*."

"Let's fix it to look like a pineapple," Maria said. "No, an airplane will be better," suggested Pablo, who loved to watch the occasional airplanes that flew high in the sky. "A star will be best," Anita said, "for Christmas."

"Yes, a star," they all agreed.

The next morning, chores done, the girls gathered at Petra's house to help stick tissue paper on the clay jug. When they got through they had a many-colored star that was quite fat in the middle, for that was the jug. They put peanuts, candy, and small oranges inside and then Miss Martinez put a long rope through the top.

"We'll let Juanito and Samuel take turns carrying the *piñata*," Miss Martinez said.

The *piñata* was hung from the sturdiest tree near their play spot. Each child was blindfolded in turn and then turned around several times. "Whack" he would go with a big stick, but usually in the opposite direction from the *piñata*. "Crack!" At last someone hit it, but it didn't break. "There, there, there," the children shouted as the next and the next took their turn. "Crash!" Samuel hit it hard this time. What a scramble, as everyone grabbed for the goodies that came tumbling down!

The confusion over, Miss Martinez brought her bag from behind a bush. "Now here's something for everyone."

"Oh, what, what?" the children exclaimed. There were paper bags tied up with a red ribbon. "Juanito, Samuel, Maria, Petra, Anita . . . ," Miss Martinez called as she read the name on each bag.

"Oh, look! look!" A car, a doll, or a ball, some candy, and a picture of Jesus as a baby and a mounted Christmas card. "Thank you, thank you, Miss Martinez," the children chorused.

"Thank you to the church," she said.

They were all at the church early next morning. "Happy Christmas!" they greeted each other. The grown people were there to help. Juanito and Samuel climbed a ladder to hang the pine needle garlands across the church. Petra's father secured the tree in a barrel of dirt. Miss Martinez pinned the star at the very top and the girls hung the Japanese lanterns, bells, and paper garlands on the branches.

Juanito's father fixed a hook from the ceiling right in the middle of the church for the lantern. Oh, how proud the children were of it. They could hardly wait to see it burn that night.

"How beautiful our church is," they all sighed. "This afternoon we will all bring chairs and benches from our homes to use for the program tonight," Miss Martinez told them.

Everyone hurried through supper to get to the church. The pastor and members of the church in town had come in on the afternoon bus. Everyone in the community had been invited. Some people would come that night who had never been to a Protestant church before.

It was nearly midnight when Juanito and Maria got home. As they went to bed they prayed, "Thank you, God, for your Son who came to earth to save us. Thank you for our new church and for Miss Martinez. Thank you for such a lovely Christmas. Help us remember your gift of your Son through all the days of the coming year. Amen."

"Here Is Joseph and Here Is Mary"

ANNIE B. KERR

THE LITTLE GROUP OF MEXICANS who lived near the Settlement House had looked forward eagerly to the sixteenth of December, when they would celebrate *Las Posadas,* their very own Christmas. But, alas! the search for a shelter for the holy family must be crowded into one short evening, instead of lasting the nine days which it took Mary and Joseph to travel from Nazareth to Bethlehem.

Miss Bradley had planned to have an International Christmas, with many different countries represented. Early in the month she had asked Herlinda, who was one of the brightest pupils in the English class, to tell her about the Mexican customs.

"In Mexico, Miss Bradley," explained Herlinda, "we have to search for nine whole days before we find a place where we can leave Mary and Joseph—before we find the *posada*—the inn. In the city rich people go to a different house each night, but the poor people borrow somebody's house and hunt through the different rooms for the *posada*. If it is a tenement house, where lots of families live, they all get together and go to a different flat each night. As we find the *posada* for Mary we sing songs to show how glad we are that she has found a place to rest at last. Then we break the *piñata* (a jug filled with candy) and everybody hunts for the candies.

"Out in the country, in the villages, on Christmas Eve we march through the street and carry our lighted candles, and the boys and girls dress like shepherds, and all go to church to worship and to sing songs before the *nacimiento,* the manger. Presents? Oh, no, we don't have those till January sixth. Then the Wise Men leave presents for the children. In the city the children put their shoes out on the balconies and the *Reyes Magos* fill them. On Christmas Eve we have a big feast before we go to church."

Herlinda lived with Miss Cooper, who had brought her from Mexico three years before. Miss Cooper had taught English in Mexico City and was now a teacher of Spanish. Herlinda had learned to keep house the American way and to take care of Mrs. Cooper. Mrs. Cooper was an old lady who had quite forgotten that three years ago she had objected violently to having an Indian girl from Mexico as a member of her household.

After Herlinda had explained all about Christmas to Miss Bradley, her thoughts went back to her family in Mexico, and an unexpected wave of homesickness took possession of her. She had been homesick before, usually in the spring when she passed the florist shops and saw the gardenias and the lilies, the daisies and the orchids. Then it was that the remembrance of the beauty and fragrance of the flowers which she had helped to grow and later to pick, arrange, and market in old Mexico would sweep over her in an overwhelming wave of nostalgia. Once more she was a little barefooted Indian girl, helping her father gather his beautiful harvest, pulling the flat-bottomed boat through the watery lanes of Xochimilco, or drifting with the flowers down the Vega canal to the city, where she and her mother arranged their stall in the San Juan market. She could see herself strolling along the busy streets of the city with her tray of blossoms balanced on her head, or resting in the cool green shade of the park, while Rodrigo, that smart little bootblack, darted here and there after customers.

When she first went to the Settlement House and found a group of her own compatriots she had felt that her happiness was complete. With kind American friends and understanding Mexican ones there was nothing left to be desired. But even so, the homesickness would sweep over her sometimes, especially when they sang "La Paloma" and "La Golondrina" and "Cielito Lindo." For the songs brought back the moonlight nights in Xochimilco when the gay *charros* and *señoritas* came out from the city, bringing their guitars and marimbas, and floated on the mysterious waterways, singing and buying flowers from the Indians who paddled out to them in their canoes.

What were they doing at home, she wondered—father and mother and the three little boys, and Rodrigo the bootblack, who had taught her to dance the *jarabe?* And her other friends? Oh—homesickness was a very painful malady. Not that she wanted to go back to Mexico to live. The last three years had brought her more happiness than she had ever dreamed of, and the money she sent home every month was much more than she could make there, selling flowers. But if she could only see them all for a little while! Two of the boys were in school now and they sent her childish scrawls in funny Spanish, but, of course, they never told her the things she most wanted to know.

At the Settlement House, Herlinda studied English and danced and sang with other Spanish-speaking girls in the department in charge of Mrs. Beautista, who was herself a Mexican. The girls all loved "Mother B," as they called her, because she was a real mother with a charming daughter and a most polite son.

On the day of the Mexican Christmas celebration, Herlinda helped Mother B put the finishing touches to the evening's fiesta. Herlinda had converted a cardboard wastebasket into a very good imitation of a *piñata*. She filled it with candies and nuts and tied an old sombrero across the top. She had painted a grotesque face on each side of the basket and arranged some wool to look like hair.

"There, Mother B," she said, holding it up for inspection, "don't you think the old wastebasket makes a fine *piñata?*"

"It *is* a fine *piñata*, Herlinda," agreed her companion, "and I'm sure the Americans will like it better than the earthen ones we use in Mexico. It will be easier to break this cardboard one. The boys strike so hard with their sticks that the noise always annoys Americans."

"I do hope the Americans will come," sighed Herlinda. "Miss Cooper's friends will be here anyway. And surely a few of the board members."

Then she unwrapped some figures, which she placed carefully on a small table in a corner of the room.

"What a lovely *nacimiento!*" Mother B stood admiring the figures and watching Herlinda erect a pasteboard stable around them.

"Isn't it wonderful to find all these at the five-and-ten-cent store!" exclaimed Herlinda. "Mary and Joseph and the Baby Jesus. Even the Wise Men and the shepherds and the animals!"

She stepped back and viewed the little Nativity scene with satisfaction.

Mother B was opening a suitcase and taking out skirts and blouses, *sombreros* and *sarapes*.

"Your *China Poblana* costume—where is it, Herlinda?" she asked anxiously.

"Here, Mother B." Herlinda untied a box and drew out a beautifully spangled red skirt. Then she held up a white blouse heavily embroidered in bright beads. "See—doesn't it look lovely? I washed and ironed it late last night. Wasn't it kind of Miss Cooper to send to Mexico for this costume?"

"Yes—it was," agreed Mother B. "And everyone loves to see you in it, Herlinda. I only hope Diego will dance the *jarabe* as well as you do."

"He's a terrible dancer." A worried look came into Herlinda's face. "If only Rodrigo could dance it with me. He's the boy I told you about—the bootblack. He learned by watching the *charros* when they danced in the park in Mexico City. He tried to teach me, but I was too stupid then to learn. How much you've taught me, Mother B—English and dancing and singing—"

"Run along home, Herlinda," interrupted Mother B, "and be sure to be back by eight o'clock—pronto!"

As she arranged the *nacimiento* that afternoon, Herlinda had been thinking of the great cathedral in Mexico City, where her father had taken her each Christmas, to kneel before the figures of Mary and Joseph and the little Jesus. And of their own village church where they had gone to worship and to attend the *Misa de Gallo* or Mass of the Cock.

And then her mind had drifted away to that other cathedral in Guadalupe Hidalgo. She recalled the picture of Our Lady of Guadalupe and the little canary that told fortunes in the plaza in front of the cathedral. It was really the canary—"that darling *pajarito*"—thought Herlinda, that was responsible for her coming to New York. For if he had not presented her with a fortune card predicting a long journey to a distant country where great opportunities awaited her, her father would never have permitted her to leave home and go with Miss Cooper to the United States.

She was so quiet at supper that night that Miss Cooper was concerned about her.

"I'm afraid you have worked too hard, Herlinda, getting ready for tonight."

Herlinda shook her head.

"You aren't worrying about anything, are you?" asked Miss Cooper solicitously.

To the surprise of everyone, including herself, Herlinda burst into tears.

"It's the *nacimiento* and the *piñata* that made me think of Christmas at home." She sobbed. Then she saw the sympathy in Miss Cooper's eyes.

"Oh—I'm sorry," she said, smiling rather uncertainly. "Now I'm all right." She ran out into the kitchen and hurried to bring in the dessert.

By nine o'clock that evening all was in readiness for the celebration of the Mexican Christmas. The American guests joined the members of the Spanish-speaking groups in their search for the *posada*. Through various rooms and halls of the Settlement House they marched, led by Herlinda, who carried a board supporting tiny clay figures of Joseph, with Mary mounted on a mule. They all carried lighted candles and the Mexicans sang the "Litany of the Virgin." Finally they stopped before a locked door and knocked loudly.

"Please let us in, please let us in," they sang.

"No!" came the voice of the innkeeper from within—a voice which sounded very much like that of Mother B.

"Oh, please—I am a pilgrim and my wife is very tired," sang Herlinda.

"Oh, no! Oh, no! You might be robbers."

"We are good—please let us in!" they sang beseechingly.

But again came the voice from within.

"We have no room, we cannot let you in."

The Mexicans drew closer to the locked door and made their final request.

"Here is Joseph, and here is Mary, the mother of Jesus."

The lock turned in the door and it flew open. They rushed inside and blew out the candles, which they no longer needed, now that their quest was over.

The manger scene on the table in the far corner of the room drew the Mexicans at once. Some of them, like Herlinda, gazed at the scene with tears in their eyes, as they were reminded of the joyful celebrations in Mexico.

Mother B sat down at the piano and sang a welcome to the "pilgrims," and they all joined in "el Rorro," a cradle song for the baby Jesus.

"It is wonderful, Mother B, that you should play and sing like this when you are Protestant," whispered Herlinda.

"But the little Christ belongs to us all, you know, Herlinda," Mother B whispered back. "Now run and put on your *China Poblana* costume and we will hang up the *piñata*. The young people are anxious for the fun."

When Herlinda returned in her gay dress, several others had

joined the party. They were standing blindfolded with long sticks in their hands, waiting for the signal to be given for the striking of the *piñata*. It hung from a stout hook in the ceiling and swayed back and forth just above the heads of the excited crowd. They struck out wildly with their sticks, and those who were not in the game hurried to places of safety.

A young man in *charro* costume, who had arrived late and whom Herlinda did not recognize, finally struck the swaying figure a blow which ripped it open from top to bottom. The nuts and candies fell in a shower on the floor and there was a wild scramble as they all snatched the bandages from their eyes and tried to scoop up as many goodies as possible.

"Now we'll have the *jarabe*—take your seats," called Mother B. "Herlinda is to dance and—"

The young man in the *charro* costume picked up a beautiful white felt sombrero and approached Herlinda, bowing low over her hand.

"I am to have the honor of dancing with you, *señorita,*" he said.

Herlinda hesitated, amazement and incredulity spreading over her face.

"Rodrigo!" she cried at last.

"The same, Herlinda," he said, and swept her into the dance.

Later they found a quiet spot near the *nacimiento.*

"Yes, I've come to stay. Yes, I have the position with my uncle. Yes, I knew about the party here tonight. And—Herlinda, don't you know *why* I've come?"

"Why?" asked Herlinda wonderingly.

"Remember the little canary of Guadalupe?"

"Do I!" breathed Herlinda.

"Remember that you were told in the fortune he gave you, to listen to a dark-haired man?"

"My father," faltered Herlinda.

"Your father—*nothing!* Who but Rodrigo is the dark-haired man who is to play an important part in your life? *I* didn't forget, if *you* did. Herlinda—I've come to marry you!"

And right there, in that one quiet corner of the noisy room, he put his arms around her and kissed her.

NICARAGUA

Lodging Provided for the Christ-child

CHRISTMAS BEGINS OFFICIALLY ON DECEMBER 6 here, but actual activities begin on December 16 with the performance of the lodging difficulties of Mary and Joseph. The home where lodging is found supplies wine and food. Every home contains a manger scene. From December 16 until Christmas Eve Mass, prayer is held each evening in the home, followed by refreshments and the singing of carols. After Christmas Eve Mass, the Christmas dinner is consumed (only adults attend this dinner). Christmas cards are exchanged in Nicaragua, but they are white and plain and contain only the inscription:

> *Felices Pascuas*
> *Y próspero Año Nuevo.*

Christmas Day is celebrated with much fun and eating, fireworks and dancing. The main streets of the towns and cities are decorated and have loud-speakers broadcasting Christmas carols.

THE UNITED STATES
(ALASKA)

Christmas in Uncle Sam's Attic

JOHN T. FARIS

AT CHRISTMAS TIME, in "Uncle Sam's Attic," as it has been called, the glory of the day melts into the grandeur of the night, for at Christmas time, within the Arctic circle, the sun spends the hours below the horizon; there is only a brief period when there is even twilight. But what beauty this brief weird light discloses! Mountains buried in snow and ice! The mighty Yukon, as it sweeps past Dawson and Eagle, bound in its winter covering of ice so thick that it will be May before it begins to break into gigantic floes, piling them into fantastic heaps as it takes its mighty way toward the Arctic! Men, and a few— pitifully few—women, looking forward with eagerness to the days when the flowers will bloom with lavish profusion by the riverbank! Then the vegetables will attain unbelievable size in the gardens where the soil is rich above the ground—ground that is still frozen so close to the surface that every householder needs only to dig to find a place to keep milk and butter cool.

During the winter of 1899 and 1900, and for a few years later, this glorious Arctic land was sought by men who looked for gold. The Yukon and its tributaries drew them as do magnets, for the stream brought down stores of the same precious gold that the Wise Men brought to the Babe of Bethlehem more than nineteen hundred years ago. Few of them thought of their Lord, except at Christmas time, when the minds of many were turned to him as their hearts were made tender by a Christmas celebration in some humble mission station, like that at Eagle, where, on one occasion, a member of a famous New York City choir sang "The Song That Reached My

Heart," with its closing words from John Howard Payne's "Home, Sweet Home." One who was there said: "I never heard anything like the deep pathos and feeling of that song. Though those who heard it were on the banks of the Yukon, far from their homes, they were taken back to the old fireside. The husbands and fathers were with their wives and children. The young men were with their mothers, their sisters, their sweethearts. When the last cadence of the song died away, when the last chords of the piano had been struck, everybody drew a full breath. There was not an untouched heart, not an unmoistened eye in the whole company."

That Christmas Day was to live long in the memories of scores who then were lifted out of carelessness by thoughts of Christmas celebrations of long ago, and who, before they were to find their way back to civilization, were to wander on into the vast interior of Alaska, among the scores—hundreds—of mountains which lift their snow-clad pinnacles and glacier-strewn peaks far up into the heavens, as if they would seek to live with Him who sent His Son to earth that Christmas morning of long ago.

(AMERICAN INDIAN)

A Navaho Christmas

L. A. ARMER

MOTHER TOOK CARE OF THE SHEEP for several days till her little boy was strong enough to go out again. The clear, calm days of fall brought health to Younger Brother. Summer stood back to back with winter. The earth months were finished, having yielded the lambs, the wool, and the corn. Only the piñons, those sweet little nuts of the single-leafed pine, remained to be gathered.

By the time the month of Slender Wind came, Younger Brother was well and strong and able to go to the piñon forests to help fill the sacks for the trader. He went with Elder Brother and his bride. Mother and Father stayed home with Baby Sister and the sheep.

The piñon pickers traveled by wagon and horseback to the forests high in the mountains. They camped under the trees, enjoying the clear sky and the still sunshine of the month of Slender Wind.

The ground beneath the trees was strewn with smooth brown nuts which had fallen from the pine cones. Younger Brother worked with interest, hoping that Mother would take him to the trading post when she went to sell the piñons.

He wanted to see the Big Man again and tell him he had found the turquoise bead in the little pottery bowl. Uncle had told him that Hasteen Tso had put it there. Now that he shared the secret of his cave with Uncle and the white medicine man, he did not feel so lonely. He still remembered how good the sweet yellow fruit smelled.

While he was thinking about all these things, he noticed two young Navahos coming down the mountain with their arms full of spruce boughs. They loaded their horses with the spruce and rode away. Younger Brother knew there was to be a sing at Two Rivers, where the spruce would be needed for the costumes of the Yays. The Yays always wore deerskin masks with spruce collars, when they danced in the Night Chant. Younger Brother remembered how sacred the spruce was when he was initiated the year before. He was glad he knew where it grew, because some day, when he had a horse of his own, he could gather spruce boughs for Uncle.

All through the month of Slender Wind the sun shone brightly. The nights were bitter cold and the campfires were kept burning all night. In the distance the coyotes sang their songs to the clouds. Then came the month of Big Wind. Still there was day after day of sunshine and the people of the earth traveled on, gathering piñons farther back in the mountain.

Younger Brother enjoyed himself immensely. It was fun to pick up the nuts and sift the dirt from them through a wire screen the trader had sent, and when it was time to eat, his new sister always had the coffee boiling on the campfire. She made good bread in the Dutch oven and roasted the mutton over the coals on a wire door mat from the store. She was very happy with her handsome husband and they played and laughed together like two children.

Younger Brother noticed that she still wore the deer hoof on the fringe of her red belt. There were little shells tied to the fringe also. Women always wore shells. That was to make them remember the White Shell Woman of the east. She was the younger sister of the Turquoise Woman of the west and was related to the water.

When the two sisters were young girls, they were all alone on a mountaintop. They were very, very lonely. The Turquoise Woman looked at her lovely young sister and said: "It is so lonely here. We have no one to speak to but ourselves. We see nothing but the orb that rolls over us in the sky, and the silver waterfall below us. I wonder if they can be people."

"I think they are people, sister," said the White Shell Woman, "for sometimes I hear the waterfall calling me softly. I feel that I must go to the waterfall. Sister, I am going."

The Turquoise Woman watched her little sister as her slender shell-white feet sped from stone to stone. She watched her crescent body sway in the sunshine along the rainbow trail of glistening spray. For one shining moment the maiden stood in all her whiteness against the shadowed rocks. The Turquoise Woman waved good-by to her, for she knew that no more would they dance together on the mountaintops.

Her loneliness was more than she could bear and she threw herself on the hot rocks and cried to the sun, "Come to me, come."

After that the sisters were not lonely, for the waterfall gave the gentle Child of the Water to the White Shell Woman, and the sun gave the Turquoise Woman a most glorious shining young god of light. These two boys had always helped the Navahos, and Younger Brother liked the stories of their adventures the best of all, and he liked their mothers, who were so kind and beautiful.

As he watched his brother's wife laughing in the sunshine with him, he thought she was like the Turquoise Woman, but when she looked at Younger Brother, he knew she was the White Shell Woman, who loved the water and cool, quiet places of mystery. That was why he knew she would understand his innermost thoughts about his treasures.

The piñons were nearly gathered and there came a bitter cold spell. The people suffered. One little baby had its feet frozen. The young mother rode horseback for two days till she reached the post. There the trader's sister rubbed oil on the little feet and cried a bit because she loved all the babies. She loved them so much she was making Christmas presents for them.

She told the young mother to let all the other mothers know there would be a Christmas tree and gifts for all the children in seven days.

The Navahos counted how many times the sun set, and bright and early on Christmas morning, they began to arrive at the post.

Fathers drove their wagons from miles around and many little children were in every wagon. The piñon pickers were through for the year and they came with hundreds of pounds of nuts in sacks.

Younger Brother was there with Mother and Baby Sister. No one knew what Christmas meant. It was a day when white people seemed kinder and did not ask for money when they gave the children apples and candy.

Inside the store a fire was burning in the big stove and coffee was boiling for everyone. The place was crowded with children and someone was telling them that soon the door would be opened and they could see the tree. They could hear people laughing and talking in the other room. They wondered what the tree was. They were such wild little children they felt uncomfortable, even afraid. They liked trees out of doors but wondered what kind of tree grew inside a room.

Then the door opened and there stood a dark-green tree all blooming with little fires. On the very top a great star glittered. It was really enough to frighten any child of the woods who had never before seen a tree of fire, but when a terrible-looking fat Yay jumped right in front of the tree and jingled little bells, all the children began to cry.

Younger Brother was braver than the rest and he looked at everything. He noticed that the Yay had on a red mask with white hair and whiskers. His clothes were bright red, trimmed with white fur. He was taking little bags of candy and nuts off the tree. Such queer things grew on that tree that it was a long time before Younger Brother recognized it as a spruce.

When he did, he remembered the spruce boughs gathered on the mountain. He remembered how the stars shone through the trees at night and how a big star once rested on the very top of a dark tree. Then he began to feel at home. This must be the white man's way of using the sacred spruce for a ceremonial.

Navaho Yays were kindly. Probably this white Yay, whom they called Santa Claus, was all right. Thinking this way, Younger Brother became brave enough to accept a bag of candy. Then the other little children followed his example and soon everyone was eating candy and apples, and blowing tin horns or chewing the ends of them. There were pink celluloid rattles for the babies, tin buckets and shovels, and a little tin man that could walk.

The white lady at the post was very happy watching the children and had almost forgotten how lonely she was for her own little girl away at school in the city. Suddenly she remembered and before she knew what was happening, a big tear rolled down her cheek. An old Navaho man noticed that she was crying and said to her:

"Little Sister, you cry because your child is away. We know what that means. When our children go away to school, the mothers cry also."

The white lady listened in wonder as the old man turned to his people in the store and spoke to them.

"My grandchildren, our white sister is sad. She cries for her child. We will all give money to have her child brought back."

Every Navaho gave something and the old man handed the collection to the white lady. This made her cry more than ever, but when she saw that the kindly people of the earth were mystified by her tears, she smiled and called the Big Man from his office to tell them how happy she was at their thought.

Younger Brother watched the Big Man and waited for the smile. It came like a shaft of sunlight on the mountain. He thanked the Navahos for their kindness to his sister and then he turned to her. She said: "Didn't I always say the spirit of Christmas would win even a savage?"

The Big Man put his arm around his little sister, smiled and answered: "Didn't I always say that these people traveled the trail of beauty?"

Younger Brother still watched the Big Man's face and deep in his heart he knew that all medicine men are beautiful, white or brown, and he knew that spruce trees meant health and happiness to everyone who understands. He remembered hearing his uncle sing this song from the Mountain Chant:

> He brings a treasure to me,
> The holy one brings to me
> A dark spruce sapling,
> A treasure he brings to me.

(ANNAPOLIS AND WEST POINT)

Christmas Festivities

A T A TIME when the eyes of the entire nation are focused on
its fighting services, scattered as these are over the face
of the world, we may well be reminded of those two noteworthy
institutions which for decades have produced the naval and
military leaders who in no small measure have written the
prologue and the story of America's place in the sun. Many a
youth's heart has quickened at the names of Annapolis and
West Point and the ideals for which each stands—the common
ideals and traditions of duty, honor, and country that have
served throughout the years to fit every cadet and midshipman
for any challenge or emergency with which he might be confronted. And now as these men are actively and courageously
fulfilling their duties, according to the knowledge imparted to
them plus their own ingenuity and experience, not a few reveal
the same dauntless spirit characterizing those heroes whose
names are still perpetuated on the memorials and buildings on
the grounds of the academies. Undoubtedly, vivid pictures of
the massive stone edifices, majestic monuments in themselves
to the best military and character training in the world, must
return repeatedly to every man whose life has been so closely
identified with them. At no other season than winter could
these dignified sentinels stand out against the gray, snow-laden
skies in such bold relief. These are the dies which are indelibly
stamped upon the memory and seal poignant recollections of
merry Christmases in less troubled years.

At both institutions, the structures which tower above all
others and command the most conspicuous sites, are signifi-

cantly enough the academy chapels. Coming up the picturesque Hudson River, thousands of visitors look forward to
seeing the West Point Chapel, perched high upon the moun-
tainside. Designed by the renowned architect, Bertram
Grosvenor Goodhue, it is an impressive example of Gothic
architecture, standing like a spiritual guardian over the Plain.
If seen illuminated by powerful floodlights as it is during the
Christmas season, it might easily be a fitting shrine for the
Holy Grail, whose quest is so artistically depicted in the carved
ornaments that encircle the entire chapel above the clerestory.
Or imagination might envision it a castle in a modern Valhalla
wherein rest West Point's dead. For high on the plateau commanding a noble view up the Hudson lie the veterans of
America's wars—the veterans of the Revolution, of the War
of 1812, of the Seminole War, the Mexican War, the Indian
War, the Civil War, and all wars since. Soldiers in peace and
in strife of whom it may well be said:

> These be the men who kept the faith,
>   Who lived and loved thereby;
> Who fought the fight, who kept the faith,
>   Who died as men should die.

West Point

THE HISTORY OF THE ACADEMY is obviously a history of the
United States. In 1776, a farsighted congressional committee recognized the need for a "Military Academy of the
Army" and created the plans for one. No action was taken
until General Washington in his annual message to Congress
in 1783 made the plea that a military school be established at
West Point inasmuch as he felt that the place had been the key
to the whole military situation in the United States and should

therefore be fortified. In the Revolutionary War, it was the site of the stronghold which Benedict Arnold attempted to betray. The Academy was officially opened on July 4, 1802, with only ten cadets entering.

At West Point today there are now, under war conditions, approximately two thousand five hundred students whose training is threefold—military, educational, and cultural. Of this number, nearly two thousand are of the Protestant faith who ordinarily attend the services in the Cadet Chapel. The Catholic cadets attend the Chapel of the Most Holy Trinity, an impressive stone edifice, almost a replica of a church built in England many centuries ago by the Carthusian monks. The Cadet Chapel itself carries out a military motif. Over the entrance hangs King Arthur's sword "Excalibur," carved in stone and buried in a cross. Within the chapel, one is impressively reminded of other wars in our history by the color flags which adorn the nave. These are the standards—many bullet-ridden and torn—of regiments that have served our country.

The interior is particularly enhanced by the many stained-glass windows, all of which are class memorials with the exception of the two large ones at either end of the chapel. The sanctuary window represents the 'Genius and Spirit of West Point," as symbolized by the chief militant figures of the Bible. The larger window over the entrance is a World War Memorial, its concept as a whole being based on St. John's revelation, which was vouchsafed to him on the Isle of Patmos for the comfort of the early Christians in the midst of persecution and war. Discernible among the great mass of colorful detail is the Congressional Medal of Honor and the Distinguished Service Cross.

Adding to the beautiful chapel service is the music of the famous organ and the cadet choir. The organ now takes its place as being the largest church instrument in the Western Hemisphere. Music lovers from all sections of the country flock to hear the special organ recitals given on certain Saturday and Sunday afternoons. The cadet choir, numbering about one hundred and sixty-five voices, is likewise regarded as the largest church choir of men's voices. To hear the entire student body singing the impressive anthem, "The Corps," accompanied by the thunderous tones of the chapel organ and led by the cadet choir, is an unforgettable experience. The song was first sung at the dedication of the chapel in 1910. Though rarely sung elsewhere, it is sung frequently at the chapel services. It always fittingly closes the choir's singing of Christmas carols on the steps just before the long-awaited Christmas leave. But most impressive to most visitors is the Cadet Prayer, of which thousands of copies are requested annually. It was written in 1919 by Chaplain Clayton E. Wheat.

THE CADET PRAYER (*West Point*)

O God, our Father, thou Searcher of men's hearts, help us to draw near to thee in sincerity and truth. May our religion be filled with gladness and may our worship of thee be natural. Strengthen and increase our admiration for honest dealing and clean thinking, and suffer not our hatred of hypocrisy and pretense ever to diminish. Encourage us in our endeavor to live above the common level of life. Make us to choose the harder right instead of the easier wrong, and never to be content with a half-truth when the whole can be won. Endow us with courage that is born of loyalty to all that is noble and worthy, that scorns to compromise with vice and injustice, and knows no fear when truth and right are in jeopardy. Guard us against flippancy and irreverence in the sacred things of life. Grant us new ties of friendship and new opportunities of service. Kindle our hearts in fellowship with those of a cheerful countenance, and soften our hearts with sympathy for those who sorrow and suffer. May we find genuine pleasure in clean and wholesome mirth and feel inherent disgust for all coarse-minded humor. Help us in our work and in our play, to keep ourselves physically strong, mentally awake, and morally straight, that we may the better maintain the honor of the Corps untarnished and unsullied, and acquit ourselves like men in our effort to realize the ideals of West Point in doing our duty to thee and to our country. All of which we ask in the name of the Great Friend and Master of Men.

Amen.

Annapolis

W HEN CAPTAIN JOHN SMITH in 1608 was exploring the mouth of the Severn River, he was the first white man of record to see the land now occupied by the United States Naval Academy. But it was not until 1845 that a naval school was formally opened, nor until 1850 that the site was officially designated the United States Naval Academy. To midshipmen returning from sea cruises, the first conspicuous landmark to greet their watchful eyes is the familiar towering dome of the Naval Chapel. It is the building of most interest to visitors not only because it is one of the most beautiful chapels in the country but also because it enshrines the casket in which rests all that is mortal of Admiral John Paul Jones. The sarcophagus is located in the crypt under the chapel. On the marble floor in front, one reads this inscription: "He Gave Our Navy Its Earliest Traditions of Heroism and Victory." The honor of receiving the first official salute by a major power to the new colors fell to this great hero. The event took place in Quiberon Bay on the west coast of France when Jones, flying his flag from the *Ranger,* persuaded the admiral commanding the port to answer his thirteen-gun salute with nine guns, the number allotted to such a power as Holland. A short time later Great Britain was forced to acknowledge the ensign, when H.M.S. *Drake* struck to the *Ranger.* Since that day the Stars and Stripes has received its due homage from every country.

The Naval Chapel was built first in the form of a Greek cross but was rebuilt in 1939–1940 in the form of a Christian cross by adding a wing to either side. The chapel is a veritable storehouse of memorials which pay tribute to naval officers who have lived greatly and died greatly. The windows to the Admirals Farragut, Porter, and Sampson assure the visitor that the Navy has done its part in the past, and her sons in the future will seek to realize "her ideals of honor, courage, loyalty, and duty in the service of God and country." A significant window flanking the altar is the one which represents a knight in armor, Sir Galahad, as the symbol of these ideals. Since the laying of the cornerstone by Admiral Dewey in 1904, the chapel has steadily drawn to itself those associations, those traditions, and those little human touches from which spiritual values stem. About the entrance are yew and lavender from the rectory garden of the birthplace of Lord Nelson. Within the doorway is a glass case which contains the much-thumbed prayer book of Admiral Farragut, open to the page in the Book of Psalms where he had marked some of his favorite passages.

Though the massive granite buildings of the Academy are a strong reminder of the grim power of modern fighting ships, the Yard has about it an atmosphere which reflects an older Navy. Farragut Field, Porter Road, and McDonough, Sampson, Dahlgren, and Bancroft Halls honor men whose names are well known in the service. It is the exterior of Bancroft Hall which is always festively decorated for the Christmas season. On the walls on either side of the main entrance, green electric lights usually outline Christmas trees, while over the doorway a yuletide wreath is simulated in the same manner in green and red. The two living fir trees near the approach to the Hall are also brilliantly lighted with globes.

But there is a type of "Christmas tree" of peculiar acquaintance to all midshipmen and of particular concern to the plebes. For it is just before the Christmas holidays that the first posting of a midshipman's average marks is made. Upon this public posting depends every Fourth Classman's holiday leave. Since the academic mortality rate is rather high among plebes, one can easily understand why the December posting with its packages of joy and gloom is appropriately known at the Academy as the "Christmas tree." It is interesting to note that each year a special committee is entrusted with the choice and selection of the Regimental Christmas Card. This choice must be one that embodies a true Christmas Spirit with something symbolic of the Naval Academy.

There are many things out of the ordinary to impress a visitor, but there is none so indicative of the character of a midshipman's training as the sight of the Regiment in the chapel

on Sunday mornings, particularly as it sings that hail and benediction "For Those in Peril on the Sea." The first stanza of the
hymn is sung at every service and the custom is similarly employed on many ships of the fleet. The hymn dates back to
1860, its inspiration dependent upon a terrible storm on the
Mediterranean from which an Englishman, the Reverend Wm.
Whiting, miraculously escaped. So profoundly was he stirred
by the spectacle that he penned the poem which a year later
was set to music by John B. Dykes. It has become a favorite
with seafaring men throughout English-speaking nations. Now
included in various hymnbooks and frequently used on current
programs honoring the naval forces, it is becoming increasingly
familiar to the general public.

> Eternal Father, strong to save,
> Whose arm hath bound the restless wave,
> Who bidd'st the mighty ocean deep
> Its own appointed limits keep:
> O hear us when we cry to Thee
> For those in peril on the sea.   Amen.

(BETHLEHEM, PENNSYLVANIA)

The Christmas City of America

BURNETTE THOMPSON

'TWAS THE NIGHT BEFORE CHRISTMAS—exactly two hundred years ago—that a little group of Moravian missionaries, gathered in a rude log cabin in the Pennsylvania wilderness, christened their New World home for the birthplace of
the Prince of Peace—Bethlehem.

These first settlers of Bethlehem, followers of one of the oldest Protestant churches in history, had come from Herrnhut, Germany, with the altruism of true missionaries to the Indians. They had faced hardships and perils to reach this distant land which offered freedom from the religious strife of the Old World. Now, on December 24, 1741, the small band was assembled in its first dwelling to observe the Vigils of Christmas Eve. In the group was its patron-leader, Count von Zinzendorf, who had come on a visit to Pennsylvania in the hope of uniting the various religious elements there.

During the evening devotions, the imaginative Count was deeply impressed with the similarity of their shelter, housing both men and beasts, to that in which Jesus was born in the City of David. Impulsively, he seized a lighted taper and led the way to the part where the cattle were kept, singing the while an old German Epiphany hymn, "Not Jerusalem, Lowly Bethlehem!" The words of the chorale, which combined Christmas and missionary thoughts, well expressed the feeling of the hour. Thus the occasion suggested to the worshipers the name Bethlehem.

The Moravian pioneers were endowed with qualities that contributed in no small measure to Bethlehem's rapid development; they were religious, industrious, progressive, and possessed a strong love for music. Bethlehem soon became a community having its own peculiar history, more closely identified with the growth of our nation than is generally known.

Although their religious convictions did not permit the bearing of arms during the Revolutionary War, the Christian deeds of the Moravians at that time were long remembered. For a few months, part of the Continental Congress was housed there, and when the patriot army retreated from Philadelphia in 1777, it headed northward toward Bethlehem with more than seven hundred wagons carrying military stores. It was during these days of uneasiness that the historic Liberty Bell, in danger of capture by the British, was carted through from Philadelphia to Allentown to be hidden in the cellar of Zion's Church. The wagon transporting it broke down at Bethlehem; so while repairs were being made, the bell was carefully guarded by the local patriots.

It was at Bethlehem that the wounded Lafayette was nursed back to health, and that hundreds of wounded soldiers were cared for at the Military Hospital located in the Single Brethren's House. The burial spot of those soldiers who died is now the site of the only tomb in the United States dedicated to an Unknown Soldier of the Revolutionary War.

There are any number of facts which bear testimony of the cultural and industrial progressiveness in early Bethlehem. Here one finds the first girls' boarding school in the country; the first fire engine, brought over from London in 1762; the first public waterworks; and the oldest drugstore in the United States open for business every day. Just before the Civil War, a little iron works was started that was to become the Bethlehem Steel Company. With the growth of this mighty enterprise, there followed the establishment of countless allied industries. As a result, thousands of people of various nationalities were attracted to this new industrial center. Soon the quiet little town found itself being transformed into an unusually cosmopolitan city. So Bethlehem is now known, far and wide, as a "steel city," where millions of dollars' worth of steel is manufactured each year.

But the city is equally celebrated as the home of the Bethlehem Bach Choir, which, during the many years of its existence, has been famous for the excellence of its music, and for the devotion of its members. Recently, it has taken its place along with the foremost choral organizations in nationwide broadcasts of Christmas music. In the spring, music lovers from all over the country gather to hear this group of singers whose annual festivals of Bach music are a natural outcome of two centuries of a love for well-performed music.

It is significant that in Bethlehem the church cordially sanctioned the use of music as an art and as a recreation, without doubt an important factor in developing the community to the musical stature it early attained. Whereas the early Puritans of New England restricted music to psalmody and abhorred instruments of accompaniment, the Moravians made daily use of both vocal and instrumental music. Only two years after the founding of Bethlehem, a spinet arrived from London and was immediately placed in the church. It is recorded that instruments brought to America by members of the First Sea Congregation were "played for the first time in the house of God" on Christmas Day, 1743, and included viols of various kinds, flutes, and French horns. In time a symphony orchestra was organized, the first in any community in the United States.

Holding a peculiar place in Moravian life is the trombone choir, which to this day announces all festival days and the passing away of members in the congregation by the playing of chorales from the church belfry tower. Benjamin Franklin's writings reveal that when he visited Bethlehem in 1755, he heard the playing of trombones and the singing of choirs. It is believed that in this same year trombone music was the means of saving the town from destruction.

Information had been received that the Indian savages proposed to make an end of Bethlehem by the time of its "great day"—Christmas. In spite of the impending danger, excellent morale was maintained, and with the exception of the guards, the people held their usual Christmas Eve Vigils and quietly retired. At four o'clock Christmas morning, the music of trombones from the roof of the Brethren's House ushered in the day so greatly dreaded. But Christmas passed without disaster. Tradition has it that the notes of that Christmas chorale, breaking the dead silence, warded off the Indians who declared that the Great Spirit most surely guarded the white settlers. Other Indians, to whom the prowlers had spoken, afterward told of it.

Although a huge steel plant has reared its smoking chimney where once Indians lay in ambush, the old-time spirit of Christmas in its traditional purity and genuineness still prevails. Naturally, in the course of two centuries, some of the customs that were in vogue during the early days of the community have disappeared. But generally speaking, the Moravian Christmas, which has become the Christmas of Bethlehem, embodies most of those original characteristics that assist in making the holiday season in that city a time of unique significance.

Weeks are spent in preparation for the yuletide celebrations. As early as October, the pouring of thousands of pure beeswax candles is begun in Simon Rau's drugstore, the oldest apothecary shop in the United States. The candlemaking itself is a hand process using the same methods and types of molds employed by the early settlers. The tiny candles which are used in Moravian churches and homes throughout the nation are supposed to symbolize the coming of Light into the World with the birth of the Christ-child. Those used in the local congregation are trimmed by the women sacristans of the church. Paper frills of different colors are placed around the base for decorative purposes and to prevent the hot wax from burning those holding the candles. Last year nearly three thousand were used in the Central Moravian Church in Bethlehem alone.

In the Moravian home, the baking of Christmas cakes and cookies is a serious and happy business. Many of the recipes for these pastries were brought to this country by the early settlers and have been handed down from generation to generation. Included in most household stores is a kind of ginger cooky of both a brown and a white variety. Tradition dictates that the brown cakes should be cut into the shapes of men, birds, dogs, sheep, roosters, lions, and other animals, while the white ones should be cut into semblances of stars, angels, hearts, trees, and flowers. Thus, they are not only good to eat, but are ornamental as well, and may be used as decorations.

Of all the Moravian customs, no doubt the creation of "putzes" is the most appealing feature of Bethlehem's Christmas. Now, a "putz" is the Moravian version of the Christmas tree and comes from the German *putzen,* meaning "to decorate." It is a miniature portrayal of the Nativity, in which the scenes are grouped under a single Christmas tree or many trees, with moss as a base for the landscaping. In its erection the creator uses treasured figures of wood or papier-mâché, tiny fences, gnarled stumps, and rocks carefully kept from year to year; sand, earth, little trees, and sometimes even water, so arranged that the holy family, represented in a cave or thatched stable, is always the central subject.

Almost every Moravian home has its putz, which varies in accordance with the taste, the ingenuity of resources, and the traditions of the different families. Some "putzes" are very elaborate, occupying an entire room and requiring weeks to build. In one home the Nativity figures have been made in

Oberammergau by the famous wood-carver, Guido Mayer, who played the part of Judas in the Passion Play of 1922. The light, delicate figures of the holy family, the Wise Men, the shepherds, and the angels are only three and a half inches high and display a remarkable perfection of facial expression. In the collection are also four little black-coated Moravian trombonists with shiny instruments, made by Andreas Lang, who performed the role of Peter. In another home, all the figures were made in Dresden, and some of the scenes include characters from legends of the Black Forest. One family treasures a wooden cow, carved and colored by the hand of an ancestor who used it in the earliest family putz of which there is any definite knowledge in Bethlehem.

In days gone by, the putz was lighted with wax candles, but now little electrical bulbs are usually used which are really more effective, for, by means of various switches, the scenes can be lighted up in sequence as the Bible story is narrated. Side attractions such as mill wheels, waterfalls, bridges, fountains, villages, log cabins, replicas of the Moravian church and old Bethlehem are permitted, but all are subordinate to the Nativity scenes. Electrical and mechanical toys have no place in the true Moravian putz, whose single purpose is to tell the children, pictorially, the story of the little Christ-child. All during Christmas week it is customary to go "putz-visiting" at friends' houses—a time of genuine neighborliness and a time of hearing the age-old story told and retold.

Originally the children were not permitted a glimpse of the putz until their return from the Christmas Lovefeast in the church on Christmas Eve afternoon. But that is not necessarily true today. The Christmas Lovefeast is primarily for the children. They sit in a body at the front of the church, which is pleasantly fragrant with the scent of evergreen decorations. After the congregation has sung several hymns, the Lovefeast, always consisting of a sweet bun and steaming coffee, is served by the sacristans to each child. Toward the close of the service, the sacristans and their assistants return, this time with the trays of lighted beeswax candles. While the congregation sings a hymn of rejoicing, they pass down the aisles giving each child a candle. The tapers, casting a soft glow on the happy faces, burn steadily until the benediction has been pronounced.

After the service there is an interval for family celebrations in the home. But at seven thirty the congregation reassembles for the Christmas Eve Vigils. (There are now two of these services to accommodate the crowds of visitors as well as the growing congregation.) After the church has been packed, the lights are dimmed with the exception of one lighted star hanging in the center, and the soft glow over the large picture of the holy family in the upper pulpit. Then begins the most beautiful service of the year, a service devoted almost entirely to music, performed sometimes by the choir, sometimes by the children, and sometimes by the congregation. At one point, a child chosen from the Sunday school sings antiphonally with the other children that hymn which to every Moravian is the keynote of the Christmas season:

> Morning Star, O cheering sight!
> Ere Thou cam'st how dark earth's night!
>   Jesus mine, In me shine;
>   Fill my heart with light divine.

Near the close of the service, the doors open at the front of the church. As the choir begins to sing, "Behold! A great, a heav'nly light, From Bethlehem's manger shineth bright," the sacristans enter with trays of lighted candles as at the Lovefeast. This time the entire congregation is served with the candles, which soon transform the room into a veritable sea of lights. Again the Christmas Vigils have been kept! Again the spirit of Christmas has indeed been born anew in Bethlehem in Pennsylvania!

The sincere appreciation and practice of these beautiful traditions by the Moravians today as in the early days has caused Bethlehem to be widely known as the "Christmas City of America." The citizens are proud of their priceless heritage, and duly conscious of the mighty challenge the very name of the city presents. And so they feel it their duty to keep alive the true spirit of peace, love, and fellowship when war, hate, and oppression seem ready to extinguish all that is held sacred. This motive, and this motive alone, inspired Bethlehem's civic leaders to organize a gigantic community Christmas program a few years ago. The combined efforts of the entire community brought this enterprise to a successful conclusion. The results are now enjoyed by thousands of visitors to Bethlehem each yuletide season.

These modern pilgrims are impressed by the "Christmas City's" elaborate street lighting, the magnificent Hill-to-Hill Bridge display, the candles in a thousand windows, and the huge Star of Bethlehem atop South Mountain. The electrified star, visible for nearly twenty miles, is a permanent fixture one hundred feet in height. It is a symbol of the star in the East to all visitors who see it, but to the citizens of Bethlehem, a reminder of the ideals they have set up for themselves. The official city seal is this same star, the five points representing the city's major interests: religion, music, industry, recreation, and education.

Thousands of persons hear the Nativity story as it is narrated again and again at the community putz, no doubt the most elaborate one in the country. The assemblage of the parts for the putz and the erection itself is no small task. An idea of the work involved can be imagined from the fact that one year the crib required no less than eight hundred pounds of sand, twelve bushels of moss, sixty-four stumps of trees, forty Christmas trees, forty-eight angels, two hundred animals including sheep, camels, and leopards, sixteen lighting effects, twenty-nine lamps, seven hundred feet of rock earth, four hundred feet of various other materials, and several paintings in oil. The putz varies yearly, but the theme is the same.

Though the putz is unveiled Christmas Eve, the turning on of the city's Christmas lights is accompanied by an impressive ceremony earlier in December. A Moravian beeswax candle is placed in the path of an "electric eye" which automatically illuminates the forty-odd blocks of myriad-colored lights and the Star of Bethlehem on South Mountain. Before the turning on of the lights, the same prayer is offered that inaugurated the Christmas lights several years ago.

And so in today's frantic bustle, modern Bethlehem pauses reverently at Christmas time, as did its forebears two hundred years ago—to celebrate the birth of Christ. Its citizens do not endeavor to set themselves up as the only true Christmas people; neither do they intend to say that Bethlehem created Christmas. Instead, they say that Christmas created Bethlehem. In anticipation of the city's bicentennial, one of its citizens must have adequately expressed the thoughts of his fellow townsmen when he said: "From Bethlehem, the Christmas City, we hope to reflect abroad a beam, be it ever so small, of that everlasting Light, of that Light of Life which, in the heart of men, is joy, love, gentleness, kindliness, and mercy. May we never cease to pray that prayer sung by the herald angels on the first Christmas Day:

"'Peace on earth, good will toward men.'"

(HAWAII)

The Christmas Ship Brings Santa and the Trees

HAWAII has its own natural Christmas decorations—festive poinsettia and red, waxy anthuriums bloom on byways and decorate homes. A Matson freighter, nicknamed the "Christmas Tree Ship," comes each year with a stock of fir trees from the U.S. Northwest. Arriving about the same time on the beach at Waikiki is Santa himself. Whether he surfs in on a board or paddles to the sand in a canoe, children marvel at his lengthy trip from the North Pole.

With water all around them, it is not surprising that Santa comes by boat, for he would not neglect the little folks of the islands in the Pacific. They look for him as eagerly as do the boys and girls in the lands of snow and ice.

From this point on, beaches and streets are alive with carolers, singing to the accompaniment of ukuleles. Nativity pageants with Chinese, Japanese, Hawaiian, Filipino, and Caucasian children playing the Biblical roles are numerous, and yuletide luaus, featuring *Kailua* pig, are painstakingly prepared.

Before the missionaries and the American settlements went to Hawaii, the natives knew nothing about Christmas, but now they celebrate the day much as do the Americans who live there.

The most striking difference between Christmas in Honolulu and Christmas in New York is that in Honolulu in December it is like June in New York. Birds are warbling in the leafy trees; gardens are overflowing with roses and carnations; fields and mountain slopes are ablaze in color, and a sunny sky smiles dreamily upon the glories of a summer day.

In the morning, people go to church, and during the day there are sports and games and merrymaking of all sorts. The Christmas dinner is eaten in the shade of the veranda, in happiness and contentment.

(NEW ENGLAND)

A Vermont Christmas

ANNE BOSWORTH GREENE

O N CHRISTMAS NIGHT a brilliant full moon rose, shining on
the icy crust. It was twelve below zero. The rolling hills
were like a silver sea. Moonlight gleamed on their tops and
made shining paths. The belts of woods were black as ink. Riding home from a festive dinner at the Chickadee's, we gazed,
though with teeth chattering; the horses galloped along the
lighted roads, but even that exhilarating motion could not keep
out the bite of the cold, and we turned gladly down the path to
the barn. Before I could dismount, Polly quickly steered me to
the watering trough, with her little chivalrous air of "Oh, do let
me save you the trouble of doing this later!" . . . But she
bumped her nose on it! It was frozen hard; *and* the fence beside
it shivered into bits!

Not a pony was to be found. They had had a kicking bee by
the fence, laid it flat, and departed. The crust was hard; they
could go anywhere.

"Elizabeth—out at this hour!" I cried.

"And Donny—she'll freeze!" mourned Babs. The moon,
though big, was still low above the hills; so we brought a lantern and scurried through the orchards (magically beautiful,
with their purples against shadowy silver). There we discovered
a stream of tracks on the hard crust.

It was dreadfully slippery on that crust; we slid along, holding the lantern at the tracks, and feeling every sword-sharp
breath of air a stab in our hearts. . . . Would Elizabeth's little
round furriness withstand this bitter night? So we hurried peril-
ously over the slopes, where birch clumps sketched enchanting

shadows, and the moon, soaring aloft, shone brightly down. The dark-blue sky was thick with northern lights, flared tongues of greenish fire upward behind the mountains. A night of celebration above, as well as on earth! and in the midst of such beauty our anxious quest seemed a bad dream. . . . It was Elizabeth's first Christmas! and we had brought her home a lump of sugar tied up with red ribbon. . . .

At the lane, tracks went in both directions, one stream into the dark woods. So we darted into a birchy hollow. Tracks were everywhere now, and round dig-places in the snow, where a hoof had scraped for food. We were both escorted by columns of steaming breath; " 'Valleys where the people went about like smoking chimneys'—remember?" I panted, holding on to my nose, which seemed of a strange numbness. . . .

The bushy lane turned here, and in its shadows we perceived clusters of deeper blackness, from which a certain *breathing* quality arose . . . and then somebody very kindly sneezed!

"I'll get over the fence," whispered my child, with strategy learned of old, "and you go back to the turn and shoo 'em in when you hear 'em coming! I'll yell if I need you!"

Before I could even nod assentingly (as an obedient parent should) she was bobbing away. I dashed desperately back. If they got there before I did—and if the wrong pony was leading—all was lost! They would go tearing downhill into the woods. . . . If steady little black Fad had been with them, she would swerve into the home field; but, alas! Fad was now far away, dragging a cart in Connecticut, and Ocean Wave, the swift and tireless, was leader of the gang. Mischief is the spice of Ocean's life. I could just *see* her dashing the whole crowd down into those shadowy depths, like the swine that dashed into the sea. Only it needs no especial devil to inspire my darling children; once get them in a mob, and out jump a dozen busy little devils ready for use—devils that a pony ordinarily keeps tucked away in the back side of his clever little head. And that pitch into the woods was a divine dash place, geographically—and psychologically; being both a lovely downhill *and* the exact opposite of the direction in which they knew—*ad nauseam!*—they ought to go. How often had they galloped along that very lane and shot piously in at the opening! And Shetlands, like people, can't bear being good *too* long.

Awaiting the onrush, I listened intently. All was still. The moon shone down through the trees, and lay in patterns on the frozen snow. Tiny sounds stole into the night stillness: a rustle, a crisping of crust, a frost-snap from a tree, the fritter of a dry beech leaf; and, behind all these, the slow rise and fall of a murmur, a vast, slow murmur as from forgotten winds. . . . But from up the lane—silence. I grew anxious. Had they eluded my questing child and careered away? Should I stick to my post, or run and help?

Just then a crunching came to my ears; the crunching became a crashing, and round the corner of the birches dashed an agitated black mass, diving into the hollow, surging up over its crest, and roaring straight at me in full flight—a laneful of wildness! The woods for them! and midnight, and freedom, and frozen ears—hooray! Into the slivers of moonlight came a gallant blink of white; two silver knees flashing, an ink-black mane waving—Ocean Wave, simply going it!

"Hi!" I yelled, swinging my lantern in mad circles, and dancing furiously from one side of the lane to the other. Just as I caught the flash of Ocean's eye, and thought she was going straight through me, she swerved past—into the home field. A clot of others followed, galloping their best, swinging on desperate small legs around the sharp turn; then a single pony, shining golden against the shadow—Marigold; after her a string of slower yearlings, breathing loudly; then Queenie, a little black galloping blot on the moonlit snow; and last—not to be hurried—the mare Thalma, at a laborious trot, with Elizabeth beside her. Finally, out of the darkness grew two attached but wrestling forms, about which expostulations hovered. "Stop, Superb! . . . Superb, don't be an ass!" and my child appeared, mightily restraining an agonized parent whose son had run on without her. Superb was knit into complete curves, her whole self a tense half-circle of suspense. Once safely in the field we let her go—and a chestnut streak shot into the valley, then up among the frisking mob of homegoers. We smiled at each other. Then our faces sobered.

"My! this cold bites!" muttered Babs.

"Got any nose?" I asked anxiously.

"Not much!" said she cheerfully, clasping it in a mittened hand. "You got any?"

In front of us were roofs and cuddling orchards; and tonight a single light shone out—that light I always longed to see. It made the whole picture; . . . even if one knew it was candlesticks on a side table under my child's portrait! . . . And the softness of the orchard darks, above clear lines of silver fields— oh, dear! what a thing to draw—at twelve below zero and ten o'clock at night! Things are always gorgeous just when it's impossible to get at them. . . .

By the door stood a huddle of forms, meekly awaiting us. As we buttoned the door upon them, a sudden shock struck me.

"Where's Kindness?" I gasped.

"And Donlinna!" breathed Babs.

We had forgotten them completely! After a rueful glance at the freezing hills, we looked at each other and burst into shouts of mirth. Seizing the lantern, we set off, and nearly a mile from home came upon them standing disconsolately before a gray wayside barn, its front brilliant silver in the moonlight. Donlinna sprang to meet us.

"Bless you, Missises!" she nickered, running her nose into my coat front.

"Why didn't you come home then, idiot?" I said crossly, petting her; and started to put a halter on her. None of that! With a bound and a flourish she and her tributary pony were off, tails up, for home. Toiling in their wake, we had just one glimpse of them flying along the moonlit lane. . . .

At exactly eleven fifteen by the kitchen clock we sat down to a Christmas supper. How marvelous the fire heat felt; how joyfully the kettles steamed! Which was the greater luxury, to bask or to eat, we did not know. The candles gleamed among the holly; Boo-boo purred like a happy cello; and Goliath, on the hearth rug, stretched out with a groan of content.

(PENNSYLVANIA DUTCH)

A Pennsylvania Dutch Christmas

JEAN LOUISE SMITH

ROSY-CHEEKED from an afternoon of gathering greens for the putz, two small children fling open the kitchen door.

"We put the greens in the shed with the moss and rocks and tree stumps that we got in the fall! Can we start fixing the putz after supper?" one of the children cries.

Mother wipes her floury hands on her ample apron. "Enough for a whole roomful of greens?" she questions.

"Yes, oh, yes, a whole roomful of greens for the putz!" the children chorus.

"Take your wraps off and give me a hand with these cookies," Mother says. "We'll get out the manger."

"And the little houses and the pan for making the pond—" one of the children interrupts merrily.

"And the electric train—and—" the other adds excitedly.

"Yes, yes," laughs Father. "I'll go to the attic now and hunt up the boxes so we can unpack them right after supper. But now, help your mother."

The kitchen is fragrant with the smell of baking cookies. Every inch of table and shelf space is taken up with old-fashioned tin cooky cutters or finished cookies done in delightful shapes: lambs, stars, hearts, angels, and figures of people.

This is but a hint of Christmas in Pennsylvania Dutchland. It but partly suggests how these colorful and charming people have kept alive Old-World Christmas customs which they brought to America two centuries and more ago.

Who are the Pennsylvania Dutch? In general, they are the

descendants of the German and Swiss immigrants who came to Pennsylvania before the Revolution. Some, also, trace their ancestry to the Moravians who fled religious persecution in Bohemia, Silesia, and Moravia.

To be counted a true Pennsylvania Dutchman, one must cling to "Dutch" patterns of life, whether his family settled in Pennsylvania, Ohio, or other parts of the Middle West. Also, certain religious groups characterize the Dutch: the Mennonites, Amish, Brethren, Lutherans, Reformed, and Schwenkfelders. The pattern is complex and interwoven; like a loomed counterpane or patchwork quilt, it is comprised of many different parts, which, all together, make a lovely and beautiful design.

Early Customs

When these German farmers and tradesmen came from the Old to the New World, they turned willing and skilled hands to the land. They built sturdy and beautiful homes. They thought well of their adopted country. But when Christmas time came, they found to their amazement that their English and Irish neighbors paid little attention to the holy day. Shops and schools were open as usual. No trees graced the living rooms, no gifts were lovingly prepared for children. There was no Christmas cooking. Even in church, only a brief reference was made to the beloved day.

But in Pennsylvania Dutch homes children were kept home from school on Christmas Day. The traditional German custom was cherished of going to the forest to cut an evergreen tree and bringing it into the house to trim with homemade ornaments. Fragrant odors of cookies and Christmas cakes permeated Dutch homes. Old legends, such as the one which told how cattle talked on Christmas night, must have sounded strange indeed to English neighbors. Strange, too, must have seemed the custom of setting out hay on Christmas Eve so that it would catch dew from heaven—guarding from ill health and misfortune the cattle who would eat the hay.

Primarily, though, Christmas was celebrated as a Christian

religious festival among the early Pennsylvania Dutch. The "Plain People," who are comprised of the Amish and Mennonites, disapproved of "worldly" observances. They thought of Christmas as a time to be observed with solemn dignity in church. Their Moravian neighbors, however, brought glorious music, the soft light of candles, the putz, and many another embellishment to their church celebration. Other groups centered as much of Christmas around the home as around the church.

In the Home

Christmas in a Pennsylvania Dutch home today is, in many respects, not unlike it was two hundred years ago. Except for the Plain People the tree is the center of the home celebration. Settlers in the New World brought the Protestant love of the Christmas tree from the upper Rhineland in Germany. There, the custom of the Christmas tree had been cherished for some two hundred years before the rest of Germany took it up.

On rolling Pennsylvania hillsides, the pioneers found beautiful evergreen trees to cut and bring into the farmhouse just before Christmas. Children kept busy for days beforehand stringing popcorn and cranberries to hang on the trees. Eggs for the cookies and cakes were carefully blown. Children then pasted strips of colored paper on the shells to make festive and gay patterns. By attaching string, the decorated egg became an ornament to hang on the tree.

Under the tree a "yard" or "garden" was set up. This miniature landscape had for its focus a Nativity group, the figures of which often came from the Old World, or were hand-carved by members of the family. Elaborating this setting, a "pond" might be made from a mirror and around it would be grouped some pine or moss. A "hill" might be created on which grazed carved figures of sheep or other domestic animals. The "yard" grew larger from year to year as new objects were added. Many Pennsylvania Dutch families today are fortunate enough to possess some of these original scenes made by their ancestors many years ago.

Gift-giving in Dutch rural homes has always been kept simple. Because children are important members of the household, it is they who receive gifts rather than the grownups. The young set out hats, baskets, or stockings to be filled with presents brought by the Christ-child, whom they call the *Krischkindel* or *Kindlein*. The child who behaves best during the year receives the most nuts and cakes, these being traditional gifts of olden times. Today gift-giving also follows more modern patterns, but even so, the current elaborate emphasis on expensive and numerous gifts is missing in most Pennsylvania Dutch households.

Belsnickel and Belsnickles

In the olden days in certain of the Pennsylvania Dutch communities there came to the homes on Christmas Eve a frightening person known as *Belsnickel*. How the children dreaded his visit—especially those who had misbehaved! A tap or sound of a switch on the window and the children would cry out *Der Belsnickel!* The door opened and in came a tall male figure, usually an uncle or another relative. He was dressed in a sheet and thoroughly disguised by a mask. In his hand he carried a hickory stick. In a gruff voice *Belsnickel* asked each child if he had been good. Truthful answers were expected and he who admitted to wrongs was often switched smartly on the knuckles. Then came questions on the catechism or about schoolwork. If the answers were satisfactory, candies and nuts were taken from the folds of *Belsnickel's* mysterious costume and tossed on the floor. While the children scrambled for these, the visitor made for the door.

In some of the Pennsylvania Dutch homes an older child, robed in white, impersonated *Krischkindel*. He would come with *Belsnickel* to light the candles on the tree and scatter the goodies. *Belsnickel* then assumed the role of the "checker-upper" and punisher.

Belsnickel gradually faded out of the picture and gave way to Santa Claus after Clement Clark Moore wrote his poem, *Visit from St. Nicholas,* in 1822. In some way which cannot be wholly accounted for, *Belsnickel* became *belsnickles* or *belsnickling.* It seemed as though the idea of masquerading could not be given up, but instead of one person's disguising himself, entire groups dressed up and wore masks, going from house to house, from farm to farm, to visit and to celebrate Christmas Eve with friends. Those who stayed at home prepared for the company by popping huge quantities of corn and laying out enormous stacks of cookies. When the dressed-up masqueraders arrived, everyone congregated in the kitchen to eat and to sing carols. Because visiting is greatly loved in Dutch communities, this quaint custom persists in many places with modifications.

Christmas Morning

Today, as long ago, everyone goes to church on Christmas morning. There, the story of Bethlehem, beloved German carols, and Holy Communion comprise the service of worship. Whole families go together and after church they return to fragrant-smelling homes for a great and wonderful feast. Though the Plain People frown on feasting, their less conservative neighbors have a traditional meal. This has always consisted of turkey with potato filling or stuffing, dried corn and stewed onions, and mince pie. Sometimes baked ham, roast pig, or "hog maw" (roast stuffed pig's stomach) is substituted for turkey, and fresh sausage, a standard item in Pennsylvania Dutch diet, is often added. Cookies and leftovers are consumed for the evening meal.

Christmas Cookies

One can reconstruct in imagination what went into the making of Christmas cookies in the early days, for much the same sort of thing goes on today. For days and days before Christmas the cast-iron stove was fired to just the right heat for the cooky baking and the women of the household got to work in no uncertain terms. Each family had its own set of cooky cutters: rabbits, fish, roosters, and other animals were among the designs. *Belsnickel,* angels, figures of men and women, stars, tulips (the hallmark of Pennsylvania Dutch folk art) and numerous other designs were fashioned into cooky cutters by the local tinsmith. Measurements went up to a foot in many instances.

With these cutters the housewives fashioned thinly rolled butter or ginger cookies, sprinkling them with red sugar or nuts "just for nice."

There were other kinds of cookies too, chief of which was the well-known sand tart, "wonderful rich" with butter, sugar, eggs, and flour. The better the cook, the thinner the sand tart! Beaten egg white was brushed over the top and crushed peanuts or a half a hickory nut garnished these cookies.

Lebkuchen and *springerle* were other favorites. From the Rhineland the early settlers had brought their *springerle* boards, wooden molds, beautiful in their intricate designs.

To delight the children, the mothers made enormous ginger cookies, cutting them into fascinating shapes. Many of these were put on the tree as ornaments.

It is said that in olden days a housewife and her daughters made enough cookies to last until Easter. Christmas cookies are still an important part of Pennsylvania Dutch Christmas festivities.

Not only cookies, but Christmas cakes were important items in the early days. The day before Christmas was baking day. The big, glowing ovens attracted the children, who were put to work cracking nuts. The cakes were mixed and poured into bake pans the shape of birds, horses, lambs, and stars. The fragrance of these baking cakes filled the house, and what an array they made when, all finished, they were spread out on long trestle tables!

Second Christmas

In some, but not all Pennsylvania Dutch groups, a "Second Christmas" was observed on the day after Christmas. It took the form of a rowdy day with pranks and general cutting up. At one period preachers sternly advised against it, with the result that it was modified. Gradually "Second Christmas" became a day for visiting and for continuing the family celebrations of

Christmas, stretching out the beloved season as long as possible. With the Amish and other Plain People who frowned on the old boisterous Second Christmas, the day was always one of visiting from farm to farm and sampling various goodies.

Barring Out the Schoolmaster

A completely prankish aspect of Christmas that developed in some communities was the custom of barring out the schoolmaster. This was the one time in the year when the children might conspire against their teacher. They would choose a day just before Christmas to shut themselves up in the schoolhouse. When the schoolmaster arrived, he would find the doors and windows tightly locked. Often as not the children, terrified at heart, were peering out from the windows. Finally, after repeated efforts to get in, the teacher would receive demands for a truce. He would be told by an older child, or by a note slipped under the door, what he must do to "buy" his entrance. When he conceded, he was allowed to enter. Usually the children asked for small gifts of candy and nuts and various indulgences that amounted to a day of greater freedom and fewer restrictions in schoolwork. The long-suffering teacher would send two older boys to the village store to purchase sweets and other treats. From then on, the day proceeded in a happy fashion with a general good time.

(PLYMOUTH ROCK)

A Pilgrim Christmas, 1620

M UNDAY, THE 25 DAY, we went on shore, some to fell tymber, some to saw, some to riue, and some to carry, so that no man rested all that day, but towards night, some, as they were at worke, heard a noyse of some Indians, which caused vs all to goe to our Muskets, but we heard no further, so we came aboord againe, and left some twentie to keepe the court of gard; that night we had a sore storme of winde and raine. Munday the 25 being Christmas day, we began to drinke water aboord, but at night, the Master caused vs to have some Beere, and so on board we had diverse times now and then some Beere, but on shore none at all.

One ye day called Christmas-day, ye Gov'r caled them out to worke (as was used), but ye most of this new company excused themselves, and said it went against their conscience to worke on ye day. So ye Gov'r tould them that if they made it a mater of conscience, he would spare them till they were better informed. So he led away ye rest, and left them: but when they came home at noone from their worke, he found them in ye streete at play, openly; some pitching ye barr, and some at stoole ball, and such like sports. So he went to them and tooke away their implements, and told them it was against his conscience that they should play, and others worke. If they made ye keeping of it matter of devotion, let them kepe their houses, but there should be no gameing or revelling in ye streets. Since which time nothing hath been attempted that way, at least, openly.

(PUERTO RICO)

Christmas in Puerto Rico

FRANCES M. HILL

IF YOU WERE SPENDING CHRISTMAS in Puerto Rico, you would say Merry Christmas this way: *Felices Pascuas!* This is in Spanish, the language of Puerto Rico, and it means Happy Christmas!

Christmas is celebrated for many days in this beautiful island. The celebration begins on Christmas Eve, *Noche Buena,* and continues until Three Kings' Day, which is the sixth of January. Christmas Eve in the Roman Catholic churches is the time when the birth of Christ is dramatized. There is the stable, the sheep, the oxen, and Mary with the baby Jesus. Christmas Eve is also the time for special feasts in the homes. Elaborate preparations are made for these. Homes are lighted and decorated. People dress in their very best clothes. In the homes of the well-to-do financially there will always be found a whole roasted pig, barbecue style. People who cannot afford such a sumptuous feast will at least try to have *arroz con pollo,* which is rice and chicken. This Christmas feast is a time for all the family to gather at one of the homes, making a sort of family reunion of the occasion. The feast comes late at night and the service in the Catholic church follows the feast in the homes. Many of the families spend the evening in merriment and in singing the old Christmas carols. It also is a time when young men serenade their young lady friends to the accompaniment of a guitar. Groups of musicians go from place to place singing their greetings, expecting gifts of money or food. Sometimes they take with them a representation of the Bethlehem scene.

The most exciting time for the children is Three Kings' Day.

One person, in writing about this day, says that no stockings are hung on Christmas Eve. There is a reason for this. It seems that the Puerto Rican children believe that the Three Kings come from the Orient each year riding camels. On the night of the fifth of January, the children fill boxes with grass and place cups of water beside them for the camels. They expect the kings to leave them gifts.

Another author has something different to say about this custom. Puerto Rican boys and girls would be frightened if Santa Claus should come to them in a sleigh drawn by reindeer. In Puerto Rico the children say that Santa Claus just comes flying through the air like a bird. The children make little boxes which they place in the courtyards or on the roofs and old Santa Claus drops the gifts into them as he flies around at night with his bag. According to custom, Santa Claus does not come on Christmas Eve only. He may come every night or two during the week. This is very exciting for the children and each morning they run out eagerly to see if Santa has left anything more in their boxes during the night.

On Bethlehem Day, the twelfth of January, groups of children parade through the streets of the town. The first three children in the procession are dressed in robes to represent the Wise Men from the East, bringing their gifts to Jesus. Following them come the angels and shepherds and flute players. These are dressed in lovely costumes and carry garlands of flowers. Processions such as these are very beautiful and mean a great deal to the children who take part as well as to others who watch the festival.

In Evangelical or Protestant churches Christmas also is celebrated as a joyous festival. Children and grownups alike dramatize the age-old Christmas story. Christians go from home to home singing the beautiful Christmas carols. Christian families have happy times together in their homes. One way in which Puerto Rican Christians honor Jesus on his birthday is to share with others. This is the real meaning of Christmas in any land, not just on the island of Puerto Rico.

SOUTH AMERICA
BOLIVIA

Christmas, a Harvest Festival

PREPARATION FOR THE BIRTH of the Christ-child begins on December 1. Children gather flowers, particularly the *pastora*, the national flower and much like a poinsettia, in the mountain valleys, to decorate the Nativity scenes in home and church. In the churches, gold and silver figurines are used for the Nativity scenes. On December 24, people attend a midnight Mass or pray in their homes and place gifts about their sleeping children. In the towns and cities, Christmas celebrations last until January 6. The working classes participate less in these celebrations.

The natives of Bolivia (50 per cent of the population) celebrate Christmas more as a harvest festival. Thanks are given for completion of the year's work. Labor leaders give an account of the work done during the year and propose what is to be done during the following year. Chiefs and tribes gather to organize their work. Christmas tends to become a feast of adoration of the Goddess Mother Earth, who is asked to bring a fruitful harvest, to keep away plagues, and to give a prosperous year, though these customs are frowned on by the authorities.

BRAZIL

Creches but No Trees

IN BRAZIL Santa Claus is little known, and those who do know of the jolly fellow call him *Papa Noël*. He enters through the window on Christmas Eve, as many of the houses have no chimneys in the warm climate.

An old legend says that the animals have the power of speech on Christmas night. The children are told that the cock crows in a loud voice at the stroke of twelve, *"Christo nasceu"* (Christ is born). The bull in a deep voice inquires *"Onde?"* (Where), and the sheep answer in chorus, *"Em Belem de Juda"* (In Bethlehem of Judea).

The children have no Christmas trees, but they do have a *creche* or *presépio*, representing the Christ-child's birth, with the holy family, the shepherds, and domestic animals. It is commonly found in private homes as well as in public hospitals, and it is left standing until Epiphany. Gifts and toys are exchanged during the holidays, after which the *presépio* is put away until the following Christmas.

Christmas at Campinas

RIDE WITH ME over dusty roads and then paved ones back to the city of Campinas, home from a trip of three thousand kilometers through the territory of the West Brazil Mission. Go with me to sing with the Protestant Evangelical choral choir of the city of Campinas. The largest theater in the city is filled with about three thousand people who have come to hear the music of the *Messiah* and other Christmas carols. Listen with joy in your hearts as the choir sings: "Hallelujah! Hallelujah! for the Lord God omnipotent reigneth, . . . and he shall reign for ever and ever, King of kings and Lord of lords." Listen to the beautiful hymns of Christmas telling the story once more of the coming of God himself to man. The Christ coming to tell of God's love for man, coming to bring forgiveness and life to all who believe.

It is just such scenes that take place within a period of twenty-four hours here in Brazil that remind one in a dramatic way of the need of all men everywhere of every social stratum— of the need to understand the birth, life, and death of Jesus Christ.

Many Christmas activities in Brazil are much like those in the United States. Store windows have been full of decorations; Santa Claus, called *Papa Noël,* visits little children. Many Christmas trees, both artificial and real, are found in homes and churches. Churches hold pageants and candlelight services. The poor are cared for by churches and clubs. Colored lights are found in the city streets, maybe in the towns of the interior—only the city square will have colored lights. In all of this activity the Protestant Church is busy giving out literature, holding programs, and preaching the Christmas message. Each Protestant church carefully takes care of her poor and many others.

As the New Year letter comes to you, I want to ask you to pray earnestly for two people. I ask that you earnestly pray for a young university student now studying at the University of São Paulo. This student is struggling to believe. Pray that God will give to this student a faith that is real, deep, and vital in Christ.

Pray also for a neighbor of mine who is an electrician by trade. He owns a shop close to where we live in Campinas. I have taken him a small Christmas gift and a Gospel. This man has read the literature of the Catholics, Protestants, and Spiritualists. He believes nothing at the present. Though I still speak poor and little Portuguese, he speaks some English. Pray in your own private prayer time and in the different meetings of the church for these two people. Let us see what God will do in two lives as you pray.

Many, many letters and Christmas cards have filled my mail box this Christmas from my friends in the U.S., and from other countries. Thank you each one; your thoughtful remembrance of me has made my Christmas happy in every way.

Each day I am thankful more and more for God's unending love and may each of you come to know his abiding love in this New Year. Remember faithfully the two prayer requests.

—Mary Lee Smith (Presbyterian Church in the U.S.), December 28, 1960.

COLOMBIA

The Christmas Guest

KENNETH IRVING BROWN

THERE ARE TIMES when new scenes pall and strange faces affright, when a man yearns for his home and the companionship of his friends. I had reached such a state of mind after four months in South America, during which I had ravaged the Guianas, Venezuela, and Colombia in search of flora for my botanical museum. My collection was complete except for a specimen of the *Cocos comosa,* and I was loath to leave the country until I had secured it. All of my search for it had been fruitless. As a final endeavor, I set out with Pedro, a native Carib guide whom I engaged at Cartagena, down the Gulf of Darien to the mouth of the Mulatto River, and up the Mulatto into the Colombian wilderness, hoping that here at last I might find that *rara avis*.

I lay back in the native dugout, lost in pleasant thoughts of home and a land where nature was tamed. Pedro, between the lazy strokes of his paddle, had told me, in lingo of distorted English and incomprehensible Spanish, of Cispatia, a tiny Carib town inland on the Mulatto which he knew, of the villagers' "heart warmness," which I interpreted to mean hospitality, and of their isolation. If I understood him correctly, no white man had visited them for twenty years. I smiled to myself at the thought of the fright I should cause them with my pale complexion—pale in comparison, in spite of the tanning of the sun—and my American clothes, for the town was ahead and we should be there by nightfall.

"And this is the day before Christmas," I mused half aloud. "We shall spend our Christmas Eve at Cispatia; I shall be their Christmas guest."

The thought was ironical, and I smiled bitterly. Pedro smiled in return; I doubt if he understood my words, but his sympathy and good nature were apparent.

The Mulatto is a sluggish stream, mud-brown, with a current whose movement is barely perceptible. High, luxuriant tropic growth lines both sides of the winding river, vegetation in fullsome abundance, and yet its very voluptuousness suggests stagnation. The air seemed heavy with that stillness, that impenetrable calm, which is so characteristic of the southern lands. The sun rose high and glared with fury; passed meridian splendor and slowly sank. Pedro paddled on leisurely; the great muscles of his bare black back moved with lazy regularity. For a long time neither of us spoke; the silence was broken only by the shrill calling of some wild bird in the palm trees.

It was approaching twilight—the twilight of Christmas Eve —when the camp enclosure of Cispatia came into view. From the coast the river had meandered willfully and vagrantly; each turn had revealed a new turn only a few rods ahead; but when the tiny village came into sight the stream ran in a straight course for several hundred yards, as if, near this oasis in the midst of yawning stretches of forest land, its conduct must be circumspect.

The first view of the enclosure was not prepossessing. The village consisted of a score or more of small huts with their novel grass roofs, many of them built on stilts for protection against the attack of wild animals. An area of some two or three acres, containing the buildings, was surrounded by a high wooden stockade and on the fourth by the river. There was only one man visible: an old father, bent low with age. His grizzled hair fell over his misshapen back like an enveloping cloak, and his beard reached to his knees.

He espied us and stood as if rooted to the spot, staring intently at us. Then with a wild shout, such as I have never heard from beast or human being, he cried: *"¡Hombres, hombres! ¡Venid!"* and straightway running from the huts came men and women. They stopped abruptly when they saw us; with one accord they fell upon their knees and bowed their faces in the dust, all the while making a rhythmic moan, uncanny at first, and then strangely harmonious and beautiful.

I knew not what to make of this strange performance and my guide offered no information. Our canoe came nearer and as it hugged the bank I stepped ashore. Not a person stood, nor even peered at me through half-closed eyes; evidently that which I had taken for a moan was a prayer.

"Can you give a night's lodging to a weary traveler?" I asked.

The old man I had first seen raised himself on his knees and extended his arms to me, but he uttered not a word.

"They no speak English," my guide said.

"Tell them we want to spend the night here," I answered.

He turned to them with my message, and no sooner had he spoken than their prayer—if such it was—ceased, and they rushed toward me. In no human eye have I ever seen expressed such a wildness of emotion as was written in theirs—amazement, fear, childish simplicity, and passion. They seemed to be searching for something in me, some special quality, for their eyes scanned my face with a hunger and avidity quite disconcerting. When I raised my arms to them to signify that I would be their friend, they fell at my feet; one even kissed my sandals and another my trousers.

When a second time my guide explained that we would spend the night with them, their delight was pitiful, and one and all ran to the largest of the several huts to make ready my bed.

The entire performance was incomprehensible to me. The hamlet's reputation for hospitality, of which Pedro had told me, failed to explain their strange actions; even amazement at the presence of a white man hardly accounted for the apparent worship. I recalled stories, from grammar-school readers, of Romans who were taken to be gods when they were cast shipwrecked upon an unknown shore; but I laughed aloud. Did they take me for an Olympian? How far was an academically sheltered botanist from qualifying as a relative of Jupiter and Juno! Rather this must be their way of paying respect to the white man's superiority.

The ancient Carib chieftain, the old man whom we had seen on the shore, came forward and bowed us to a bench before a narrow table near the steps of the main hut. We seated ourselves—Pedro and I—but our host was troubled. He made strange motions to my guide, and then came to whisper something in his ear. Pedro rose solemnly and, with a gaze half of regret and half of reverence, moved to another table, leaving me alone. Then the *muchachas* brought the food; but while they served Pedro, all the dishes intended for me were given to my host, who himself served me. Although I dared not attempt to thank him in my meager Spanish, I tried to show him by smile and friendly nod that I appreciated his generosity. The dishes set before me were many and, to a wayfaring man, delicious: a soup of beef, fried plantains, and a roasted bull steak. I was hungry and ate greedily. When I had finished I strolled down to the bank of the little stream and sat in wonder, while the shadows of twilight thickened, and the matted growth across the river, higher than the height of a man, assumed strange forms as it swayed in the gentle night breezes.

I could see the *hombres* and *mujeres* in the distance. They were talking in low soft tones. Suddenly from the group I saw a figure emerge. It was one of the *muchachas,* young and slender, but she walked with difficulty, leaning heavily upon a staff at each step. She was partially shrouded in the dusk, so that I could not see her distinctly, but as she drew nearer I thought her left side was paralyzed. Her foot dragged as a leaden weight, and her arm hung useless. She came forward alone, stumbling and with visible hesitation. No one moved among the group in the background, and yet I could see they were watching her intently. What could it mean?

The young girl was too much in earnest to be acting a part in any heathen ceremonial. She was trembling violently and now I could see that she was coming toward me. I rose, wondering what was expected of me, and even as I did she stumbled. Her staff fell from her hand and she pitched forward, her right arm stretched out for help. I caught her easily, and held her trembling body for a moment. Eyes like the eyes of a young lioness when first entrapped—soft, yearning, wondering, before she knows the cruelty of her position—met mine in a look which years of scientific training had brought me no means of understanding. Then, with a cry of ecstasy, the young thing leaped from my arms and flew back to the shadows. As if waiting for this moment, her friends raised their voices with hers and there arose on the night air a solemn chanting, crude and unmusical, yet beautiful in its absolute sincerity and resplendent in its recurring note of joy. I watched, listening, and waited, longing to know the secret of the mystery.

The *muchacha's* staff lay at my feet. Could it be that these poor people, hearing of our progress in medicine, believed in the white man's miraculous power to heal? Faith is the ability to believe the incredible, I had heard it said. Was this the solution?

I did not see my guide again that night. I was so astounded at what had taken place, and so disconcerted by the plaintive chanting, that I hurried to absent myself and made signs to my host that I would retire. He understood and led me to the hut, where they had prepared a spreading of fresh palm leaves with a blanket covering—the choicest sleeping accommodation the camp offered, I knew—and I accepted with gracious heart.

I was weary from my journey, and the cool night air brought refreshing sleep. It was dawn when I awoke.

Christmas Day—yet how unbelievable! What was Christmas Day in a land of wilderness and black folk? What could it mean to these dark-skinned Carib Indians? Not even a name, I suspected, to them who would worship a white man as they would a god, who instinctively bowed before a stranger from the fairyland of success.

It was with a feeling of wretchedness and discontent that I recalled the past Christmases, and knew that for the love of leaves and grass I had deprived myself of another such exquisite pleasure. My thoughts were willful truants: a jolly Christmas Day; outside, the ground white with snow, inside, the tree bulging with gifts and tempting eatables; the children were probably shouting as they opened their presents, and their mother—she too was lonely, even as I was lonely, for she had expected me to return before the holiday season. And all for a *Cocos comosa.*

The dream was dispelled as I became conscious of the voices which had awakened me, harsh and untuneful, even as the night before, yet they stirred something within me which quieted the loneliness of my heart. I bethought me of the old Christmas minstrels—but the very unlikeness of their carols to the present crying caused me to smile. I rose from my pallet; there about the hut were gathered the inhabitants of the camp, with their arms laden. At sight of me they bowed themselves to the ground; then slowly one by one they came and laid their offerings at my feet. I stood as a man in a dream, insensible to what was going on. I looked for my guide to explain, but Pedro was nowhere near. At the foot of my ladder were heaped great skins of tiger and lynx, bananas and plantains, curiously carved images, and a reed basket woven in intricate design and filled with stone charms. In my amazement I wondered if this were my Christmas dream come true!

I did my best to express my thanks by smiles and gestures,

and the natives appeared to understand, but my confusion was turning to puzzled incredulity. I wanted to get away from it all; I wanted to question my guide. Was this Cispatia's tribute to civilization and nothing more?

They brought me food, when I had thanked them as best I could; and when I had eaten I sought my guide.

"Pedro, we must away."

He looked at me in awe and surprise. "¿Hoy, señor?"

"Yes, today; at once."

He acquiesced and went to my host with word that we were going. The old man hurried to my side and through Pedro and pantomime begged me to stay. Then, seeing I was resolute, he motioned me to remain for a moment while he called the villagers together.

They came quickly, for at no time did they seem to be far away, and, grouping themselves about me, they fell on their knees. My host stood before me, and by frantic gesticulation, spreading his hands out in front of him, endeavored to communicate an idea to me, but I could not understand. I turned to Pedro for assistance.

"Bless," he said.

They wanted me to bless them. I, an old, homesick botany professor, with theological notions too vague or too radical to be bound by creed or formula, was called upon to bless this little community which had housed me in the best of their homes! I lifted my hands and, with eyes raised to heaven, I repeated over them the words which came to my mind from childhood days, like a voice heard from afar: "*The Lord watch between me and thee, when we are absent one from another.*" Then, turning to my companion, I entered the dugout, and we pushed off.

Pedro took his place at the fore and began to paddle with his long, lazy strokes. By a turn in the stream the tiny enclosure was soon lost to sight.

"Pedro, what did it all mean?"

He looked at me with eyes filled with amazement and doubt. "You know."

"I don't know; tell me."

He hesitated, but something in my face must have warned him that I wanted an answer, for at last he spoke.

"Christ come."

No white man ever uttered such words with deeper reverence.

"Christ come!" I echoed, as I remembered their greeting and the incident of the night before.

"Yes, old miss'nary tell—Christ come. He come day 'fore Christmas; come up river at shade time in dugout with *hombre*. He stay all night at Cispatia. They know at Cispatia."

I sat stunned by the thought. This then was the reason for their reception and their gifts: this the reason for the *muchacha's* confidence.

It was an idea which made me tremble. How inconceivable their childish faith, how perfect their adoration! And I had taken their *homage* as a white man's due!

Very, very silent I sat, awed and oppressed by an overburdening sense of impotence. If only the King might have come to receive his Christmas tribute!

The canoe moved on. The tall grasses rustled in the breeze; in the distance I heard music. It was the solemn chant they had sung for me when I came; they were singing it again as I left them. Clear, sometimes shrill, ever tuneless, and yet motivated by a strangely recurring theme of joy, it came to me on the morning air. Fainter and fainter it grew, as the recessional fades in the anteroom of the cathedral; then the hushed pause, silence, and that sense of unutterable loneliness, of loss, even as when a star falls from the heavens and the light of the world seems dimmed.

Pedro leaned toward me.

"It is true ¿*no es verdad?* You are, you are—He?"

ECUADOR

Christmas, the Universal Feast

CHRISTMAS AND THE NEW YEAR are celebrated as the same festival, not separately as in North America. Rich and poor prepare new costumes for Christmas, as we do for Easter. Church and state co-operate in collecting money to purchase toys for the children of the poor.

Children write letters to the Christ-child and place shoes in the window in which he may place toys as he passes by on Christmas Eve. Noise-making toys are common and are used with much energy on the streets on Christmas morning.

Since the weather is very warm, most celebrations are in the streets. There are firecrackers, brass bands, and dancing. At midnight everyone goes to Mass, after which the family dinner is enjoyed.